MEDITERRANEAN SEA

WHITE STAR
PUBLISHERS

Contents

Texts
Angelo Mojetta

Literary coordination
Valeria Manferto De Fabianis
Laura Accomazzo

Graphic design
Patrizia Balocco Lovisetti
Clara Zanotti

Color plates
Monica Falcone
Roberta Vigone

Illustration of the fish
Alessandra Arnoletti
Monica Falcone
Sabrina Moscatelli
Roberta Vigone

1 An intricate tangle of amazingly varied and colorful forms of marine life. Jewel anemones, hydroids and crinoids mask the substrate on which they have established their colony, making it totally unrecognizable.

2-3 Transparent turquoise and blue stream up from the floor of a sun-drenched Mediterranean bay. These are the typical colors of a sea which thrives on light.

4 A wall of bicolored, red and yellow sea fans offers just one of countless breathtaking vistas that lie beneath the surface of the Mediterranean. Sights like this more than explain this sea's irresistible appeal to divers.

5 top Along the Mediterranean coasts rugged cliffs, carved by wind and waves, alternate with long sandy beaches. And these alternating features of the shoreline have helped shape the rich variety of marine environments and organisms.

5 bottom A large brown grouper (Ephinephelus marginatus) appears to be observing a group of other fish, as if to make the diver aware of the profusion of life-forms to be found in the Mediterranean.

© 2005 White Star S.r.l.
Via Candido Sassone, 22/24
13100 Vercelli, Italy
www.whitestar.it

ISBN 88-544-0048-3

REPRINTS:
1 2 3 4 5 6   09 08 07 06 05

Color separation: Graphic Service, Milan
Printed in China

THE HISTORY AND EVOLUTION
OF THE MEDITERRANEAN

The sea of gods and men alike. How else could one define a sea like the Mediterranean? Peoples with different cultures and histories, each with their own sea-faring traditions and their own underwater gods, have succeeded one other around its shores, have lived side by side, as they live side by side today, in a marvellous balance between the universal and the particular. Neptune, Aeolius, Scilla and Charybdis, Glauco and Gilgamesh: nowadays the Tritons and the Nereids have now been replaced by elaborate forecasting systems and sophisticated mathematical models or diagrams to placate our urge for knowledge and our need to have the answers, just as once we demanded of the ancient gods that they should. After coalescing , the great civilizations of East and West seem now to be running the risk of becoming opposing blocks, thus contravening one of the main rules of the Mediterranean world: unity in difference, the same rule, fundamentally, which is at the basis of the phenomenon we call life. There is no doubt that these are negative symbols, but anyone who

spends some time on the shores of the Mediterranean, in places where man still interacts harmoniously with nature, sometimes leaving no traces at all, discovers in the end that this sea has not lost its magic, or its power to cast a spell. The Mediterranean, and it was the destiny of the name that its significance should transcend the purely geographical meaning, was the cradle of the Western world, a cradle which from above looks like a narrow blue stain, transformed by the shape of its coastline into a chain of huge lakes shared by Europe, Africa and Asia. It looks such a natural setting, amidst the shorelines of surrounding lands and at the same time at the center of the Earth. Which is as it should be, if we believe that everything has a beginning and an end. This is where "things" were first given names; here ideas found a fertile ground on which to take root and here man, perhaps, first asked of himself the elementary questions whose answers we are still seeking today, setting off a unique evolutionary process whose traces have been visible on the shores of the Mediterranean for over a million

years. From no other of the planet's mediterranean seas, by which I mean seas surrounded by land and with similar hydrological and dynamic characteristics, can you see three continents with the naked eye, separated as these are by straits (Gibraltar, Suez, the Bosporus). Only the first of these is a natural phenomenon. Suez was created by man and the Bosporus is crossed by a bridge which fulfils Xerses' intention of travelling into Greece without getting his armyís feet wet. But the Mediterranean is not just a meeting place for mankind, animals and plants. Nature herself would appear to have chosen it as her ideal crucible, not just of her living parts, but of her inanimate parts too. Into its waters, with their dominant lapis-lazuli tones, flow the waters of the rivers of Africa, the Alps, central Europe and far away Russia, and there they mix. Here, where according to the mythology of the ancient world, stood Aeolius's Palace of the Winds, blow winds which are icy and winds which are torrid: the Mistral, the Bora, the Meltemi, the Khamsin, the Scirocco and the Libeccio, they all stretch out from the roots of their distant origins to the center of the Mediterranean. The waves and the currents they create shape the distant shores, carrying detritus of all kinds from one part of the sea to another, maybe providing a rudimentary guide for the coastal settlers of this tight circle, suggesting it was possible to cross their sea, where no two points are ever separated by more than 400 kilometers. The entire world was here, within the columns of Hercules, beyond which the immense and uncrossable river Ocean totally surrounded the earth.

In medieval drawings of the known world the Mediterranean was attributed center place. For centuries the history of Europe and its bordering nations developed along the shores of this sea which, in terms of size, had a "human scale". Ships sailing its waters took advantage of familiar winds, known to all Mediterranean seaboard peoples. Trade and insights into different cultures encouraged men to look further afield: they eventually discovered other seas and peoples, and voyages and trade extended from the Mediterranean to the oceans.
But knowledge acquired in the Mediterranean was sufficient to allow astronomers like Paolo Toscanelli - whose planisphere can be seen on the left - to maintain that the Earth was round, and to influence the projects of Christopher Columbus.
The picture on the right shows the planisphere by Giovanni Leardo.

THE ROOTS OF THE MEDITERRANEAN

The Mediterranean Sea occupies a huge depression which reaches a depth of 5,093 meters at its deepest point and measures almost 4,000 kilometers from east to west, covering a surface area of around 3 million square kilometers. Of these, 2.5 million belong to the Mediterranean proper and 423,000 make up the Black Sea, a tributary sea. Its coastline is 22,500 kilometers long, of which 13,000 belong to Europe, 5,000 to Africa and the rest to Asia. But on a planetary scale the Mediterranean is only a small sea, accounting for less than 1% of the total surface water, but the roots of the genesis and evolution of this environment, a natural laboratory which has drastically changed appearance more than once, even in the last 10-20 million years, lie in the beginnings of the big oceans and have a central position in the history of the world as we know it. Tethys, for the Ancient Greeks, was the symbol of the fertility of the sea, the wife of Oceanus and the mother of all rivers. Geologists have given her name to a huge, hot, primordial sea which in Mesozoic times stretched across the middle of the single block of continents, called Pangaea. It had some shallower marginal basins, like gulfs or lagoons. Life in this single sea swarmed: reptiles, fish, molluscs

and crustaceans swam or crawled amongst massive coral cliffs of which the only remaining clues are the fossils. But the gigantic Pangaea did not remain a monolith for long and under the thrust of powerful tectonic forces it began to break up. The reciprocal movements of the huge continental blocks gradually changed the planet's entire physiognomy. At the end of the Jurassic era (around 165 million years ago), the partial opening up of the northern Atlantic Ocean, which resulted from the breaking away of North America from Africa and the formation of the big tectonic ditches, was a second step in the transformation of the Tethys Sea,

which communicated with the new ocean through a series of straits. The Tethys became a border sea between the northern block, which comprised North America, Europe and Asia and the southern continent of Gondwana (Africa, India, Antarctica and Australia). It stretched northwards over part of central Europe, dividing itself up into numerous basins, while southwards it constituted a large oceanic basin, whose bed featured a series of plains separated by creases which would give rise to the earth's main mountain ranges. The passage from the Jurassic period to the Cretaceous period (140 million years ago) coincided with a rise in sea level and the

Some 200 million years ago the continents were more or less united and formed one gigantic land mass called Pangaea. The tectonic forces which still govern movements of the Earth's crust today caused the continents to slowly break apart, thereby creating primeval seas and the nuclei of the present oceans.

Continuous movement of the Earth's mantle led to the formation of huge continental blocks separated from one another by a single ocean, the Tethys Sea, which once girdled the Eastern hemisphere from the Americas to the regions of the present Pacific. It was an enormous, warm sea, with characteristics not unlike those of the tropical waters where corals thrive today.

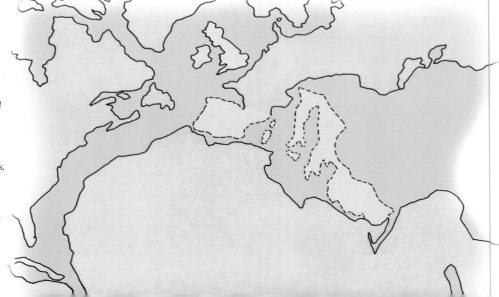

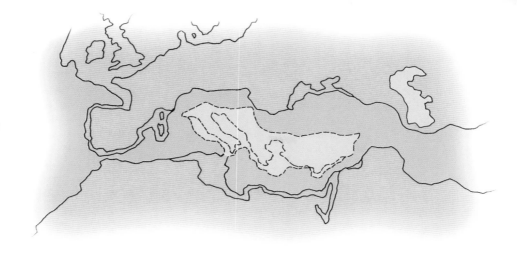

With the slow drift of the continents the blocks of Africa and Euroasia gradually converged. The initial point of contact occurred between the Iberian peninsula and the northern coast of West Africa. The primeval Mediterranean thus started to take shape.

formation of new, shallow, basins above the European regions, part of Asia and the Americas. It was one of the biggest marine invasions in the history of the Earth, involving a large part of the Sahara too. Around 125 million years ago the southern Atlantic began to open up, but for a long time it was a separate basin, wedged between America and Africa. Between the Middle and Late Cretaceous periods (100 million years ago) Europe began its definitive separation from North America, making way for the opening up of a deep waterway which joined the Tethys and the Atlantic, turning them into a gigantic tropical ocean with high beds and trenches, separated by rocky thresholds which rose thousands of meters towards the surface. The end of the Cretaceous

period was a period of profound change for the entire planet, characterized by mass extinctions, not just on land, where the dinosaurs disappeared, but in the oceans too. The fossils and sediments of that period 70-65 million years agobear witness to drastic changes in the populations of the ocean deeps: the big-shelled molluscs such as the ammonites and the belemnites disappeared, along with the big marine reptiles such as the plesiosaurus, the ichthyosaurus, the mosasaurus and entire types of fishes, as well as many plankton. Maybe it was a meteorite, or a succession of powerful volcanic eruptions, which changed the overall picture of the environmental characteristics of the earth, both above and below the water. Currents in the oceans increased and red clay sediment

of continental origin covered the black rocks, which were rich in the organic substances left by the explosion of life in the previous period. The environmental changes coincided with a resumption of the drift of the continental masses and with a broadening of the Atlantic between the Azores and Gibraltar. Meanwhile, Africa and the small Mediterranean plates (Iberian, Adriatic, Aegean, Turkish and Arabic) began to move towards Europe, lifting it up and creating the long series of mountain chains which still stretches across southern-eastern Europe, from the Pyrenees to the Alps, forming a perfect barrier around the Mediterranean, from where they carry on to join the heights of Asia Minor and until at last they reach the Himalayas.

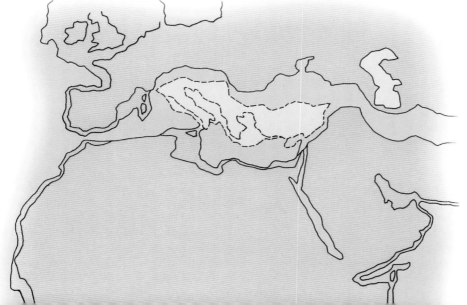

Points of communication on the eastern and Pacific sides became fewer and fewer until eventual complete breakaway, caused by the counterclockwise rotation of Africa and the Arabian peninsula which became joined to Eurasia. These movements also contributed to the formation of the mountain range which stretches from the Pyrenees to the Alps and down on into south-eastern Europe, creating a barrier that protects the Mediterranean from the cold of the north.

THE BIRTH AND EVOLUTION OF THE MEDITERRANEAN

The formation of the Mediterranean basin up until the present has been by no means a simple process and, as we can see from the earthquakes which occur along its shores and the slow but constant increase in sea level, is definitely not yet completed. In the Mediterranean, ancient and recent history are superimposed upon one another, revealing a dynamic sea, more like a mosaic

A, B - The life-forms that now inhabit the Mediterranean owe much to its long history. As well as species living in this sea alone, like red gorgonians (Paramuricea clavata) and yellow gorgonians (Eunicella cavolinii), there are species of Atlantic origin and even others found in distant tropical seas.

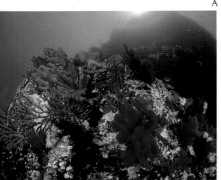

C - The rocky floor of the Mediterranean with its eye-catching colors and stunning light effects provides a home for organisms whose presence here is all part of the long and complex evolution of this sea.

composed of interlocking ridges, trenches, basins and islands, born of a succession, sometimes protracted and sometimes sudden, but all on a geological scale whose commonest units of measurement are intervals of a million years. Once again, the main agents responsible for the creation of the Mediterranean were the movements of the plates which make up the earth's surface. Floating like huge rafts above the earth's mantle, over time they changed the shape, the dimensions and the position of both land masses and oceans. The mechanism has remained unchanged for billions of years and, judging by the movements still going on on the earth's surface - where continents are still drifting together, moving apart and breaking up, new oceans are being formed - is still going on today. The titanic jigsaw puzzle of the plates led, around 65 million years ago, to the formation of the ancestral Mediterranean, made up roughly of the intermediate part of the Tethys, between the Atlantic and the Pacific. At the beginning of the Palaeocene the seas began gradually to retreat, leaving huge areas out of the water, but they were destined to be submerged once again during a new phase of encroachment in the Eocene (55 million years

D - This perfectly preserved fossil was found in the "Pesciara" at Bolca, Verona, Italy where rock encloses the remains of organisms which lived some 50 million years ago in a warm shallow sea. The shape of the fish,

now given the name of Eoplatax papilio, bears an amazing resemblance to that of the bat fish (Platax sp.) which live in tropical waters today, from the Red Sea to the Indo-Pacific Ocean.

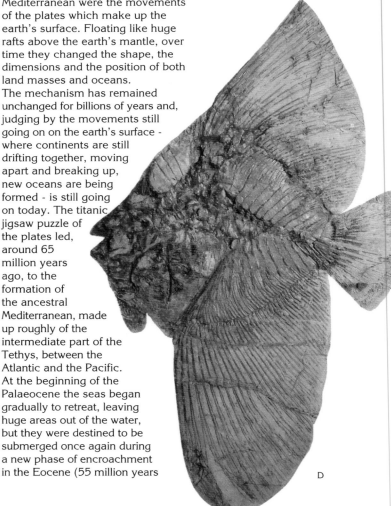

E

of tropical-type vegetation lead to the hypothesis that the Mediterranean of the time had a hot climate, where coral fish swam and the aquatic algae and plants were like those of the present Indo-Pacific area. The "Pesciara" at Bolca, in Verona, Italy, is in fact a petrified sea of the Eocene era, as its famous fossil deposits show. If we could transport ourselves back to the shores of the primordial Mediterranean and dive in its waters, it would feel very similar to diving on the seabed of the Red Sea or the Maldives or the Great Barrier Reef in Australia. The scene before our eyes would be one of sections of coral reef made of colonies of stony corals such as *Goniastrea*, *Goniopora*, *Euphyllia*, *Stylophora* and blue corals like the *Heliopora* amongst which would swim Nautilus with their triangular shells, batfish *(Platax sp.)*, rabbitfish *(Siganus sp.)*, carangids, burrfish, surgeonfish, trumpetfish and soldierfish.

ago) period, when Europe was once again invaded by shallow seas. This was not a rapid phenomenon, but a continuous series of oscillations in the sea level, similar to gigantic tidal waves, which drew the waters into areas like present-day Germany and Russia, which up until then had always been out of the water. Fossils show that these aquatic and continental areas were inhabited by organisms similar, or even identical, in shape and biology, to the ones which live in our planet's seas today. In fact in that period the Mediterranean was one of the centers of differentiation and of the diffusion of marine molluscs, both bivalves and gastropods, which were able to spread throughout the whole of the Tethys, thanks to the equatorial currents from the east and those heading in the opposite direction which bathed the African and Asian shorelines. By comparing ancient and current flora and fauna, it has been possible to reconstruct the climatic and environmental conditions of that geological period. The distribution and the abundance of coral barriers and the remains

E - Hard shells of sea urchins are perfectly preserved in rock formed from the seabed on which they once lived. By studying and comparing these fossilized remains it has been possible to establish that, way back in the eons of time, the Mediterranean was a tropical sea.

F, G - As well as allowing man to reconstruct an environment which disappeared from the face of the Earth almost 50 million years ago, the fossils discovered at Bolca offer tangible evidence of the many enormous changes undergone by the Mediterranean through the ages.

F

G

A GREAT SALT DESERT

The appearance of the Alps and the progressive detachment and distancing of Sardinia and Corsica from southern Europe (30-25 million years) marked the end of the circumtropical Tethys, even though the basins which made up the Mediterranean continued to be connected to the Atlantic and the Indo-Pacific for several million years more.
The union with the latter ocean first came to an end in the Middle-Eastern regions in one of the Miocene periods, between 22 and 13 million years ago. During this period the relationships between water masses and land masses were established and the process of differentiation between the marine fauna of the Atlantic-Mediterranean and that of the Indo-Pacific begun.
However, the evolution of the two populations was neither totally independent nor distinct.
Fossil deposits reveal similarities modern Hungary, Rumania and southern Russia, forming a vast, shallow sea (Paratethys) with little circulation and few contacts with the Mediterranean proper.
In a short time (3-4 million years) these eastern basins were cut off, following the huge sedimentary deposits which closed off communication between Northern Italy and the nearby Balkan regions and turned into lakes of varying degrees of salinity, of which the Caspian Sea, the Balaton and Lake Aral are the last

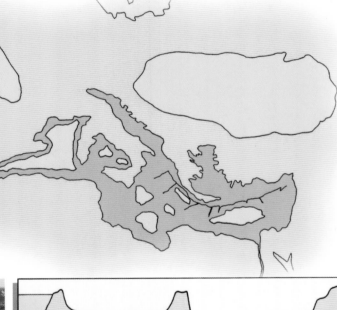

During its evolution the Mediterranean experienced a long period of total isolation. This was caused by the convergence of the continental blocks which eventually cut off the Mediterranean basin from the Atlantic Ocean. As a result huge lakes formed, which gradually turned into immense salt-encrusted flats (top).

A
This sketch shows the situation that existed in the Mediterranean when its waters had no exit into the Atlantic through the Strait of Gibraltar. The sea floor was occupied by lagoons, separated at the center of the basin by the ridges across the Sicilian channel.

A - The sight of these rugged Mediterranean shores emerging from the sea may elicit thoughts of times when these coasts were washed by an isolated, slowly receding sea.

between the two environments over long periods, which can only be explained by the theory of repeated encroachments which re-established connections between the bordering basins at intervals. However, during the early phases of the Miocene the Mediterranean was well-established in the north-eastern sector. Its waters had submerged part of Europe, forming a narrow stretch of water wedged between the newly-emerged Alpine chain and continental Europe, then widening out in the area which is now Vienna. From here its waters moved further eastwards into remaining examples. It is, perhaps, difficult to believe that the process of sedimentary deposits alone could create what is almost a continent, but this is easily explained considering the period of time involved and using examples closer to our own times. The Adriatic basin alone has, in the last 1.8 million years, received deposits of around 1600-2000 meters, originating from the surrounding mountains.
The river Po alone carries on average 14 million tons of solid material annually, consisting of 77% silt and clay and 23% sand. As I mentioned earlier, at almost

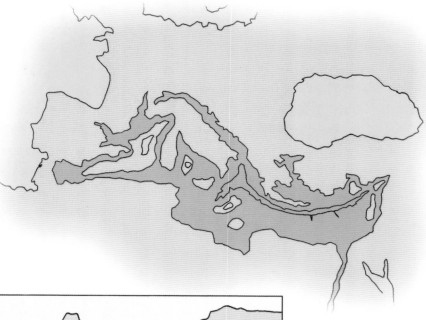

Prolonged isolation resulted in almost total disappearance of life-forms and the formation of immense salt deposits which reached a thickness of 2000 meters in places (top). The drawing below (to be compared with the previous one) highlights the effects of the almost total absence of water in the Mediterranean basin.

B - During the evaporation period high rocks on the sea floor were *exposed, towering above the water which had previously submerged them.*

B

the same time (14-13 million years ago), the eastern passage into the Indian Ocean was also being sealed off as a result of the African continent's slow but continual clockwise rotation and movement. In the meantime the new water/land balance had also led to modifications in the climate which were to have important consequences in the future, but which were initially apparent in a slight cooling in respect of earlier periods, even though the climate was still similar to that of today's Canary Islands, and the consequent disappearance of tropical plants and the increase in deciduous species such as willow, poplar and plane.

The closure in the east was followed by a reduction during the central Miocene period (12-10 million years ago) of contacts between the Atlantic and the Mediterranean in the Gibraltar region, where there had been series of straits which crossed southern Spain in the Cordillera Betica and northern Morocco through the Rif mountains.

The achievement of geographical autonomy was not without consequences for the Mediterranean. During this period

it underwent the greatest and most drastic of changes, which was to be responsible for its transformation into the extraordinary sea it is today. Having become a virtually closed sea, its survival depended , then as now, solely on the equilibrium between fluvial input, rain and evaporation and the existence of a contact, and a continually shrinking one at that, with the Atlantic Ocean.

This led to a gradual lowering in the level of the Mediterranean, which eventually became a series of large lagoons of varying salinity, populated by organisms whose number decreased progressively, but which were increasingly able to tolerate gradually worsening environmental conditions.

This process continued until it peaked between 10 and 6 million years ago - proof of this was gathered in 1970 by the oceanographic ship the Glomar Challenger during the international DSPD (Deep Sea Drilling Project) expedition - with the definitive sealing off of every contact with the Atlantic and domination of evaporation phenomena which followed, peaking during what is

known as the salinity crisis of the Messinian period. In actual fact, the possible disappearance of the Mediterranean towards the end of the Tertiary was put forward in the 1950s and ë60s by an Italian scholar called G. Ruggieri, whose geological and palaeontological research in the southern regions of the Italian peninsula led him to put forward the theory that the Mediterranean had partially dried up. Both the core boring carried out on the sea bed by the Glomar Challenger, which was equipped to function at over 3,000 meters below sea-level, and the physical surveys, revealed the existence of superimposed salt strata, as thick as 2000 meters in some places and in some cases shaped like gigantic spires buried in the

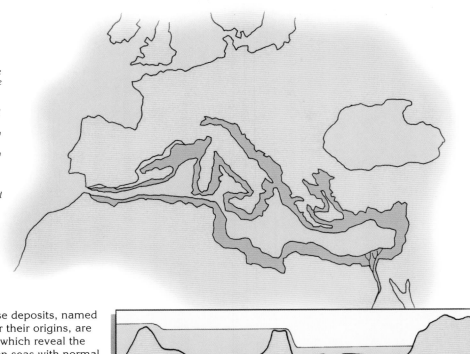

The collapse or further sinking of the Gibraltar threshold led to the formation of a huge wall of cascading Atlantic water which slowly filled the Mediterranean and brought it new life (top). The diagram below shows how the cascading water first filled the western basins and then - once it had passed the ridges across the Sicilian canal - flowed on into the eastern basins.

sediment. These deposits, named evaporites after their origins, are made of rocks which reveal the absence of open seas with normal salinity and are composed of saline compounds whose dominant elements are either sulphates, potassium salts, chalk or rock-salt (halite). These different salts, originating either in oversalt or saline environments and alternating here with deposits of fossil flour, tellurian mud and

A

A - The hollow along this wall - the result of erosion by waves - indicates the level once reached here by the sea. Through the ages the level of the Mediterranean has often changed as its waters have either receded or risen.

the remains of living organisms, some similar to the ancient stromatolites formed from carbonates of monocellular algae and the bacteria found in warm, saline seas, suggested a drying-out process of the Mediterranean occurring over several stages, with alternating phases (up to 40 according to some scientists) of flooding and evaporation. This is the only possible explanation for the enormous depth of the evaporate deposits, because even the entire Mediterranean could not have contained enough salt to account for the phenomenon. It has been calculated that the drying-up process led to 6% of the salts dissolved in all the world's oceans being accumulated in this basin and that if Gibraltar was transformed back into an insurmountable dike, under current climatic conditions, it would take from between 1000 to 1500 years - an insignificant period on the geological timescale - for the whole of the Mediterranean to evaporate. Some scientists put forward the theory that the Messinian crisis actually brought about the change towards a colder climate which occurred at that time: the reduced

salinity was responsible for a simple physical phenomenon i. e. the formation of ice at a temperature closer to zero. This furthered the expansion of the Antarctic polar caps and an increase in the albedo effect i.e. the amount of incident solar light they reflect. The increase in the ice must then have led to a lowering of the sea-level and therefore to the increased isolation of the Mediterranean, increasing the evaporation rate in a succession of reactions which, as well as affecting almost half the planet, were definitely connected, although it is as yet difficult to be sure as to the prime cause. The spectacle presented to the eyes of a hypothetical observer can only be described in terms of seeing the Grand Canyon, Death Valley and the Dead Sea grouped together in a few thousand kilometers. Nowadays, the closest in appearance to that far-off, desertified, basin, would be the arid plains of the Arabian Gulf where there are vast saline areas called ìsabkhaî which geologists equate with those ancient seabeds. In the west, they would have been vast and sunny lifeless plains, covered in deep layers of salt, dotted with oversalt lagoons, edged with beaches and deep canyons; to the east, the seabed of the modern Mediterranean consisted of brackish or fresh water like the alkaline lakes in Africa, fed by the Lake Sea, the descendant of Paratethys.

Over mountainous coastlines set much further back than today's, the waters of the great rivers plunged downwards to swirl along the bottom of the deep canyons geologists have discovered underneath the sediment at 2000-3000 meters below sea-level, along the coast of the western Mediterranean, where the beds of modern rivers still run. Because of the change in their equilibrium profile, the Nile, the Rhone and the Ebro flowed towards a plain which was 1000 meters below current sea-level, carving out the surrounding areas and carrying away tons and tons of sediment, which would then fill up the basins downstream, carved out by the rivers themselves, with wide fans of layered detritus mixed with marine sediments which can be found today at the edges of the continental slope.

About 5.5 million years ago a gigantic earthquake, probably associated with eustatic movements, was responsible for the rebirth of the Mediterranean. The dike which separated the sunny but by no means monotonous Mediterranean panorama from the Atlantic Ocean, broke.

The Gibraltar threshold collapsed and a mass of water estimated by scientists at 1000 times that of the Niagara Falls, began to pour inwards. It took thousands of years and a 10-20 meters lowering of the mean oceanic sea-level to fill our sea and make it what it is today. Since then the Mediterranean has been a temperate sea and has strengthened its association with the ocean by which it was, and still is, fed. Despite this its level is a long way from constant. In the last million years, for example, it has changed several times, falling and rising around 80-100 meters in the last 18,000 years alone, covering caves once inhabited by man and which can only be explored by underwater speleologists today.

Finally, the Quaternary glaciations had important consequences for the Mediterranean.

The effects seem to have been particularly notable not so much on the water temperature as on the changes to the currents around the Strait of Gibraltar, which ushered in alternating currents of cold, deep water from the Arctic and warm, surface, water from the tropics. Each of these acquaeous masses brought with it each time ecologically opposed fauna and flora, whose limits of diffusion were determined by the adaptive capacity of each individual species and the continued existence of conditions which were favorable to their installation.

B

B - Many of the grottos found along the coast of Italy were formed as a result of karstic phenomena which could occur only where land emerged from the water: they therefore offer further evidence of the variations in sea level.

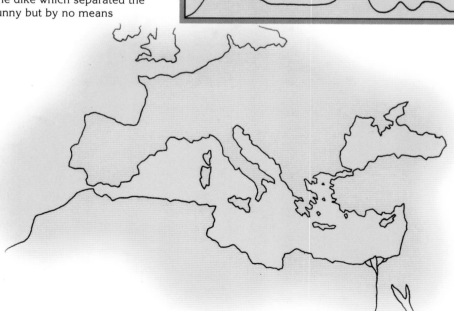

Shown here is a simplified section of the floor of the Mediterranean, stretching from Gibraltar through the Sicilian channel to the Levantine basin.
This map illustrates the Mediterranean as we know it today, with its familiar boundaries, islands and straits.

PHYSIOGNOMY OF THE MODERN MEDITERRANEAN

The movements of the plates which still collide on the Mediterranean seabed and which were the cause of the birth of this historically complex sea, are responsible for the fragmentation of the entire basin and how it would look if the conditions which led to the almost total disappearance of the waters in the distant past were ever to be repeated. Although it is possible to sail from one end to the other without touching land, the layout of

A - Underwater exploration could be said to have originated in the Mediterranean and it has certainly helped make many more people familiar with this sea.

B - The clear warm waters of the Mediterranean have undeniably played an important part in bringing man to know and love the sea.

C

A

B

D
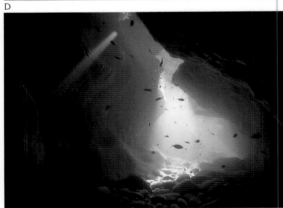

the continental and coastal masses means that the uniformity of the Mediterranean is only apparent and that two main basins can be identified, not only geographically, but climatically and biologically too: the western Mediterranean and the eastern Mediterranean. The western basin, separated by the Sicilian Channel, is characterized by large, abyssal, plains, while the eastern is more uneven and is dominated by the Mediterranean Ridge system. Nautical charts of the Mediterranean show that below the surface the

C - A lighthouse and a diver swimming in transparent waters are both symbols of the long-standing relationship between man and the Mediterranean.

D - The light outlining the entrance to the caves is like a distant memory of when part of the Mediterranean sea bed was above the water level and subjected to erosion by atmospheric agents.

E - Underwater rocks are often the result of the erosive action of waves and atmospheric agents. The latter have been able to perpetrate their action for hundreds of years, especially during the great glaciations of the Quaternary, when the level of the sea was many tens of meters lower than it is now.

seabed is incredibly irregular, with a succession of intersecting ridges, valleys, trenches and canyons from Gibraltar to the Bosporus. A feature common to the whole basin is the smallness (about 20% of total the seabed) of the continental shelf i.e. the strip of land which extends the continents below sea-level to a depth of 150-200 meters, making it the most interesting part for us. The main such areas are in the Northern Adriatic, off the Tunisian coastline, between Sicily and Malta, around Sardinia and Corsica and, last of all, in the Aegean. The two

G

H

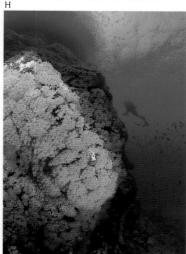

E

F

F - The Mediterranean's favorable geographical position and the fact that it is a closed sea are both factors in maintaining a constantly mild temperature throughout the basin. Even the minimum winter temperatures, caused by the rising currents and the mingling of the waters, rarely go below 13 degrees Centigrade and only then in a few places.

G - The colors of the Mediterranean are the most obvious demonstration of the wealth and variety of life forms which live on and colonise its bottoms. The common red star (Echinaster sepositus) can be considered one of the Mediterraneanis symbols: it is found close to the surface, on rocks or amongst the posidonia meadows.

H - Twenty-five kilometers from the island of Lampedusa, Lampione reef is one of the wildest and most isolated spots in the Mediterranean; it is also frequented by large sharks. The water all around is so clear that the outline of the towering rock can be seen from a depth of even twenty or thirty meters. This part of the Mediterranean, with its warm water, offers an ideal habitat for organisms of practically tropical origin and color.

biggest depressions in the Mediterranean (the Balearic and the Tyrrhenian basins), on the other hand, are separate from the islands of Sardinia and Corsica. Although many islands are constituted by parts of the seabed which has risen up above the surface of the water, as is the case with Cyprus for example, it should not be forgotten that underneath the Mediterranean runs a system of ridges originating from the compression of the rocky seabeds of the opposing masses of Africa, Europe and Asia. This was the origin of the big ridge situated south of Greece, Crete and Turkey and the two lesser ridges to the east and the west of it, one close to the Italian peninsula and one near Cyprus.

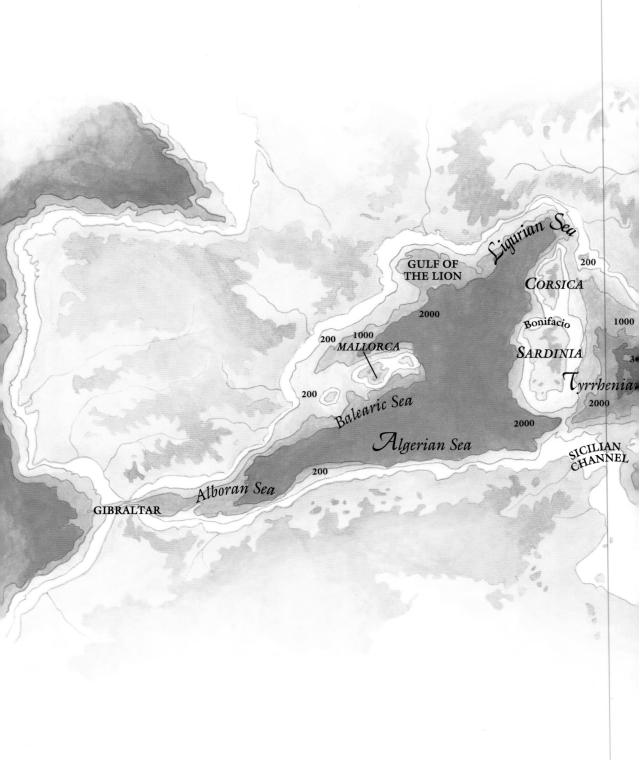

GULF OF
THE LION

Ligurian Sea

CORSICA

200

2000

200

1000

1000

MALLORCA

Bonifacio

SARDINIA

200

Balearic Sea

Tyrrhenian

3

200

2000

Algerian Sea

2000

Alboran Sea

200

SICILIAN
CHANNEL

GIBRALTAR

The rapid geographical, climatic and geological changes which are observable across the Mediterranean and the considerable variety of seabed topography make it possible to divide the basin into distinct units which can be considered semi-sealed. The western region, for example, includes the Alboran Sea and the huge depression of the Balearic, or Algerian-Provençal, basin. Corsica, Sardinia and Sicily mark the perimeter of the Tyrrhenian basin which is separated in its turn from the Adriatic Sea by the Apennine mountain chain. The Ionian and Aegean Seas and the Levant Sea, cut off by deep trenches and archipelagos, make up the eastern Mediterranean.

Adriatic Sea

200

1000   2000

Black Sea

2000

STRAIT
OF OTRANTO

Bosporus

Dardanelles

Aegean Sea   *Sea of Marmara*

Ionian Sea

3000

PELOPONNESE

1000

SICILY

MALTA

5093

200   3800   4800

4000

2000   1000

3000   *CRETA*   3000   *CYPRUS*

2000

3000   *Levant Sea*   2000

200   2000   200   3000   1000

2000

1000

SUEZ
CANAL

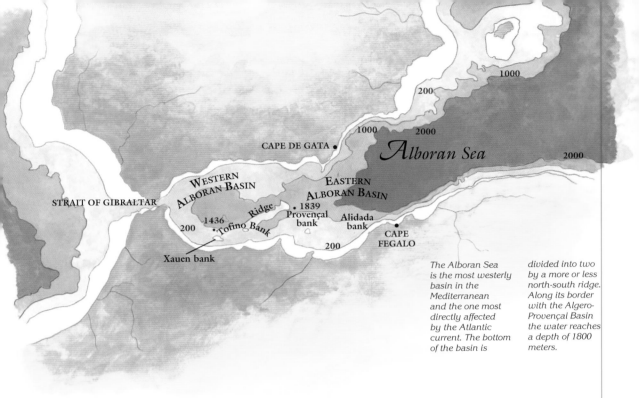

200
1000

CAPE DE GATA •
1000   2000

Alboran Sea

2000

2000

WESTERN
ALBORAN BASIN

EASTERN
ALBORAN BASIN

STRAIT OF GIBRALTAR

200   1436
Ridge
• Tofino Bank

• 1839
Provençal
bank

Alidada
bank

CAPE
FEGALO

200

Xauen bank

The Alboran Sea is the most westerly basin in the Mediterranean and the one most directly affected by the Atlantic current. The bottom of the basin is divided into two by a more or less north-south ridge. Along its border with the Algero-Provençal Basin the water reaches a depth of 1800 meters.

A

B

A - Down its whole length the Spanish coast known as the "Costa del Sol" overlooks the Alboran Sea.

B - A small bank of clouds hangs over the narrow arm of water which separates Spain from Morocco. This channel, the Strait of Gibraltar, was the equivalent of Hercules' pillars which, for the ancient Greeks, marked the extreme edge of the known world. The slight difference in the color shows where the waters of the Atlantic flow into the Mediterranean.

THE ALBORAN SEA

The Alboran Sea opens into the Mediterranean at the mouth of the Strait of Gibraltar and extends right to the Balearic basin, from which it is separated, according to the International Hydrographic Organization, by an ideal line joining Cabo de Gata in Spain and Cape Fegalo in Algeria. Bordered by Spain, Morocco and Algeria, it covers a surface area of 54,000 square chilometers and has a maximum depth of approximately 1500 meters in the western sector and 1200 meters in the eastern sector. The continental shelf which extends to the 100-200 meters bathymetric line, the most interesting part for scuba divers, varies in width from 2 to 10 kilometers along the Spanish coastline and to the south, along the North African coast, has a maximum width of 18 kilometers. The island of the same name lies in the center of the Alboran Sea; it is a small volcanic island, no higher than 10 meters at any point, surrounded by a seabed which plunges to a depth of 1800 meters in the Alboran trench, which is connected to the Algerian basin.

C - The Rhone Delta, where this important river meets the sea is an area of great interest in terms of natural environment and scenery.

D - Along the rugged coast of Liguria the folded, rippling surface of the rocks was produced by the uplifting action of forces deep in the bowels of the Earth.

GULF OF THE LION

Rhone coniod

Ebro conoid

CORSICA

VALENZA DEPRESSION

BALEARIC ABYSSAL PLAIN

SARDINIA

MENORCA

MALLORCA

IBIZA

2801

ALGERIAN-PROVENÇAL BASIN

200

1000

2000

2000

1000

200

2000

2000

1000

200

THE ALGERIAN-PROVENÇAL BASIN

This is the largest physiographical area of the western Mediterranean, roughly triangular in shape and lying between the Gulf of Valencia, the Ligurian Sea and the Alboran Sea. It has a surface area of 240,000 square chilometers and a maximum depth of 2800 meters. In several points, off the mouth of the Ebro, for example, the continental shelf is as wide as 60 kilometers and even 72 kilometers in the Gulf of Lions. Its point of minimum width (from 3 to 9 kilometers) is found in the area between Toulon and Genoa, a coastal strip distinguished by many deep canyons, extending for many kilometers into the open sea. The islands of Mallorca and Menorca share a common shelf, but Ibiza is separated by a seabed which falls to depths of up to 800 meters. The threshold between Sardinia and Tunisia separates the Tyrrhenian basin from the Algerian one. In the center of the basin is the vast, Balearic plain, surrounded by a seabed varying in depth from 2600 to 2800 meters, inside which is wedged the fan of sedimentary deposits created by the Rhone.

This is the largest physiographical area of the western Mediterranean, roughly triangular in shape and lying between the Gulf of Valencia, the Ligurian Sea and the Alboran Sea. It has a surface area of approximately 240,000 chilometers and a maximum depth of

2800 meters. In several points, off the mouth of the Ebro, for example, the continental shelf is as wide as 60 kilometers and even 72 kilometers in the Gulf of Lions. Its point of minimum width (from 3 to 9 kilometers) is found in the area between Toulon and Genoa, a coastal strip

distinguished by a series of numerous, deep, canyons, extending for many kilometers into the open sea. The islands of Mallorca and Menorca share a common shelf, but Ibiza is separated by a seabed which falls to depths of up to 800 meters. The threshold between Sardinia

and Tunisia separates the Tyrrhenian basin from the Algerian one. In the center of the basin is the vast, abyssal, Balearic plain, surrounded by a seabed varying in depth from 2600 to 2800 meters, inside which is wedged the fan of sedimentary deposits created by the Rhone.

21

A

B

A - The white cliffs of Bonifacio plunge into the waters of the strait, one of the main shipping routes between the Tyrrhenian Sea and the Provenáal Basin.

B - Vulcano, one of the Eolie islands, is the exposed summit of a submerged volcano, part of a small volcanic chain which is a feature of the Tyrrhennian Basin.

communicating passages with the adjacent basins. To the north a deep channel leads to the Ligurian Sea, rising to a threshold at 300-400 meters below the surface. The Strait of Boniface between Corsica and Sardinia gives access to the Algerian basin across a seabed whose depth never exceeds 50 meters. The strip between Sicily and Sardinia which communicates with the Algerian basin is much wider and the channel descends to depths of 2000 meters. The Strait of Messina, which provides a passage to the Ionian Sea, has a threshold of approximately 100 meters.

The Tyrrhenian Basin is the deepest in the western Mediterranean. Considered by many as a kind of still-developing, small-scale ocean, it has a chain of volcanoes - some on land, some submerged - in its south-eastern corner

THE TYRRHENIAN BASIN

The Tyrrhenian basin is almost 3800 meters and is the deepest part of the western Mediterranean. The seabed is dominated by a large number of structural ridges and volcanic heights which correspond to underwater mountains like the ones named after Marsili, Vavilov and Magnaghi between Sardinia and Calabria. These summits, once above water, climb to heights of 2900 meters from the surrounding abyssal plains which in ancient times were real plains. Some of these abyssal plains have been revealed as beaches from 15 million years ago. The abyssal plains cover very small areas. An arc of terrestrial, insular or submarine volcanoes, including Vesuvius, Etna and Stromboli, occupies the south-eastern part of the basin and is connected to the seismic area which traverses Calabria in southern Italy.
The width of the continental shelf off Corsica and Sardinia varies from 5 to 25 kilometers, while along the coastline of the Italian mainland between La Spezia and the Gulf of Policastro it varies from 5-10 kilometers to over 65 kilometers in the Tuscan archipelago section. The basin is closed except for four

GULF
OF
VENICE

ADRIATIC
CONTINENTAL
SHELF

MID-ADRIATIC
TRENCH

200
200

200
1000

ADRIATIC
SHELF

1230

STRAIN OF
OTRANTO

200
1000

1000

Jonian Sea

The Adriatic Sea is divided into three areas of increasing depth: the deepest is in the bottom south-east, closest to the deep throughs of the Ionian basin.

of irregular ridges which could be old coral reefs which have been covered with more recent sedimentation. In the center of the basin between Apulia and Albania lies the Adriatic plain, which has an average depth of around 1000 meters and a maximum of over 1200. From here the seabed rises towards the Otranto threshold, at 800 meters below

THE ADRIATIC SEA

The Adriatic Sea covers an area of approximately 135,000 square kilometers, has a maximum depth of 1230 meters and lies in a wedge between Italy and the coastline of the ex-Yugoslav Republic and Albania. It communicates with the Ionian through the Strait of Otranto. It can be divided into three distinct parts based on the main features of its seabed: a continental shelf to the north and the center and a southern basin. The northern area is entirely under the influence of the Po delta and from the north right down to the Ancona barrier slopes slowly and very gradually to a maximum depth of just 75 meters. The central part (from Ancona to Gargano) on the other hand features a closed, jointed depression known as the Central Adriatic trench (depth 266 meters) which stretches southwards in a channel whose average depth is 160 meters. The southern part is more varied, with a continental shelf which widens south of the Gargano to a width of 80 kilometers then narrows to 20 kilometers at the most southerly point of Apulia. In this section the edge of the shelf has a small series

C - The Adriatic is known for its low-lying coasts and sandy shores.

D - Parts of the rocky coastline of the Gargano region are covered with stands of Aleppo pine (Pinus halepensis), a tree typically found around the Mediterranean.

C

D

Geographically the Ionian Sea is the largest of the Mediterranean basins, extending from Europe to Africa. It is here - at the so-called Hellenic Trench - that the Mediterrean reaches its deepest point. In its most profound depths flows the deep current of the Eastern Mediterranean.

A

A - Lampedusa is an island formed of limestone. Although politically part of Italy, geographically it has more in common with Africa. It is separated from the African continent by shelves rarely deeper than 100 meters; closer to Sicily the water's depth drops to more than 800 meters.

THE IONIAN SEA

The Ionian Sea is in the central Mediterranean and stretches from the African coast of Libya and Tunisia to Southern Italy and Greece. It covers an area of approximately 616,000 square kilometers and reaches a depth of 5093 meters in the Hellenic Trench, the maximum depth surveyed anywhere in the Mediterranean. It has the largest abyssal plain in the eastern Mediterranean, but it too is divided into smaller plains separated from each other by underwater mountains and plateaux. It is, therefore, possible to identify a Sicilian basin, with a maximum depth of around 3600 meters with a peak of 4013 m, closed in the north by the Messina threshold and broken in the south by part of the Mediterranean Ridge. The southern region includes the plain of Sirte where the seabed reaches depths of 3847 meters The Hellenic Trench runs alongside the Mediterranean Ridge towards the east. It lies at the base of the edge of the Greek continental shelf and stretches for over 300 kilometers at an average depth of 3000 meters. The Herodotus Trench lies along the edge of the Libyan continental shelf at 3000 meters and is separated from the threshold of the same name by the underwater peak, also of the same name, at 3400 meters. The continental shelf comprises two main sectors. The first begins with the Avventura Bank between Sicily and Tunisia, continues along the Sicilian coastline until it joins the Maltese elevation, from where it plunges eastwards. The larger of the two parts, the biggest in the Mediterranean, lies along the Tunisian coast (the Gulf of Gabes) and extends right to the Italian island of Lampedusa, which geologically is part of Africa. The northern sector of the Ionian continental shelf gradually narrows along the Libyan coastline to a little under 4 kilometers wide at Cape Raís al Hilal.

B

C

THE AEGEAN SEA

The Aegean Sea, which separates Greece and Turkey, is the start of the eastern part of the Mediterranean. It covers an area of over 180,000 square kilometers and is characterized by the presence of over 200 islands stretching like a necklace across the whole of its surface. It is connected to the Ionian Sea by the shallow (56 meters) Gulf of Corinth. The Crete sub-basin is in the south of the Aegean and is bordered by the islands of Kythera, Crete and Rhodes. The many passages through these islands into the Mediterranean vary in depth between 300 and 800 meters. The principal feature in this sector is the Cretan Trench, an arc which runs from the Gulf of Argolis to Rhodes, reaching a maximum depth of 2500 meters. To the north-east of the Aegean basin is the Sea of Marmara, 10,350 square kilometers, which communicates with the Mediterranean through the Dardanelles Strait and via the Bosporus with the Black Sea. There is a trench in the middle consisting of three small consecutive depressions, the deepest of which reaches 1389 meters and is connected to the Anatolian Trench, which is the continuation of the North Anatolian fault.

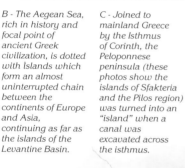

B - The Aegean Sea, rich in history and focal point of ancient Greek civilization, is dotted with islands which form an almost uninterrupted chain between the continents of Europe and Asia, continuing as far as the islands of the Levantine Basin.

C - Joined to mainland Greece by the Isthmus of Corinth, the Peloponnese peninsula (these photos show the islands of Sfakteria and the Pilos region) was turned into an "island" when a canal was excavated across the isthmus.

The Aegean Sea is famous for its countless islands, big and small. In the very center is the almost legendary island of Santorini, rocked by a tremendous eruption which has been linked with the disappearance of Atlantis.

200

200
1000

DARDANELLES

200

Sea of Marmara

200

1000

200

PELOPONNESE

200   1000

1000

Aegean Sea

200

4000   2000

RHODES

3000

1000   1000   4000   2000

CRETAN TRENCH   3000

CRETE

2000

THE LEVANT SEA

This region of the Mediterranean includes the most eastern part and is bordered to the west by an ideal line running from Cape Raís al Hilal in Libya to the island of Gavdos facing Crete. It covers a surface area of 320,000 square kilometers with a maximum depth of 4384 meters and is closed to the north by Crete, the Dodecanese archipelago and by Turkey. The continental shelf is particularly developed both off the Gulf of Iskenderun, due to the presence of numerous rivers which together form a wide delta and off the Nile delta , but it is very narrow between Turkey and Syria. The continental escarpment has many canyons: the Pliny (4834 meters) and the Strabone (3720meters) trenches run between the Mediterranean Ridge and the underwater peak Ptolemy. In the Sea of Levant the ridge runs east-north-east and rises to 700 meters above the surrounding abyssal plains. It, too, can be divided into several sub-basins, according to the nature of its seabed: Herodotus, Cyprus, Anatolia, Cilicia and Rhodes.

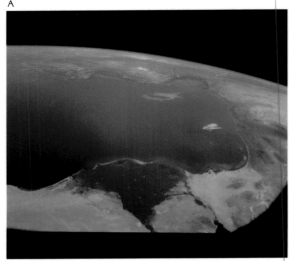

The Sea of Levant is the hottest part of the Mediterrean. It receives the inflow of water carried by the Atlantic current and part of the intermediate-layer current originates here.

RHODES 3000 4000

ANTALYAN BASIN

ADANA BASIN 200

CRETE

CYPRUS 1000

Levant Sea

Herodotus Mountain

MEDITERRANEAN RIDGE 1620 2550

2680 LEVANT ABYSSAL PLAIN

1850

2200

1000

1000

2000

1000

200

1000

200

200

Nile conoid

Azov Sea

200
1000
1000
2000 *Black Sea*
2243
1000
200
1000
1000

BOSPORUS

Sea of Marmara

A distinctive feature
of the Black Sea is
its low salinity,
caused by fresh.
water runoff.
As a result its water
is stratified and
layers of practically
de-oxygenated water
form below 150-200
meters. A weak
surface current flows
in the direction of the
Mediterranean.

THE BLACK SEA

The Black Sea is even more of an
inland sea than the Mediterranean,
to which it is connected by the Sea
of Marmara and the Bosporus Strait
(depth 40 meters). In part at least
this relationship can be compared
to the one between the main
Mediterranean basin and the Atlantic
Ocean. Bordered by the countries
of eastern Europe and Asia Minor,
the Black Sea covers a surface area
of 423,000 square kilometers and
has an average depth of 1272
meters, with a maximum of 2212
meters. It is greatly influenced by
the fresh water of the Danube, it
can in fact be compared to a huge
estuary, and by its considerably
stratified waters, which are the
result of the difference in salinity
between the surface and the deeper
layers. Within the Black Sea the
continental shelf is wide on the
western and northern coastlines.

C

D

C - The Bosporus
has played an
important part
in the history of
the Mediterranean.
This arm of land
divides two
continents and two
seas: the Sea of
Marmara and the
Black Sea.

D - The Strait
of the Dardanelles
separates the
Gallipoli Peninsula,
in Europe, from Asia
Minor. It also links
the Sea of Marmara -
and hence the Black
Sea - with the
Aegean and entire
Mediterranean.

A SEA AT THE COURT OF THE SUN

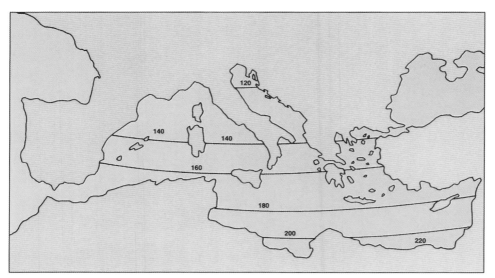

This diagram shows the intensity of the sun's rays (in calories per square centimeter) in the Mediterranean basin in December. The differences evident between the Mediterranean's northern and southern regions play a fundamental part in biological and other cycles of this sea.

A

B

A - Stormy seas send waves crashing onto the shore. The swell has important effects on marine environments since it stirs up the water and performs the essential function of redistributing nutrients.

B - The cooling of the Mediterranean's waters marks the onset of a period of renewal for its resources. Due to thermal inertia however the lowest seawater temperatures are recorded only towards the end of winter on land.

SUN, WIND AND RAIN

However strange it may sound, it is not Neptune, god of the sea, who is the protecting deity of the Mediterranean, but Apollo the sun-god, born on the sparkling, floating island of Delos which he ordered to be anchored ever after in the center of the Aegean Sea.
Since drying up the Mediterranean in the past, this bright heavenly body has never ceased to exert power over it as the determining influence on everything which gives it life and mobility. The currents, the temperature, the salinity, the density of its waters and, consequently, all the forms of life it hosts, depend exclusively upon the sun and certain favorable features of the water. Water is an extraordinary compound: two hydrogen atoms and one oxygen atom combined made it possible for life as we know it to exist and even now condition its survival. The compound born of their union is the best natural solvent there is and has the capacity to dissolve many substances; it can accumulate and store heat, it unites many points on the planet through the water cycle, but it is actually the sun which provides the conditions for many of these phenomena to work.

The Mediterranean has a charmed climate and this is reflected in the fact that since time began it has been a magnet; it abounds in relics left behind for us by those who have seen the passage of the classical civilizations along the shores of the Mediterranean as a fundamental stage of life and for life. Less poetically, but more practically, at the summer solstice, solar radiation on the Mediterranean shores and the sea which bathes them is one of the highest in the world, at over 22 kilocalories per square centimeter in the Levant Sea and 18 in the Western Mediterranean. Such high values, in association with the Mediterranean's relative isolation, make the waters pleasantly warm but, curiously, they do not increase the rate of evaporation much, as there is little wind in the summer and the air is warm and humid. During the winter on the other hand, the water is warmer than the air above it (cooling and heating always come from above) and the winds are relatively dry and off the land. Mistral, Bora, Vardarac (a wind which blows in the Aegean Sea), Scirocco and Meltemi are the winds which influence the rate of evaporation most and which, together with the sun, transform more than 3000 cubic kilometers of water into water vapor every year, a much greater quantity, on average, than over similar areas

28

of the world's other oceans. But the heat exchange with the atmosphere does not just cause water evaporation. It also sets off a series of mechanisms by which the entire Mediterranean is moved and transformed into a gigantic machine, capable on the one hand of modifying its chemical, physical and biological properties, depending on the particular basin in question and on the other of making them remarkably uniform on a global scale and endowing them with their very Mediterraneanity.

Once again the key to everything is the sun, although the sea is the indispensable element which makes its action manifest. Thermalinertia is a property of water, which means that it can absorb heat slowly and release it just as slowly. The surface of the sea can, therefore, take the energy from the sun's rays and store it in the water underneath, which acts as an immense storage heater. Of course, not all the sun's energy is transformed into heat. Most of it is reflected as soon as it hits the sea's surface, while another part is lost by irradiation during the night. But what remains becomes in some ways part of the sea's assets, especially in the spring and summer. The size of this column of heated water increases gradually until it reaches a maximum which coincides, on average, with the end of the

summer. Of course, it is the coastal waters which are most affected by the seasonal rhythms and the daytime/night-time alternation, for despite its smallness, the surface temperature of the Mediterranean varies widely: more than 25°C between the warmest and the coldest points. After reaching its maximum size at the end of the summer, the deep layer of heated water begins to shrink and to lose its heat in the autumn and winter and the thermal equilibrium is inverted during these seasons. So the waters are warmer than the atmosphere above them and have a pleasing effect on the coastal towns, which are distinguished by the famed "Mediterranean climate". One of the effects related to the heating of the water is a change in its density. This effect is not felt directly by humans but it has enormous repercussions on the Mediterranean's physics and biology. This change is not equal all over the water, which once more reveals itself to be an anomalous compound, reaching its maximum density at -4°C and not at 0°C, its solidification point, as demonstrated by gigantic icebergs. As a result, the increase in temperature reduces the density of sea water which proceds to float as a natural consequence of this. The action of the winds further modifies this equilibrium and causes a mixing of the upper

C - Rough seas over a prolonged period of time speed up redistribution processes triggered by the lowered water temperature in winter.

D - Once winter has set in, the appearance of the sea-bed changes as many species vanish or "shrink": only the stalk of the mermaid's cup (Acetabularia) remains visible while Cystoseira lose their fronds.

Illustrated here is the situation resulting from the intense rays of the sun in in July. As can be seen, light and heat are uniformly distributed over much of the basin; paradoxically, however, the areas where luminous intensity is greatest are the coldest ones in winter.

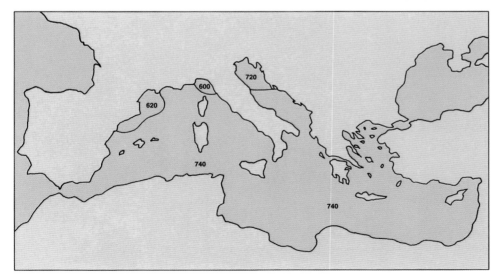

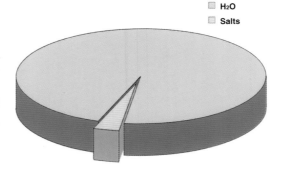

☐ H₂O
☐ Salts

Sea water contains 3.5% dissolved salts on average. However, salinity is usually measured in salts per kilo of water, so the average salinity of sea water is expressed as 35 per thousand.

A

B

layers which transmits the heat to the water beneath, which then heats up in its turn, at least until the thickness of the heated layer is excessive and other forces, particular those connected with friction and viscosity, come into play to halt its diffusion at the limit marked by the thermocline.

This is the name given to the layer which separates the warm waters from the more thermally stable zones, which are only slightly influenced by the sun's rays and are therefore colder and denser. The deeper the thermocline becomes, the weaker the action of the wind and the greater the tendency of the hot and cold layers to remain separate.

The existence of the thermocline is easy to prove and a discovery every scuba diver can make personally during any summer dive without needing to have any knowledge of the physics of water.

At a depth which varies, depending on the area, between 20 and 30 meters, a sudden change in temperature will be felt. Sometimes the change is so definite that different temperatures can be felt in the body's extremities. In other cases the thermocline causes a definite variation in light transmission and the limit between warm and cold water, which also differ in density, can actually be seen with the naked eye as a thin, indistinct and trembling layer which forms, rather like the evanescent cushion of air which rises from the tarmac on roads grilled by the summer sun. The superimposition of layers of water of decreasing temperature, initially gradual and then becoming more rapid, determines highly stable conditions which can block convection and exchanges between the surface water and the

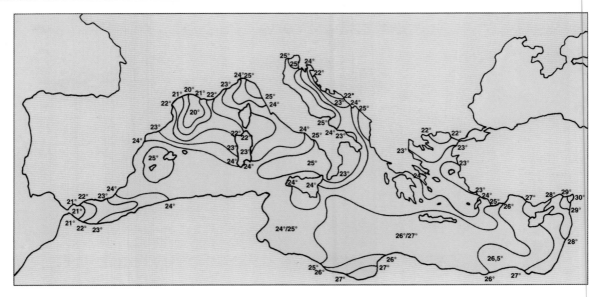

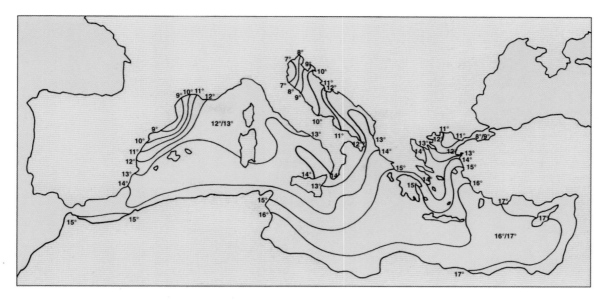

deeper masses, not only of heat, but also of nutrients and forms of life (see Chapter 3). When the direction of the prevalent flows of heat is inverted, the surface water cools and increases in density. It then tends to sink and the vacuum it leaves is compensated by the influx of deeper water. This causes convection, starting off a kind of huge merry-go-round which mixes the whole column of water. This happens more markedly at the onset of the cold season, but during the summer too periods of bad weather can cause a temporary cooling of the surface water. The influx of cold water from the deeps is also influenced by the stronger winter winds, which not only bring about more rapid cooling and increase the density of the water, thereby increasing evaporation, but also increase turbulence and mixing. In these conditions the thermocline rises progressively towards the surface until it disappears.

In winter the temperature of the Western Mediterranean becomes uniform from the surface to the seabed at 13°C, a unique homothermal situation which characterizes our sea and which makes possible an almost total, mixing of the water over vast areas, bringing the deep, nutrient-rich layers to the surface and carrying precious oxygen down to the bottom.

Thus the joint action of the winds and of the sun produces a heat cycle in the Mediterranean whose mechanisms, although their absolute values might vary from year to year and place to place, have remained constant for thousands of years and had a determining influence on all forms of life, both aquatic and terrestrial, in its basin.

The waters of the Mediterranean heat up during the summer, creating numerous areas in the different basins where temperatures are the same. These thermal "subregions" are of enormous importance: not only do they influence man's way of life, they also affect the ecology and biology of all living creatures.

In winter the thermal barriers separating the various basins become less accentuated and in some cases allow redistribution of species, horizontally as well as vertically.

- ■ Other
- ■ Potassium
- □ Calcium
- ▫ Magnesium
- ▫ Sulphates
- ▫ Sodium
- ▨ Chlorine

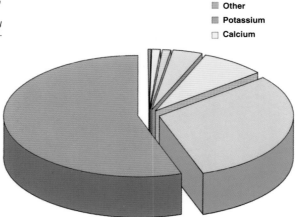

Of these dissolved salts (diagram 2), the largest percentage consists of chloride and sodium, the elements which make up common sea salt (sodium chloride).

CIRCULATION OF THE MEDITERRANEAN WATERS

The Mediterranean, by definition, is a sea enclosed by land, but the series of alternating beaches and steep cliffs, sand dunes and pine forests are not its only boundaries. Sonar soundings reveal that underneath the surface too there are marked boundaries which delimit the different basins described in the previous chapter. All of these are separated from the waters of the rest of the globe by the 13 kilometers of the Strait of Gibraltar and the threshold beneath, the last stage of an obstacle race which the waters of the Mediterranean have to embark upon before being reunited with the waters whose children they are, although the Atlantic Ocean would be hard pushed to recognise them.From a quick glance at the charts of the Mediterranean seabed it is easy to see there are several obligatory passages to be made in order to cross it from east to west. Starting with the furthest boundary of the Bosporus, the first in the sequence of eastern basins is the Dardanelle Strait. From here, the search for a westwards passage involves following the heights and valleys of the Aegean Sea before being pushed into the Ionian, bordered by the Strait of Otranto between Italy and Albania, moving on to the Sicilian Channel and the Strait of Messina which open up into the western basins.

Then come the seabeds of the Strait of Sardinia or the Corsican Channel which point the way out of the Tyrrhenian towards the vast plain of the Balearic basin and the heights of Alboran, the outpost of Gibraltar. However much of a labyrinth this visual itinerary across the charts may seem, it is only a simplified version of the complicated itinerary followed by the Mediterranean currents which are, once again, influenced by the sun. The Mediterranean can be viewed as a sea going downhill or, paradoxically, like a huge tank which is never full. Its intense evaporation rate is the cause of a shortfall in water which is compensated almost totally by

a constant influx of water from the Atlantic, which flows through the Strait of Gibraltar like a huge river as wide as the strait and more than 70 meters deep. At a speed varying in different points from 60 to 100 centimeters per second, the Atlantic pours from around 36,000 to 38,000 cubic kilometers of water into our sea - an astonishing quantity, indeed one where the enormous figures involved make it difficult to comprehend.

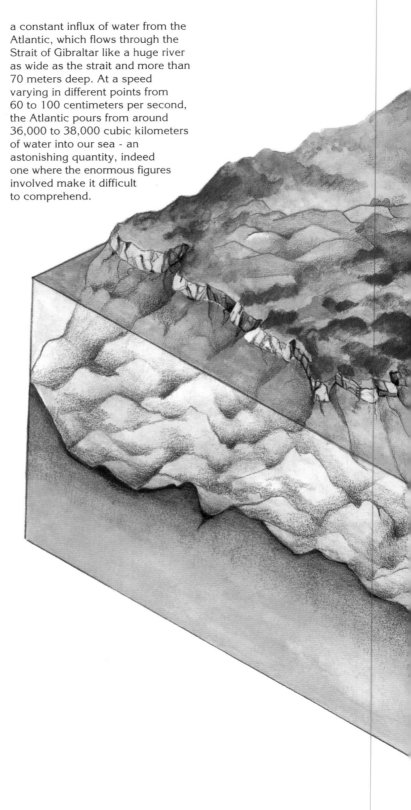

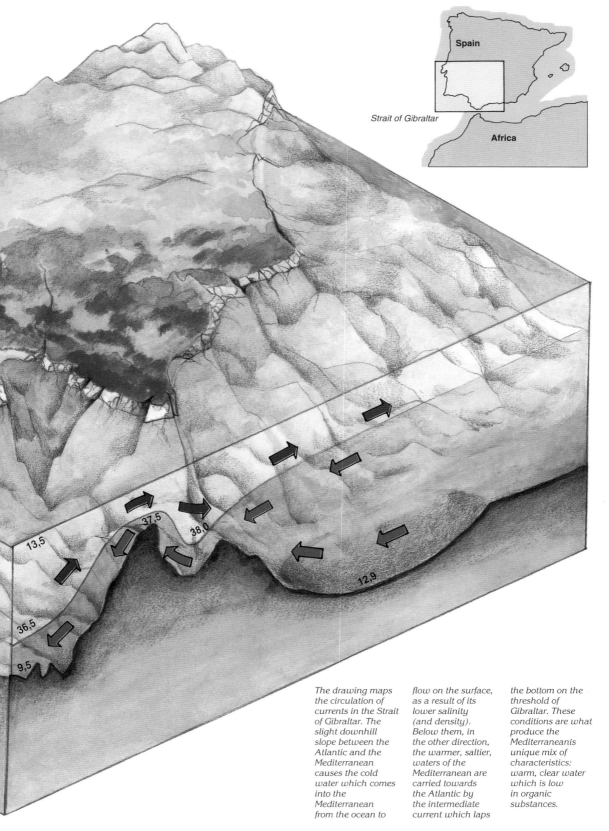

Spain

Strait of Gibraltar

Africa

13,5

37,5

38,0

36,5

9,5

12,9

The drawing maps the circulation of currents in the Strait of Gibraltar. The slight downhill slope between the Atlantic and the Mediterranean causes the cold water which comes into the Mediterranean from the ocean to flow on the surface, as a result of its lower salinity (and density). Below them, in the other direction, the warmer, saltier, waters of the Mediterranean are carried towards the Atlantic by the intermediate current which laps the bottom on the threshold of Gibraltar. These conditions are what produce the Mediterranean's unique mix of characteristics: warm, clear water which is low in organic substances.

33

A

B

C

We can get an idea of it, however, when we realize that one cubic kilometer alone corresponds to around one billion cubic meters which corresponds to a thousand billion litres. The influx of these Atlantic waters is aided by a slight anomaly: a tiny step which lies between the two sides of the strait. Not only is the average sea-level between 10-15 centimeters lower in the Mediterranean, but as the water travels east the difference in level tends to increase until it reaches 30 centimeters as a result of the greater density of the waters in the Levantine basins.

It is difficult to calculate the real flow rate of the river which feeds the Mediterranean, a concept which immediately recalls the river Ocean of the Ancient Greeks, and the calculation is rendered even more complex by a series of seasonal and meteorological factors. Not only does it peak at the end of the summer and reach its minimum in winter, but it is also influenced by the alternation of pressure on both sides of Gibraltar, which influences the exchange of water in both directions.

The Mediterranean not only fills up, but also empties at the same rate, thanks to a current which flows beneath the Atlantic current carrying just 5% less water, due to the reduced salinity, in the opposite direction.

The Phoenicians appear to have been aware of the existence of this counter current, because it was a widespread practice to lower their sails tens of meters under the surface of the water to take advantage of the current flowing out of the Mediterranean. In this way they countered the thrust of the surface current which was hard to sail against with boats powered only by oars and by sails unsuited to sailing against the current.

As with much historical knowledge, and due partly perhaps to the transformation of the Mediterranean away from being the center of the known world, the Phoenician sailors' knowledge of such phenomena was lost and it was only at the end of the 17th century that the Bolognese nobleman Luigi Ferdinando Marsili, considered to have been the father of oceanography, hypothesised them. It was not until 1870, during the exploratory mission by the English ships the Porcupine and the Shearwater carrying numerous scientists charged with investigating the Strait of Gibraltar, that it was rediscovered.

The waters which enter the Mediterranean have different characteristics, however, from those of the sea they fill up. The mixing process is slow and gradual - the Mediterranean is in no hurry. Recent estimates put at 150 years the time it takes for a drop of water from the Atlantic to pass back through the Columns of Hercules from whence it came and in this long period of time it loses its identity: it becomes loaded with salt and with heat, changing into the Mediterranean. Such a slow time scale is, of course, a risk, as the evacuation of the ever-present pollutants is very slow, but were it not so, the sea which bathes three continents, 17 countries and more than 200 millions of inhabitants, could no longer be referred to as "ours".

D

E

F

G

D - The Otranto Channel is another crucial point in the complex division of the Mediterranean into submarine basins. Here the Adriatic narrows and the sea-bed starts to slope towards the very deep shelves of the Ionian basin.

E - The currents which pass close to the coastline of Puglia and through the Otranto Channel, the barrier separating Italy from Albania and Greece, flow on with undiminished strength towards the open seas of the Ionian Basin.

F - The Strait of the Dardanelles is one of the last channels through which the Mediterranean Sea passes and one of the points separating Europe from Asia. The Mediterranean is the only sea bordered by three continents.

G - The Bosporus marks the extreme eastern limit of the Mediterranean. Beyond this point is the Black Sea, which could almost be considered a smaller-scale Mediterranean.

A - Encompassed by land, the Mediterranean Sea depends on inflows and outflows of water through the Strait of Gibraltar.

B - The Strait of Bonifacio - the first example of an international protected area - separates the islands of Sardinia and Corsica. This narrow channel has a direct influence on the hydrodynamism

of the water here, which is often rough and swept by strong currents.

C - Land masses form obligatory passages not only for man but for the waters of the Mediterranean too. The Strait of Messina separates the Tyrrhenian and Ionian Basins. Inflows and outflows of water masses between the two create currents known to man since antiquity.

THE SURFACE CURRENTS

The surface of the Mediterranean is marked by liquid roads which are not just there for the use of sailors and oceanographers, but for the many organisms which move, actively or otherwise, following currents which travel the high seas, or move along the coastline or insinuate themselves into one of the basins. Whatever their destination and their itinerary, these surface currents mainly follow cyclonic-type routes i.e. they travel clockwise.
The main current circuits are in the Balearic Sea, the Ligurian Sea, the Ionian Sea and the Adriatic Sea. There seem to be many of them and they appear a long way from each other, but they all originate in the same mass of Atlantic water, whose destiny can be followed almost kilometer by kilometer after it enters the Mediterranean. Modern telemetric techniques carried out by the

B

A

sophisticated sensors of satellites specialized in geographical studies have allowed scientists to visualize and follow the water of this ocean as it flows in through Gibraltar. Thanks to its different temperature and density it shows up as a muddier, darker, current driving a wedge into the blue of the Mediterranean.The waters of this current acquire volume and strength as they run first along the Atlantic coastline of Morocco and then upwards toward Gibraltar. Part mixes straight away with the exiting water, but more than 80% flows into the Mediterranean, rapidly losing speed after the acceleration of the Venturi effect

in the funnel-shaped strait and flowing mainly on the surface, because although it is colder it is also a good deal less salty. At the beginning of its Mediterranean journey the Atlantic Current follows the African coast, although less closely than one might expect and in spite of the Coriolis effect which tends to push it southwards, because the rocky spur at Punta Almina and Ceuta is too sharply angled for the enormous mass of water to follow its outline. Practically "spat"out from Gibraltar, the current continues its course, flowing up towards the Spanish coast, helped by the strong anti-cyclonic (i.e. anticlockwise) current centred in the Sea of Alboran.
Soon after its meeting with the Mediterranean the shape of the sea-bed and the meteorological conditions combine to split the current: one part moves north towards the Balearics and the other, larger, part continues along the north-African coast forming the Algerian Current heading towards the Sicilian Channel. However, a part of this current

is diverted north towards south-western Sardinia, before heading back towards the southern sector of the Balearic Sea. Another part influences the north-western sector directly, travelling right up to Corsica where it mixes with the part of the Atlantic Current which has been heading for the Balearics right from the start. Once rejoined, the two flows, together with other, secondary currents, form the current known as the Ligurian-Provençal-Catalan current, which runs west along the Ligurian coastline from France to Spain. This current crosses the Gulf of Lions, one of the most dynamically complex areas of the whole of the western Mediterranean, not only because of the effect of the Mistral and the shape of the seabed, which are uneven and studded with canyons, but because of the presence of the Rhone and other, minor, rivers, which during periods of heavy rainfall bring about a marked dilution of the water, with important consequences on local oceanographic conditions. Meanwhile, the Algerian Current loses little or nothing of its power and continues its journey eastwards, although it is once more forced to branch before entering the Sicilian Channel. The shallow seabed of the Sherky Bank diverts around one third of the volume of water in the current towards the Sardinian Channel and into the Tyrrhenian, where it forms a cyclonic current which varies widely over the course of the year. Part of it hits the Ligurian coastline and joins up with the Ligurian-Provençal-Catalan current. In the Western Mediterranean these main currents are associated with other, weaker, ones, mostly in the southern zones, which form cyclonic vortices about 50-250 kilometers in diameter. These vortices are present all the year round, although their characteristics do change from season to season. Some of these marginal currents, like the ones originating along the Algerian coastline, can affect water up to several hundred meters deep and in many cases they tend to move out towards the open sea where they gradually lose their identity. The remains of the Algerian current which passes through the Sicilian Channel enters the Eastern Mediterranean running centrally between Africa and Sicily, its flow rate differing according to the seasons. In winter it is almost double its summer volume. It runs centrally

because the new current is wedged between a homogeneous mass of cold waters driven upwards by the winds which blow on the south-western coast of Sicily and the huge vortices of the anticyclonic currents which dominate the coastlines of Tunisia and Libya, occupying virtually the whole of the Bay of Syrte. At 20 degrees of longitude it forms the African current, which runs along the coastline of the Levant Sea, where it becomes the Asia Minor current and affects the Turkish coast as far as the island of Rhodes, where it borders a cyclonic current extending to Cyprus. There are other cyclonic currents in the Aegean, the Adriatic and the Ionian Seas. In addition to these currents, which are to varying degrees all coastal, the Central Mediterranean current, which flows above the Mediterranean Rdige, is of considerable importance in the Eastern Mediterranean. This current, blocked in the south bythe powerful vortex of the Marsa Matruk anti-cyclonic current on the Egyptian coast, travels mainly towards the Sea of Crete and Cyprus, strengthening the Asia Minor current, while a secondary branch first heads east before turning south.

C - The whirling foam and eddies caused beneath the surface by passing waves can help us imagine the effect of huge waves on the water masses below.

D - Currents play an important part in the luxuriant growth of Neptune grass: on one hand they ensure the meadows are constantly supplied with "fresh" water; on the other, they carry sediment which is caught in the leaves and falls to the bottom, ready to contribute to the further growth of the grass.

C

D

This map shows the direction followed by the Mediterranean's surface current which originates from water masses flowing in from the Atlantic through the Strait of Gibraltar. As it proceeds eastward, this uniform mass breaks up and is transformed, some of the water reaching the furthermost basins of the Sea of Levant

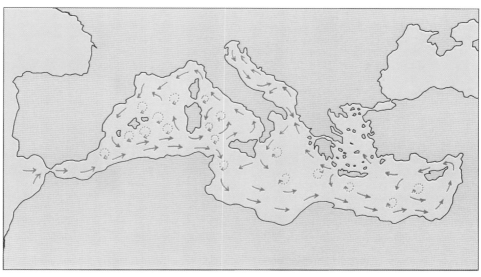

INTERMEDIATE CIRCULATION

The currents which form in the Mediterranean as a result of the influx of the Atlantic and of evaporation do not only affect the surface. There is an intermediate layer of water which lies in a band between a depth of 200 to 600 meters. It is in continual movement, following the route of the surface currents, but in the opposite direction. This "counter" current is manifest right from its origin in the Sea of Levant at the opposite extreme of the Mediterranean from Gibraltar, where the highest levels of salinity are recorded as a result of the gradual transformation of the chemistry of the Atlantic water as it crosses the Mediterranean. The Mediterranean climate increases its salt content, terminating in the east at 39.1 grams per thousand, equal to 39.1 grams of salt in every 1000 grams of water. In view of the fact that the average salinity of the Atlantic when it enters the Mediterranean is a little above 36 grams per thousand, this increase is a marked one and, given the volume of water involved denotes tons more salt. Water with these characteristics tends to be unstable and sensitive to changes in the winter temperature, when the sea's surface temperature falls below 17 degrees under the influence of north winds.
Thanks to the mechanisms described at the beginning of the chapter, this causes an increase in the density of the surface water and the formation of a layer 100-150 meters thick comprising the warm salty water from the summer and the Atlantic water which has stayed below the summer thermocline. The lower limit of this mixture of waters of differing origins borders on a colder and more homogeneous intermediate layer, formed during the previous winter and capable of spreading more or less horizontally over the entire eastern basin, where it forms a layer at between 200 and 700 meters, feeding a flow heading towards the Western Mediterranean

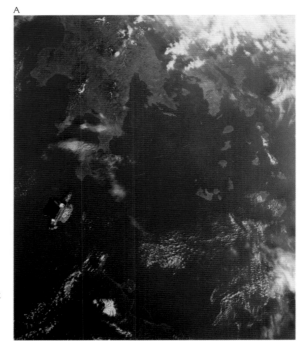

A

B

at an estimated 0.7 million cubic meters per second, which is equal to 2/3 of the water which flows out at Gibraltar. The flow towards the Atlantic seem therefore to be equal to their area of provenance, as the eastern basins occupy around 2/3 of the entire Mediterranean basin. After looking at the origin and the fate of the intermediate current, it might be interesting to study the stages of its journey westwards. Driven by the new winter water, the water of the Intermediate Levantine current goes deeper, widening out into broader sections. Scientists who have followed the route of the current over long periods have discovered the existence of a main branch which crosses the entire

Mediterranean and two secondary branches: a weaker, southern current, which hits the Gulf of Syrte and a larger, northern one in the Ionian Sea, which travels along the eastern coastline of the Adriatic, past the Strait of Otranto, at a depth of around 300 meters.
In the Adriatic the current mixes with the cold winter waters from the north of the basin and then exits towards the Ionian. On the threshold of the Sicilian Channel, the cross-roads of the main currents and the demarcation line between the Western and Eastern Mediterranean, the intermediate current's main flow is held close to the bottom by the Atlantic water above it and is channelled between

A -This satellite picture shows the tract of sea surrounding Greece and the island of Crete, where the Aegean Sea meets the Ionian and Levantine Basins. From an oceanographic standpoint this is one of the most interesting areas of the Mediterranean: here the flow of surface currents ends and intermediate currents form.

B - The intermediate currents which circulate in the Mediterranean at depths between 200 and 500 meters. originate in the Levantine Basin. Here the warm, saline water of the surface layer cools and sinks, moving other masses of water westward.

two long, narrow passages which run alongside each other but at different depths: 430 and 365 meters respectively.

The wider and deeper of the two, closer to the Sicilian coast, faces north and it is through here that the eastern water flows into the Tyrrhenian.

The part of the current which goes through the other channel is initially diverted west and then north towards Sardinia. This way the Tyrrhenian is the beneficiary of the greater part of the Intermediate Levantine current, whose denser and colder waters rise up the basin in a long, anti-clockwise, movement.

Locked between the Italian peninsula and the block of the larger Mediterranean islands, the waters from the east lose some of their original characteristics before exiting along the southern coast of Sardinia and joining up with the secondary branch heading north. The intermediate current, transformed but still homogeneous and recognisable, once more heads north-west, driving along the Spanish coastline and forming a single liquid lode which, compressed between the surface waters and the deep waters, is forced to head upwards towards the Gibraltar threshold and out into the Atlantic, closing the cycle started such a long time earlier.

The arrows indicate the direction of flow of the intermediate Levantine current of the Mediterranean. At depths between 200 and 700 meters, this current moves practically as a counterflow to the surface current. It carries warm water, rich in nutrients, out of the Mediterranean and is thus one of the factors that contribute to the low productivity of this sea.

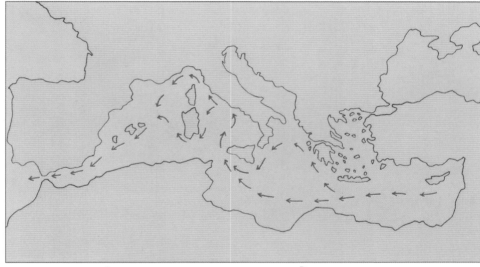

C - Intermediate currents originate from transformation of the chemical and physical properties of surface water as a result of evaporation and winter cooling.

D - The intermediate layer flows across the Mediterranean through the same straits and over the same sills which regulate the flow of surface currents.

C

D

On account of their characteristics, the water flows that form the deep currents of the Mediterranean remain in the very deepest and coldest basins, as can be seen in the sketch.

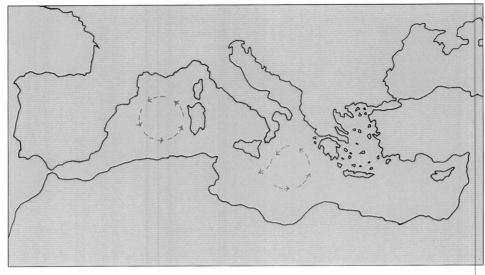

A

A - The origin of deep currents is connected with the cold winter winds that blow in the Upper Adriatic and in the Gulf of Lion. The mistral can whip up violent storms - like the one in this photo - which cause enormous water masses to rapidly cool and move to deeper layers.

DEPTH CIRCULATION

Below the Intermediate Levant current, protected by a barrier hundreds of meters deep, the waters of the Mediterranean seem to tire of the continual coming and going to and from the ocean and look for a niche in which they can rest in a situation of relative calm. The thresholds which divide the different basins finally come into their own, functioning as barriers and no longer as obstacles to be overcome, isolating the masses of cold, homogeneous water which hardly ever mix with each other and which are once again separated by the two great blocks of seabed which rise up between Sicily and Africa. Yet, despite this isolation, in spite of the fact that it is identifiable and has a physiognomy of its own, the liquid kingdom which occupies the bathymetrical 1000-meter band cannot be cut off from the rest of the Mediterranean's waters and is subject to the same laws. Once more, in fact, it is the reduction in water temperature and its increase in density that create these particular deep waters originating in the Western Mediterranean, prevalently in the Ligurian-Provençal basin, in the center of the Gulf of Lions. The formation of the deep waters is not, however, as simple as that. It requires the joint action of strong and prolonged winds and of severe winters to produce water which is sufficiently cold and dense to fall down to the bottom of the Mediterranean without the intervention of other forces. And it is the unique meteorological conditions found in winter in the Gulf of Lions, which did not lightly gain its infamous reputation amongst sailors as one of the most feared of all patches of sea, which create these idealconditions. The cold surface waters coming from the coast are massed in a small area and other waters are attracted from the depths below. This accumulation process continues until the masses of water involved become like a gigantic, liquid skyscraper of dubious stability. It only needs a few days of the Mistral sometime between February and March to destroy its apparent stability, lowering the temperature the little that is necessary to transform the accumulated water into an avalanche plummeting down towards the bottom of the sea. In fact, the definitive transformation is simply a consequence of vertical up and down movements produced by the wind as it acts on the volume of water produced by the forces of nature. Some scientists have compared the movements which take place in this gigantic sphere of cold water to those which occur in a pan of boiling water. Vortices, side-slips, descents and upward surges all take place simultaneously, involving a volume of water

estimated by some scientists at 5,000 cubic kilometers - a drop compared tothe entire Mediterranean, but still 1000,000,000,000 litres of water multiplied by 5,000. The movements which take place in this mass demonstrate the size of the forces involved, which are capable of acting at depths of more than 2,000 meters on the oldest and outermost strata of the deep water, which is partially, although very slowly, replaced.
It has been calculated that the deep waters in this sector of the Mediterranean has changed over a period of 100-150 years.
The prolonged time of residence and the extraordinary genesis of these waters do affect the characteristics they reveal in chemical-physical analysis. Water samples taken at the center of the Western Mediterranean show such remarkably consistent temperature and salinity values (12.7°C and 38.40 per thousand respectively) that in 1970 a proposal was put forward to use them as the standard for oceanographic analysis. It was certainly an important discovery, but the Mediterranean was and is a changing sea, as the most recent surveys show. Analyses carried out in 1972 and 1973 in virtually the same areas led to the discovery of anomalous layers of water - slightly warmer (+ 0.03°C) and saltier (38.42 per thousand). These higher values disappeared in the years which followed, only to reappear at the beginning of the 1980s in the Gulf of Genoa and off the coast of Sardinia. The presence of anomalous masses of water like these is seen now as proof of the progressive warming of the Mediterranean, a much more

tangible sign of which is the movement northwards of the areas of distribution of many species which were until now found only in much more southern regions. These in their turn have for some time now been undergoing a partial tropicalization as far as fauna is concerned, with the Lessepsian migrations which have led more than a hundred species from the Red Sea (mainly fishes and molluscs) to cross the Suez Canal and colonise the Eastern Mediterranean in particular.
This area, which has not been sceintifically studied to the extent of the western part, has a similar reserve of deep water which accumulates and circulates in the abysses of the Ionian - the deepest part of the Mediterranean. Below the 1000-meter mark there is a homogeneous layer of cold water created by phenomena which occur on a distant part of the surface. The winter cooling and the Bora, an

impetuous, icy, wind which blows from the east of Europe, cool the temperature of the waters in the relatively shallow Northern Adriatic. The special characteristics of the waters in this part of the Mediterranean, including the tides which play such a large part in the "high water" phenomenon which affects Venice, make it the most Atlantic of the Mediterranean Seas. This extremely cold and dense water gives rise to a current which heads south along the coast of the Italian peninsula until it reaches the relatively warm, salty water from the east, with which it mixes, before its density causes it to fall, past the Strait of Otranto, towards the abysses of the Ionian.
Even in this case it is not totally segregated. Convection and internal currents moving a few hundreds of litres per second ensure that these waters are slowly replaced, a process which is completed every 120 years.

B

C

B - Deep currents circulate in permanently dark, cold zones where they help keep the water homogeneous (so much so that it is taken as the standard when conducting analyses).

C - An Alicia mirabilis *with completely extended column sees its tentacles all facing in the same direction as an effect of the current. Looking at this photo, we can imagine the possible effects of currents on the sessile organisms which populate really deep waters.*

LIGHTS AND TRANSLUCENCY

Much of the attraction of the Mediterranean seabed for divers, especially around some of the more isolated islands, lies in the color of the water. Just as a cloudy sky lets through the rays of a hidden sun, illuminating the earth with brushstrokes of light looking like symbolic images of the divine, so when the Mediterranean meets the sun it produces incredible harmonies of color and light. The effect is similar to that of the rays of light which filter through the stained glass windows of the great cathedrals, illuminating the dark naves. The light penetrates the wave curtain to create reflections

B - Together with waves and currents, light is the main form of energy that animates the sea. But not all rays of the solar spectrum can penetrate water to the same degree.

C - Light intensity can extensively condition the distribution of organisms under the water. Green algae prefer well-illuminated zones while sponges and other invertebrates make their home on poorly-lit walls.

A - The red of these starfish would be almost invisible had it not been illuminated by the flash of an underwater torch.

Because reds are filtered out of the ambient light, they tend no longer to be seen by man at a depth of only a few meters.

and bands of light which disappear into the deep blue, transforming the liquid atmospheres into a series of stage sets draped in soft silks. In shallower water the movement of the waves is transformed into a pattern of changing light which wakes and enlivens the seabed below.

But light is more than an attraction, it is the sea's main source of energy. Without it there would be none of the movements caused by heat exchange, there would be know currents and, more especially, there would be no living creatures. Light is so indispensable to the sea that not only does it absorb it, but it appropriates, it to change it into heat and life. There are three fundamental categories of light radiation which reach the sea: ultra-violet, infra-red and visible light. The first two types of radiation are invisible to the naked eye, special instruments or films are needed to reveal these "lights", which make the chromatic world very different from how we see it. Although unseen, to our eyes at least, these

two components of the solar spectrum have important effects on the sea, especially the infra-reds, for although they disappear after the first three meters, they contribute greatly to heating the water. The effects of the ultra-violet rays, which are active down to around 30 meters, are harder to interpret. What is certain, is that they are dangerous for many forms of life, to the extent that scientists believe the blue coloring of so many types of organisms found in the so-called blue layer, the shallowest part of an ocean, is not only a form of camouflage, but also a chromatic defense against ultra-violet rays. However, they appear to be fundamental for the metabolic functioning of some species. The function of visible light is more clearly understood: the sea acts first of all like a mirror and then like a huge filter. The sea's surface reflects the sun's light rays in proportion to its height on the horizon: at midday less than 5% of the sun's rays are reflected, but when the sun is close to the horizon the quantity of rays reflected rises to 40%.

These percentages increase considerably if the sea is rough. The mirror effect not only explains the different luminosity between a watery environment and a terrestrial one, but also the differences between the shorter underwater day and the longer one of the world above the water. The residual light then has to tackle the optical properties of water and of the particles suspended in it. The suspended particles modify the transparency of the water and interfere with the pathway and penetration of the light's rays, which are reflected in all directions, while the water acts as a powerful selective filter. The different wavelengths and therefore the different colors which make up white light, are intercepted and blocked by the increasing thickness of the water. The first color to disappear before

continue their journey right to their limits. In a transparent sea such as the Mediterranean this can be 800-1000 meters, a depth at which there is still enough light to fix an impression on a photographic plate - as Auguste and Jacques Piccard discovered in 1953 when diving in the Bay of Naples to a depth of 3150 meters. Despite this more than adequate explanation of what happens to light and the color of the sea, all divers are astonished when strobes or flashguns revive the bright colors of many Mediterranean seabeds. No-one has yet found the answer to why at some depths the sea looks like a splendidly colored cloth. Although biology teaches us why certain algae are still brightly colored at great depths, it has not yet unlocked the significance of other organisms which, although blind, are brightly

D

E

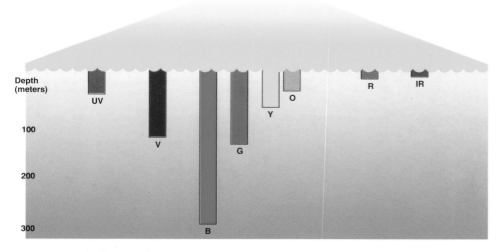

Depth (meters)

UV

100

V

200

G

Y

O

R

IR

300

B

Here can be seen how the water filters the light's rays. The different wavelengths, which correspond to the different colors of the solar spectrum, are selectively blocked at precise depths.

UV = ultra-violet
V = purple
B= blue
G = green
Y = yellow
O = orange
R = red
IR = infra-red

our eyes is red. Even in clear waters like those of the Mediterranean a starfish will look brownish once it is below the 4-meter threshold and it is only by taking it back up to the surface that its characteristic red color will reappear. Orange is no longer the same color from 20-25 meters down and yellow loses its brightness towards 50 meters. The rays which are most absorbed are the greens and the blues, the sea's own colors, which

colored, such as sponges or ascidians and many coelenterates. Perhaps fishes are capable of experiencing the same feelings as we do; but without artificial light and in a world dominated by greens and blues what could they ever see? We do not know enough about our world to answer, but the mystery of this universe, of which we form part, offers us a way out: those colors, like Everest, are there to be discovered and enjoyed and, in time, understood.

D - The sea fan forests which cover vast sections of sea bed are one of the most visible proofs of the relationships between the physical environment and living things. The development of gorgonians is, in fact, closely linked to the presence of currents and to the intensity of the light.

E - The scarcity of nutrients and the unique currents which dominate the Mediterranean are amongst the main causes of its notable transparency. In the Mediterranean, green and blue radiations, the colors of the sea, reach depths of 800-1000 meters, where it is still possible to expose photographic plates.

LIFE IN THE MEDITERRANEAN

A jellyfish followed by a group of fish pulses rhythmically through the water above rocks which are hidden by algae. A common sight along the Mediterranean coastline, uniting representatives of the three categories of marine organisms: plankton, nekton and benthos. These categories of living creatures transcend the official classification systems, by considering only the most intimate, essential relationships between organisms and their aquatic environment. Plankton includes all those plant and animal organisms which, by their size or by their structure, either do not or cannot move independently of the currents and the waves. Nekton, on the other

A - It is not uncommon for sailors crossing the Mediterranean to find themselves in the company of groups of cetaceans. These striped dolphins (Stenella coeruleoalba) seem determined to prove that the story of Arius is not pure legend.

B - The Pelagia noctiluca is one of the best known jellyfish in the Mediterranean. Many bathers have had the misfortune to feel its painful sting. If touched at night, this organism gives off a bright light.

C - The brown groupers of the Mediterranean (Epinephelus marginatus) have become a symbol of the sea's continuing struggle to survive. In areas where they are protected, these fish offer us a chance to gaze in wonder at timeless scenarios epitomizing the far-distant past of our planet and its seas.

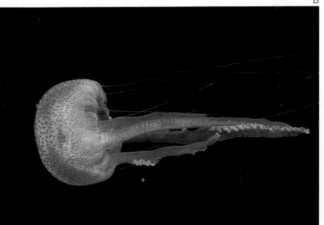

D - A large cerianthus tube dwelling anemone (Cerianthus membranaceus) reveals its double crown of tentacles in the current which sweeps the sea-floor of Scilla, one of the mythical Mediterranean sites mentioned by Homer.

hand, include only those animals such as fish, cetaceans and cephalopods, for whom the viscosity of the water and the strength of the currents represent no obstacle and which can swim thousands of kilometers from one point in the sea to another. The benthos includes immobile animals and plants, as well as ones which move on the ocean bottom or feed there. This is not a rigid sub-division, and some organisms can switch categories. For example, plankton includes the larval stages of many organisms which, in their adult forms, belong to the nektonic or benthic categories.

E - Marine life-forms do not populate only the surface layers. It is on the sea-bed that the greatest variety of species, colors and forms is to be found. The Octopus macropus is one of the most interesting and colorful cephalopods that have made the Mediterranean their habitat.

The drawing illustrates an ideal section of Mediterranean from the surface down to the greatest depths. Here is shown the wealth and variety in populations and species, by including both the small planktonic invertebrates and plants as well as the benthic organisms, right up to the big pelagic fish like tunny and swordfish and the cetaceans, from the fin whales to the sperm whales. Some of these species are commoner and more likely to be seen when diving or cruising in the Mediterranean. At greater depths, where daylight decreases until there is none at all, there are strange-shaped fish which can only be seen in museum collections or photographs taken through the portholes of bathyscaphs.

1) Stony sea urchin (Paracentrotus lividus)
2) Warty crab (Eriphia verrucosa)
3) Barnacles
4) Phytoplankton
5) Zooplankton
6) Monk seal (Monachus monachus)
7) Warty jellyfish (Pelagia noctiluca)
8) Flyingfish (Exocoetus volitans)
9) Amberjack (Seriola dumerili)
10) Sunfish (Mola mola)
11) Blackspot seabream (Pagellus bogaraveo)
12) Bottlenosed dolphin (Tursiops truncatus)
13) Dolphinfish (Coriphaena hippurus)
14) Loggerhead turtle (Caretta caretta)
15) Neptune grass (Posidonia oceanica)
16) Alcyonium sp.
17) Limpet
18) Beadlet anemone (Actinia equina)
19) Paramuricea clavata
20) Carithe (Cerithium sp.)
21) Sponges
22) Hermit crab (Pagurus sp.)
23) Octopus (Octopus vulgaris)
24) Moray eel (Muraena helena)
25) Conger (Conger conger)
26) Golden zoanthid (Parazoanthus axinellae)
27) Red mullet (Mullus sp.)
28) Pentagon star (Peltaster placenta)
29) Pelican foot (Aporrhais pespelecani)

30) Wide eyed flounder (Bothus podus)
31) Crinoid (Antedon mediterranea)
32) Prawn
33) Purple sea urchin (Sphaerechinus granularis)
34) Common red star (Echinaster spositus)
35) Scallop (Pecten sp.)
36) Songes
37) Brittle star
38) Thornback ray (Raja clavata)
39) Funiculina
40) Sea pen (Pennatula rubra)
41) Red sea pen
42) Sea cucumber
43) Brachiopods
44) John Dory (Zeus faber)
45) Little tunny
46) Pilot fish (Naucrates ductor)
47) Sardine (Sardine pilchardus)
48) Blue shark (Prionace glauca)
49) Swordfish (Xiphias gladius)
50) Bluefin tuna (Thunnus thynnus)
51) Basking shark (Cethorinus maximus)
52) Common pandora (Pagellus erythrinus)
53) Blue whiting (Micromesistius poutassou)
54) Hake (Merluccius, merluccius)
55) Fin whale (Balaenoptera physalus)
56) Blackmouthed catshark
   (Galeus melastomus)
57) Rabbitfish (Chimaera monstrosa)
58) Argentine (Argentina sphyraena)
59) Squids
60) Krill
61) Sperm whale (Physeter catodon)
62) Lanternfish (Myctophum sp.)
63) Gonostoma sp.
64) Gulper shark (Centrophorus uyatus)
65) Hatchet fish (Argyropelecus hemigymnus)
66) Macrurid (Nezumia aequalis)
67) Haloporphyrus sp.
68) Lantern fish (Notoscopelus elongatus)
69) Zooplankton
70) Sea dragon (Stomias boa)
71) Notacanthid (Notacanthus sp.)
72) Tripod fish (Bathypterois mediterraneus)
73) Viperfish (Chauliodus sloanei)
74) Zooplankton

F - The common cuttlefish (Sepia officinalis) is not easy to approach.
It beats a hasty retreat while emitting powerful jets from its ink sac. Occasionally - and especially during the reproduction period - it becomes less diffident and it is possible to take pictures that highlight its shape and color.

E

F

0

200

1000

3000

PLANKTON:
THE SOURCE OF LIFE

Summer cruising in the
Mediterranean is very likely to take
place on a perfectly calm surface,
through which the sun's rays
penetrate easily and disappear into
the blue deeps without meeting
any obstacles in their way.
This liquid mass appears to be
lifeless, but filter it through a thin-
gauge net and there is a kind of
soup, of varying density, made up
of beings whose minute details can
only be seen under the microscope.
The lens enlarges a universe of
marvels which might have come
off a designer's drawing-board,
or a out of a glassblower's
workshop, not to mention straight
from the imagination of Sergio
Rambaldi, creator of E.T. Shapes
of astonishing elegance,
geometrically perfect or strangely
composite: triangles, cylinders,
spheres, feathers, spirals, bells,
cones and flowers, fill every drop

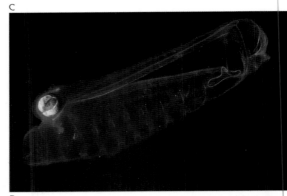

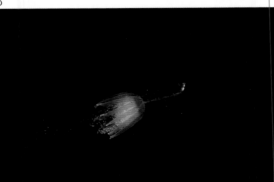

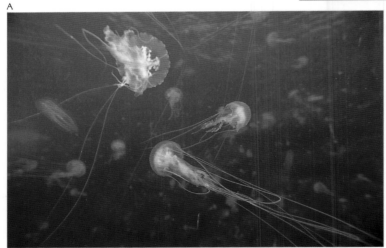

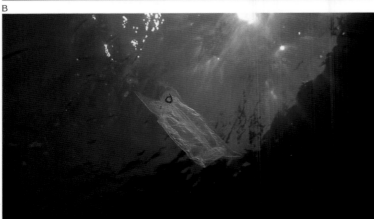

of water as they move - wriggling,
sliding or pulsing, as if driven by
invisible oars.
But it would be a mistake to
imagine that plankton is always so
small and invisible to the naked
eye. Jellyfish, siphonophores,
salps, hydrozoans, Chaetognates,
molluscs and crustaceans, which
are the most typical types of
plankton, include large species
(from a few centimeters to several
meters in the case of colonial
organisms). Nor are they invisible
and they always inspire a certain
degree of fear in humans, often
justified by their stinging defensive
weapons. However, in the majority
of cases, plankton is indeed small,
but its importance is inversely
proportional to its dimensions,
because the life of these waters
depends on it. An abundance of
plankton is considered one of the
fundamental parameters for
judging a sea's wealth and from
this point of view the
Mediterranean pays a heavy tribute
to its internal circulation and the
transparency of its waters.
Compared with other seas and a
good many oceans the
Mediterranean is, viewed overall,

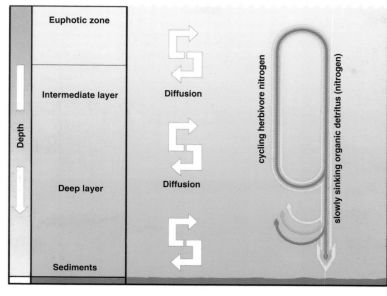

Depth

Euphotic zone

Intermediate layer

Diffusion

Deep layer

Diffusion

Sediments

cycling herbivore nitrogen

slowly sinking organic detritus (nitrogen)

The drawing illustrates the vertical distribution of some of the main dissolved salts (nitrogen and silicate) in the sea and the processes which regulate their recycling.
The diffusion processes and the rising currents in the intermediate layers permit the recycling of most of the organisms which exploit these substances either directly or indirectly. Utilization is by photosynthesis and occurs for the most part in the euphotic (well-illuminated) layer.
The sedimentation process leads to the segregation of most of these substances, which are normally only partly recycled in the deep layers and carried back up towards the surface.

a fundamentally poor sea. The Atlantic waters it receives are low in nutrients (mainly made up of nitrogen and phosphorus) while the ones which flow out at Gibraltar are much richer. The fact that most of the currents in the different basins described in the first chapter are very deep prevents the recycling of nutrients. This is especially so for phosphorus, much of which is segregated in the waters furthest from the surface and therefore from the sun, once more a protagonist in the life of the Mediterranean.

E

F

E - A fine mesh net trawled in the Mediterranean for a few minutes will capture a whole world of unknown, and fascinating, organisms. Despite their size, or lack of it, their existence is fundamental for all those macroscopic organisms, including humans, which live in and off the sea.

F - A microscopic jellyfish beats rhythmically underneath a microscope lens.

A GREAT MEADOWLAND

The most important of the components of plankton is the vegetable one. Just as one land, so underwater, plants are the first and fundamental link in the food chain which often leads to humans - just look at the lively, picturesque fish markets in the main fishing ports. But, contrary to what generally happens in our world of air, plants which grow in direct contact with the sea-bottom have their own importance in the global economy of the sea. There are very few surfaces suited to being colonised by algae and benthic

C - Detail of the feathered frond of Caulerpa taxifolia. This seaweed has only recently appeared in the Mediterranean and is one of the latest examples of how humans can cause modifications to an ecosystem.

C

D

A - The great grazing grounds of the sea are not provided, as one might think, by the big seaweeds like these laminates (Saccorhyza polyschides), but by the microscopic components of vegetable plankton.

B - The green in this meadow of Caulerpa taxifolia is of little account when compared with the amount of chlorophyll which can exist in sea water. Chlorophyll, that can be measured by special sensors lodged in satellites orbiting the earth, determines a sea's degree of

wealth or of poverty. This technique makes it possible to identify the richer, and therefore commercially exploitable, oceanic areas. In other cases, the excessive concentration of chlorophyll can signal situations of organic pollution and excessive algal growth.

plants. Sand is not always suitable, rocks are more so. Both however are dominated by the laws regulating the penetration under water of the light rays on which the life of the plants depends. It is only in the first 100-150 meters, known as the euphotic zone (i.e. well-illuminated), that plants can exploit the light to

D - The regular shape of Acetabularia mediterranea would look ordinary and rather simple if compared with the architectural perfection of some microscopic algae.

E - Apolemia uvaria, an unusual siphonophore, sometimes found caught in sea fans.

F - The trasparent tissues and broad shapes are the visible signs of the adaptation of these organisms to planktonic life.

manufacture the various substances of which they are made and which satisfy their nutritional, respiratory and reproductive requirements, starting with inorganic substances. A comparison between the volume of water in this band and the size of the sea-bottom it borders highlights the fact that the habitat available to benthic plants is much smaller than the one available to vegetable plankton, or phytoplankton, which can perform their entire life cycle in the surface waters, where they hand like a culture.

F

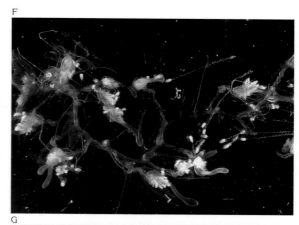

G

H

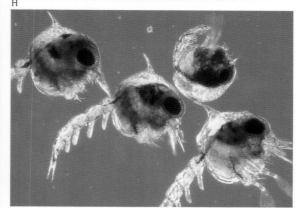

I

E

G - In many cases the tiny umbrellas of these jellyfish are the means of locomotion for organisms like hydroids, which live anchored to the bottom.

H - These planktonic crustaceans larvae, great consumers of microscopic plants, are important elements in temporary plankton (meroplankton).

I - The strange-looking organism in this photograph is destined to have a very different appearance in its adult form, as a sea worm slithering over the bottom.

THE SEASONS OF PLANKTON

Phytoplankton is compared by some to the leaves in a forest; its abundance and differentiated distribution patterns in the marine habitat depend on environmental parameters which act simultaneously, such as temperature, light and nutrient availability.

Variations in water temperature and their effect on the sea, for example, have a considerable influence on the presence and quantity of phytoplankton, especially in the upper bands; this cycle is superimposed on the heat cycle which creates the thermocline and the separation in summer of the hot, less dense, surface water, from the deeper,

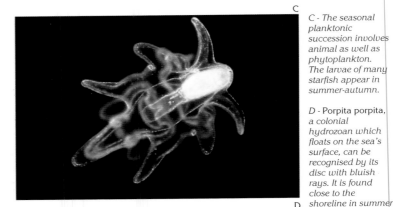

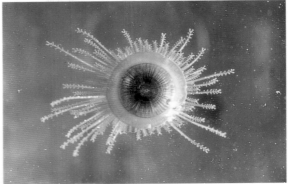

A - Padina pavonica is a brown alga found in surface waters. The surface of the thallus is encrusted with limestone, a substance used by some microscopic algae to protect themselves.

B - The stolon from which the fronds of Caulerpa taxifolia grow, looks a little like the long ribbons of monocellular algae held together by a common matrix.

C - The seasonal planktonic succession involves animal as well as phytoplankton. The larvae of many starfish appear in summer-autumn.

D - Porpita porpita, a colonial hydrozoan which floats on the sea's surface, can be recognised by its disc with bluish rays. It is found close to the shoreline in summer and autumn, when high tides sometimes drive large quantities on to the beaches.

E - The copepods are typical planktonic crustaceans, sometimes constituting more than half the total population of the Mediterranean's zooplankton.

colder strata. The summer is the least productive season in the Mediterranean.

As far as humans are concerned it is the ideal period to get to know the sea, but for the aquatic world it is a season of famine.

The stratification of the water prevents any nutrient exchange between the deeper, richer, areas and the poorer ones close to the surface. In addition, the gap between the two environments is destined to widen, as the organisms in the surface strata are forced to feed on the residual nutritive salts rapidly recycled by

bacteria alone, while deeper down the nutrients build up without being used. In these conditions scientists are sometimes faced with paradoxical situations, such as the discovery of highly productive areas where the phytoplankton are photosynthetically fully active, but where the nutrients are almost absent, just as happens in the luxuriant tropical forests.

On the other hand the intensity of the light is actually a limiting factor. Too much light blocks photosynthesis in the microalgae. The synthesis of organic

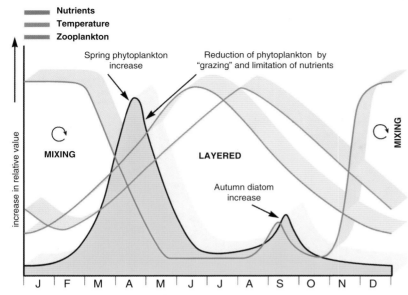

Nutrients
Temperature
Zooplankton

Spring phytoplankton increase

Reduction of phytoplankton by "grazing" and limitation of nutrients

increase in relative value

MIXING

LAYERED

Autumn diatom increase

MIXING

J F M A M J J A S O N D

The diagram illustrates the seasonal trend of phytoplankton (yellow), in particular of diatoms and zooplankton (red). It can be seen from the diagram that the spring peak in phyto concentration follows the herbivore plankton peak, which then diminishes with the decrease in resources. The green and blue lines indicate the variations which occur in the concentration of nutrients and the temperature of the sea respectively. In spring and autumn, the effect of the reduction in temperature is to bring about a mingling of the waters and, consequently, an increase in productivity. In summer, on the other hand, thermal stratification of the water prevents nutrient recycling and the development of the planktonic populations.

substances in the presence of chlorophyll, the pigment which gives the algae their color, is indeed proportional to the amount of energy available, but only up to a certain point. Above this threshold photosynthesis tends to be reduced and eventually to stop. This mechanism has very important consequences for the Mediterranean, where the transparency of the water leads to peaks of productivity (the index which measures organic substance synthesis) at depths below 50 meters, sometimes even at 100 meters - which is well over the limits posed by the thermocline barrier - where light and nutrients compensate each other.

Towards the end of the summer, with the first heavy autumn seas and the reduction in heat, the pleasant balance between hot and cold waters is upset. The hydrodynamics of the surface create turbulence and convection movements, causing vertical instability, which in its turn brings the colder, denser water, rich in nutrients, to the surface. This leads to a short, but rapid, increase in the phytoplankton. Late autumn and winter are the "fertilising" period for the marine meadows. The situation of homothermy to which the

Mediterranean tends in these months permits the water to mix easily, without any friction, from the surface to the bottom. The fertilization processes depend to a large extent upon the energy available in the form of waves and currents. It is in this way that the nutrient salts and the trace elements (copper, iron, cobalt, molybdenum, manganese) which are indispensable to the growth of the planktonic algae, are redistributed throughout the entire depth of water and removed from the segregation of the deepest layers, where they have been building up unused. This is why the coldest years, which boost the mixing of the water in the superficial and the deeper layers, tend to be the most productive too. In spring a series of favorable circumstances, especially the increase in the hours of sunlight and the availability of nutrients, create the ideal conditions for the rapid development of the phytoplankton population, with a fairly regular succession of botanical groups in the entire basin.

F

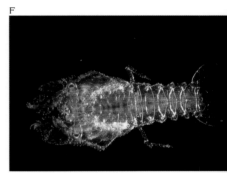

G

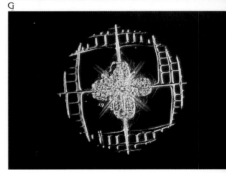

F - An advanced larval stage of a decapod crustacean (maybe a lobster or spiny lobster) caught with a plankton net. The larvae of these crustaceans tend to appear with greater frequency in springtime plankton. In winter, the most abundant crustacean larva is that of crabs.

G - Enlargement of this planktonic organism under the microscope reveals even the minutest details.

THE PLANKTON'S HARVEST

The changes to the Mediterranean during the course of the year are not, as we have seen, limited to the cycle of meteorological and oceanographic phenomena. The changing of the seasons is also reflected in the appearance of forms of certain plant life which is typical of cold and hot periods. The first to appear are the diatoms, brought by the low temperature and rough seas, both essential conditions for their growth. These regularly-shaped algae dominate the spring phytoplankton season and, to some extent, the autumn too. Rich in the silicon which is indispensable for their survival and which almost disappears from the water when they have finished flowering, diatoms have a rigid, elegantly-structured cell wall called the frustule, composed of two parts which fit together like a box and its lid. When alive, diatoms are mainly a uniform greeny-brown and under the microscope, especially the electronic scansion microscope which provides a 3-D image, they reveal a variety of shapes: stick, cigar, triangular, oval, discoid, star-shaped, step-shapes etc. Their surfaces are equally complex: pores of all sizes, thin ridges and depressions, transform the walls into works of refined marketry or cameos. All this, incredibly, on organisms which vary from a few microns to 2-4 millimeters in size. The perfection of the design is such that in the past, diatom frustules were used to check the quality of microscope lenses. Diatoms have a curious way of multiplying which looks like a forerunner of the Chinese box technique. Reproduction is by division, a rapid method and one commonly used by the smallest organisms to increase their population, as soon as conditions favorable to the species present themselves. The increase in volume of the cell contained in the two

halves or valves of the box leads to their separation. Each one of the two parts formed ends up with half the cytoplasm and a single valve. But this is by no means a problem. Each half is able to reconstitute the missing part and reform a box which is either identical or similar to the original. The terms "identical" and "similar" are not used lightly here, because each of the two parts does reform the missing valve, but with a small yet essential difference. The two halves both become lids of

the diatom box, but only the original one retains that function. The other one, which at the beginning corresponded to the (smaller) bottom of the box, can only form a smaller diatom. If this multiplication process were to be repeated thousands or millions of times - and the diatoms can multiply so rapidly that they can saturate vast areas of sea and clog the mesh of the nets use to capture them, covering them with a slippery greeny-brown mass - it is evident that the average size of a diatom is

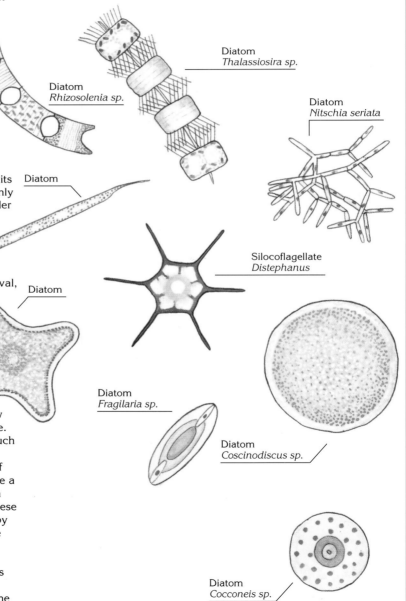

Diatom
Rhizosolenia sp.

Diatom
Thalassiosira sp.

Diatom
Nitschia seriata

Diatom

Silocoflagellate
Distephanus

Diatom

Diatom
Fragilaria sp.

Diatom
Coscinodiscus sp.

Diatom
Cocconeis sp.

54

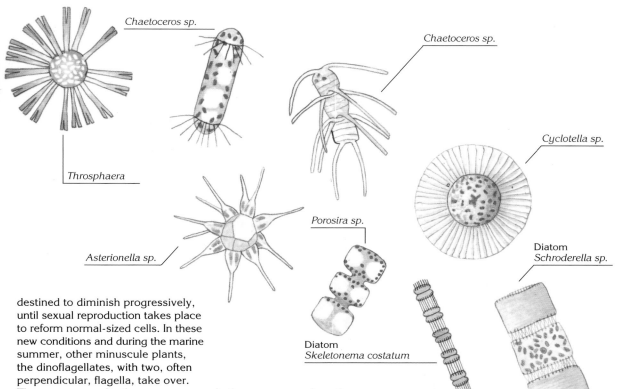

Chaetoceros sp.

Chaetoceros sp.

Throsphaera

Cyclotella sp.

Asterionella sp.

Porosira sp.

Diatom
Schroderella sp.

Diatom
Skeletonema costatum

destined to diminish progressively, until sexual reproduction takes place to reform normal-sized cells. In these new conditions and during the marine summer, other minuscule plants, the dinoflagellates, with two, often perpendicular, flagella, take over. These organs make the dinoflagellates mobile, unlike the diatoms, and within certain limits permit them to move from one place to another in the search for more favorable conditions. Often anchor-shaped, dinoflagellates also have an average of three, pointed protuberances, like thorns, one pointing forward and the others backward. Their surface is ridged like the diatom's and has differently-shaped calcite scales, between which are the two main grooves housing the flagella. The motility of many species of dinoflagellates is enhanced by the presence of sense organs which, as they can register the presence of light, can be compared to human eyes. This permits the algae to orient themselves and get to the best places for photosynthesis. However, Dinoflagellates are unusual and rather worrying planktonic organisms, physiologically a kind of Dr. Jekyll and Mr. Hyde. Some species are perfectly autotrophic and are amongst the principal primary producers of organic material in the oceans but others, although they have not totally lost their chlorophyll, are parasites of small planktonic crustaceans;

further groups, such as the luminescent *Noctiluca* are on the borderline with the animal world, as they can alternate photosynthesis with the capacity to feed on both animal and plant organisms. Dinoflagellates can multiply rapidly by binary division and give rise to sudden, quite natural, bouts of blooming as soon as environmental conditions favorable to the phenomenon present themselves.

The diagram illustrates the seasonal succession of some of the components of phytoplankton. Dinoflagellates in yellow, diatoms in blue and total volume of phyto in orange; the average concentration of the latter is marked on the axis of ordinates.

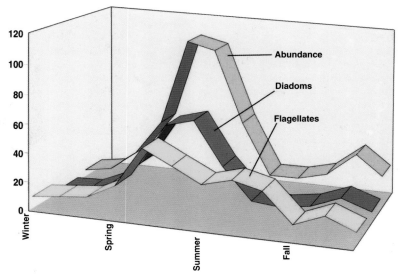

Abundance

Diadoms

Flagellates

120
100
80
60
40
20
0

Winter
Spring
Summer
Fall

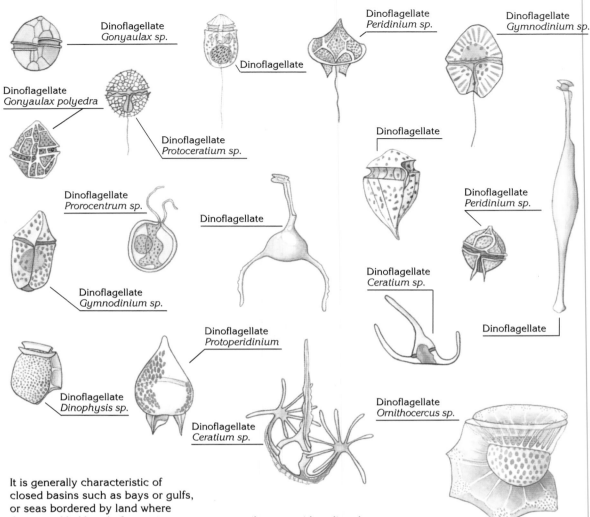

Dinoflagellate
Gonyaulax sp.

Dinoflagellate
Gonyaulax polyedra

Dinoflagellate

Dinoflagellate
Peridinium sp.

Dinoflagellate
Gymnodinium sp.

Dinoflagellate
Protoceratium sp.

Dinoflagellate
Prorocentrum sp.

Dinoflagellate

Dinoflagellate

Dinoflagellate
Peridinium sp.

Dinoflagellate
Gymnodinium sp.

Dinoflagellate
Ceratium sp.

Dinoflagellate
Protoperidinium

Dinoflagellate

Dinoflagellate
Dinophysis sp.

Dinoflagellate
Ceratium sp.

Dinoflagellate
Ornithocercus sp.

It is generally characteristic of closed basins such as bays or gulfs, or seas bordered by land where there is a likelihood of organic substances accumulating, such as the Northern Adriatic, for example. This is one of the most intensely farmed areas of the whole Mediterranean and is therefore subject to the appearance of such phenomena. At such times the sea can change its appearance in a few days, turning red, beige, yellowy-brown, grey or green, depending on the dominant species, which can achieve a density of tens of millions of cells per litre. These immense bloomings, although natural, are tangible proof of a localized alteration of the marine environment cause by an abundance of nutrients - eutrophication - which can make the aquatic environment temporarily and locally incompatible with life for many species, especially benthic and non-motile ones, either directly, by poisoning the waters, or indirectly, through the subtraction of oxygen during the respiration process of the algae and their decomposition when dead, as they are transformed into a mass of organic substance. These are not the only peculiarities of the dinoflagellates, however. Many of them contain a particular biochemical system for generating light. They wrote about it in the old logbooks - on calm summer nights, a passing boat causes lively sparks which flash in the midst of the rough water of the wave, increasingly dense, almost like sheets of fire which douse themselves in the middle of the sea until, finally, the whole of the broad, wavy, band which marks the path of the ship is lit up, a lighted path bejewelled with sparks and flashes'. The same phenomenon is sometimes seen by night-time swimmers. The impression is often one of swimming in the middle of sparks which seem to leap from the dark every time the body moves. The phosphorescence, these lights which sway and disappear as if part of a defense mechanism, is caused by the *Noctiluca scintillans*, which are similar to small globes, each with a single tentacle and other species of the genus *Goniaulax*, shaped like stylized sailing boats. These contain toxins which are potentially poisonous as they can accumulate in crustaceans, molluscs and fishes and *Peridinium*, another alga, similar to a small flask resting on a forked support. Of course, although the diatoms and the dinoflagellates are predominant, they are not the only representatives of phytoplankton in the Mediterranean. The peaks of abundance of both groups are in some way connected and are accompanied by Coccolythophora and Silicoflagellates, both minute flagellate algae. The former measure a few thousandths of a millimeter and are covered with shield-like calcite plates (coccoliths), which interlock and make these algae look like ivory balls, or bones drilled and sculptured inside in concentric circles. Coccolythophorids prefer clear waters with few nutrients, which means they find ideal conditions in the Mediterranean where, in certain periods of the year and in certain places, they constitute almost all the phytoplankton, reaching concentrations of 30 million cells per litre. It may be this very abundance which has allowed these organisms to develop their considerable adaptation variability - they can be found at depths of up to 1000 meters, where the lack of light forces them to live almost like carnivorous plants or fungi, feeding on decomposing organic substances. The Silicoflagellates are just as small. They belong to a group of algae known as the Chrysophyceae, because of their golden color, and have a siliceous skeleton made up of water-filled tubules. These create a sort of rigid frame with a polygonal base ring, with vertices extended into spines of varying length. The composition of the silicoflagellates means that their season almost coincides with that of the diatoms, but they do not disappear during the summer, but stay in the uppermost layers of the sea.

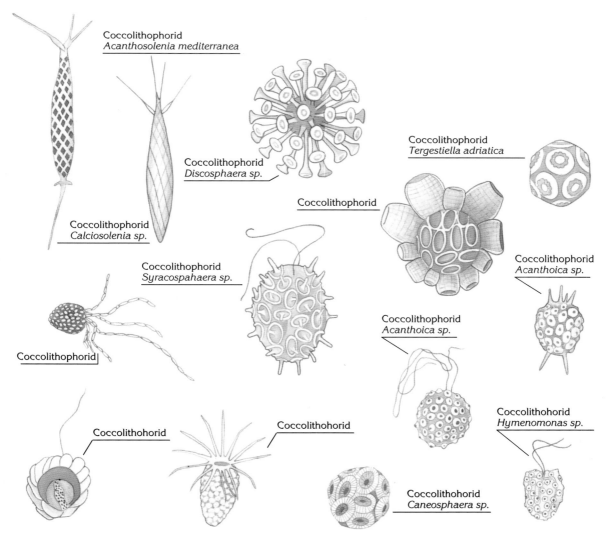

Coccolithophorid
Acanthosolenia mediterranea

Coccolithophorid
Discosphaera sp.

Coccolithophorid
Calciosolenia sp.

Coccolithophorid

Coccolithophorid
Tergestiella adriatica

Coccolithophorid
Syracospahaera sp.

Coccolithophorid
Acanthoica sp.

Coccolithophorid
Acanthoica sp.

Coccolithophorid

Coccolithohorid

Coccolithohorid

Coccolithohorid
Hymenomonas sp.

Coccolithohorid
Caneosphaera sp.

WANDERING ANIMALS

The table summarizes the average concentration of coastal plankton throughout the year. The groups taken into consideration include those organisms defined as belonging to the holoplankton, i.e. perennial plankton.

- Copepoda
- Appendicularia
- Pteropoda
- Cladocera
- Chaetognatha
- Hydromedusa
- Lamellibranchia
- Gasteropoda
- Echinodermata
- Polychaeta
- Other groups

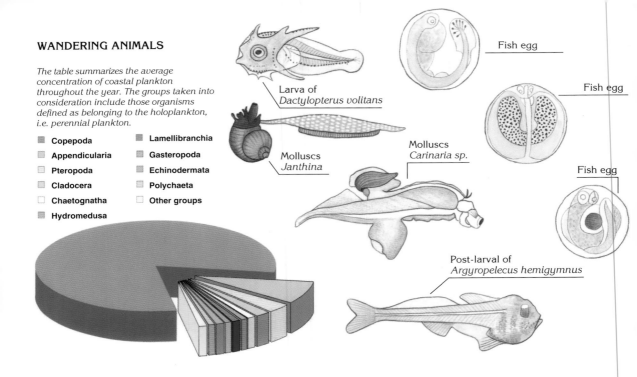

Larva of *Dactylopterus volitans*

Molluscs *Janthina*

Molluscs *Carinaria sp.*

Fish egg

Fish egg

Fish egg

Post-larval of *Argyropelecus hemigymnus*

The huge phytoplankton food resources would be largely unused were it not for the existence of other organisms which can mediate not only between the first and last food chain links, so that nothing is wasted, but also, as we saw earlier, link the vast marine dominions. What happens far out at sea can be vital to coast life, deep waters and surface waters alternate their roles and a surface diatom can determine the survival of a fish which lives in the unlit deeps. Animal plankton - zooplankton - includes representatives of organisms from all the zoological groups, from the monocellular ones which make up microplankton, to the complex, multicellular ones which belong to the megaplankton measuring more than 20 centimeters. Their alimentary habits, quite naturally, are equally varied. Alongside the herbivores, which are quantitatively dominant, there are carnivorous, predatory plankton or omnivores which feed on detritus. Some organisms, meroplankton, only belong to this innumerable series temporarily. They include the eggs and the first stages of life of many fishes, both nektonic and benthic, as

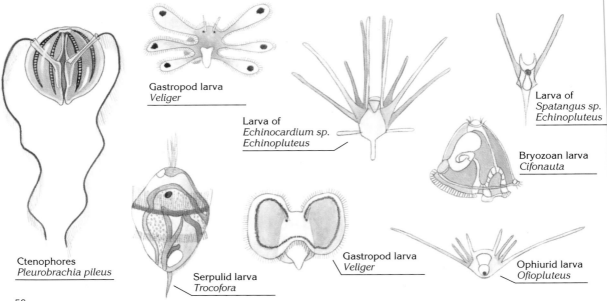

Ctenophores *Pleurobrachia pileus*

Gastropod larva *Veliger*

Larva of *Echinocardium sp.* *Echinopluteus*

Serpulid larva *Trocofora*

Gastropod larva *Veliger*

Larva of *Spatangus sp.* *Echinopluteus*

Bryozoan larva *Cifonauta*

Ophiurid larva *Ofiopluteus*

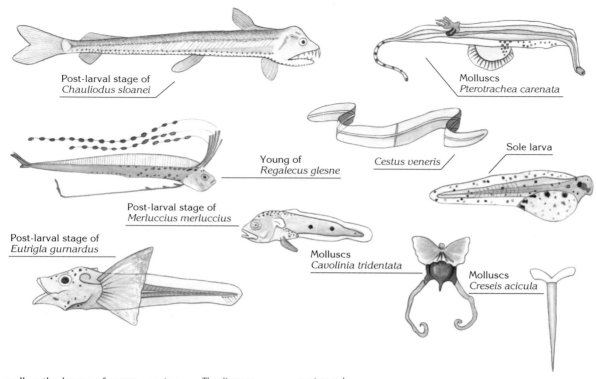

Post-larval stage of
Chauliodus sloanei

Molluscs
Pterotrachea carenata

Young of
Regalecus glesne

Cestus veneris

Sole larva

Post-larval stage of
Merluccius merluccius

Post-larval stage of
Eutrigla gurnardus

Molluscs
Cavolinia tridentata

Molluscs
Creseis acicula

well as the larvae of many species belonging to many types and classes, such as echinoderms, Ascydians, bivalves, annelids, bryozoans and a number of crustaceans, which spend a large part of their lives moving close to the sea-bottom or permanently fixed and can spread by colonising only thanks to these short periods in which they are swept up by the currents.

The diagram illustrates the average composition of coastal plankton. In addition to holoplankton, it also includes meroplankton (lamellibranches,

gasteropods, echinoderms and polychaetes) i.e. the part of plankton comprising the larval stages of species which become benthic when adult.

☐ Copepoda
☐ Appendicularia
☐ Pteropoda
☐ Cladocera

☐ Chaetognatha
☐ Hydromedusa
☐ Other groups

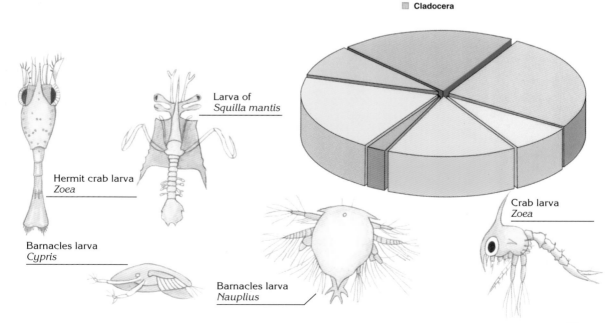

Larva of
Squilla mantis

Hermit crab larva
Zoea

Barnacles larva
Cypris

Barnacles larva
Nauplius

Crab larva
Zoea

A

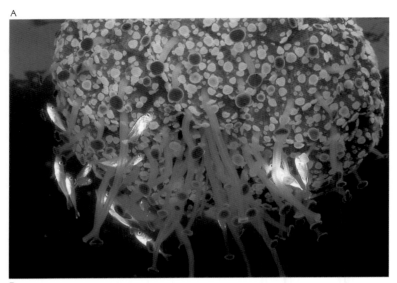

The Radiolaria, foraminifers, acantharia and tintinnids are amongst the most widespread of the marine protozoans which are part of the perennial plankton, or holoplankton, and with their beautiful shells, like stiff lace or patterned suns complete with rays, they are as beautiful as the diatoms. There are also numerous coelenterates, like the big jellyfishes which have been called sea-lungs since the time of the ancient Romans *(Rhizostoma pulmo)* and the yellow and purple *Cothyloriza tubercolata*, often surrounded by groups of small horse jack ready to take shelter when frightened amongst the stinging tentacles, in a Mediterranean version of the strange behaviour of the tropical clownfish. Then there is the relatively common pink *Pelagia noctiluca*, which give off a bright phosphorescence and is renowned for its sting. The jellyfish, perhaps the most common representatives of what is known as gelatinous macroplankton, are typical examples of how closely plankton depends on the sea's

B

D

C

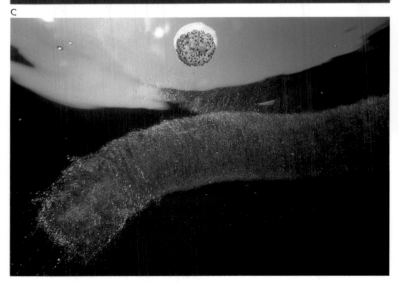

movements. A few days of wind off the sea are all it takes to drive entire swarms of pulsing organisms to the shore; there packed cemeteries can sometimes be found inside the deep grottoes where they have been relentlessly driven by the currents. Coelenterates such as the By-the-wind sailors *(Velella velella)* and the *Porpita porpita* are

A - It is not uncommon to see groups of tiny animals among the tentacles of larger. They are most often young horse-jacks which, in the early months of life, seek refuge amongst the stinging arms of the jellyfish.

B - The Pelagia noctiluca is a small jellyfish, but widely feared on account of the powerful stinging cells of its tentacles. This species has a special life cycle which enables it to reproduce rapidly, forming numerous swarms which can make swimming difficult and risky.

C - A strange tubular formation is carried along by the currents. This unusual translucent structure is an enormous mass of eggs laid by a huge squid (Thysanoteuthis rhombus), a creature which can grow to a length of 1 meter and weigh more than 15 kilos.

D - The Cothyloriza tubercolata is a jellyfish fairly widely found in summer and autumn. Its yellow float and short tentacles ending in a small bluey-purple disc make it easy to recognize.

typical surface dwellers.
With its strange shape and its rare appearances on the shoreline, the latter is a bit of a mystery.
The former, practically transparent and more like a plastic device than an animal, gets its curious name because it is shaped like a little boat, surmounted by a small sail which catches the wind, so that banks of these animals are moved from one point in the Mediterranean to another.
The porpita, a small, rigid, dark blue and light blue disc, surrounded with short tentacles, is likewise subject to the wind. Despite appearances, neither of these specimens is an individual, but like the rarer (in the Mediterranean at least) Physalia physalis or Portuguese man of war, with its long tentacles which can cause severe injury to humans, they are colonies made up of several organisms, each of which is specialized in a specific task: defense, nutrition, reproduction and keeping afloat. There are, however, some even more enigmatic plankton, sometimes

G

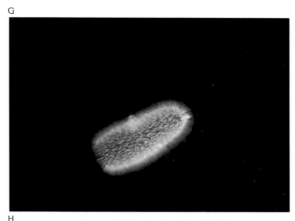

H

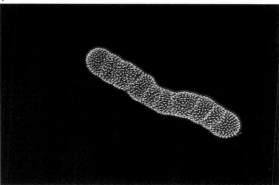

E

F

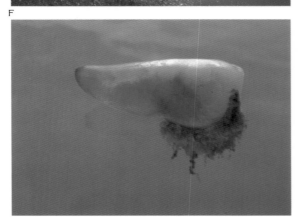

E - A closer view of the jellylike mass containing the eggs of the Thysanoteuthis rhombus. The eggs are the tiny bluey-purple dots that form the internal spiral-shaped structure. The presence of these eggs on the surface is considered accidental since they normally remain in deep water.

F - Like a bubble afloat, a Portuguese man-of-war (Physalia physalis) is swept across the sea by the wind. This siphonophore may look harmless but its stinging tentacles - sometimes as long as 10 meters - can cause mortal injury to man.

G - Pyrosoma are macroplanktonic tunicates of the Thaliacea class. They owe their name to their brilliant bioluminescence: derived from ancient Greek, pyrosoma means "with a body of fire".

H - This strange creature is a planktonic organism: a colonial radiolarian (Collozoum sp.). Radiolars have a very complex skeleton mainly made by sylicium.

A

found in relatively shallow waters, which divers will sometimes come across, especially during a decompression stop when they have time and more opportunity to look around. Most times this kind of meeting arouses strange reactions in those present, as the *Ctenophora* and the *Tunicata* have unusual looks. These animals are quite far apart on the evolutionary scale (the *Tunicata* come just before the vertebrates while the *Ctenophora* are similar to the coelenterates) but they share many features, foremost amongst them their almost perfect transparency. For example, the shape of the Venus' girdle *(Cestus veneris),* a ribbon-like ctenophore which can grow to 2 meters in length,

A - A fin whale of the Mediterranean (Balaenoptera physalus). Although the Mediterranean is a poor sea, it is able to support a fairly large population of fin whales. Their ideal habitat and safe-haven is the Upper Tyrrhenian basin.

B - Fishing-boat, net, seagulls and sea. This picture sums up the complex cycle of events in which the sun's rays are transformed into increasingly sophisticated creatures. Among the most prominent examples of the rich variety of

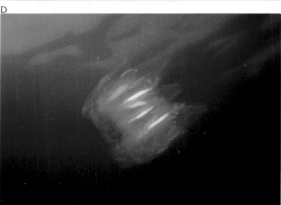

B

C

E

D

can only be picked out by light reflecting on it, its more compact internal structures and the rows of iridescent cilia which it beats. Completely translucent, it oscillates at the slightest impulse and is as intangible as a cloud. Other examples are the *Beroe,* similar to glass balloons, or the *Pyrosoma,* luminescent animals like glass vases, lit up by interior flashes of light, or the barrel-like salps, totally transparent tunicates except for a central red blotch, and filled with reflections which transform the glassy body into mobile shafts of light. Pushed by the currents, these big plankton show up to observers like UFOs lost in space, ready to disappear into the blue with the accompanying waters they comb to find their food. The arrow worms

underwater life-forms are the species which, through the ages, man has learnt to exploit. But exploitation by man is not always compatible with the replacement cycles of marine resources.

C - The flattened helmet combjelly (Beroe ovata) is a large ctenophore which resembles a translucent, elongated bubble. The longitudinal bands noticeable when it is viewed against the light are in fact formed of countless vibratile cilia which transform light into a play of iridescent flashes.

D - A planktonic tunicate is carried along by the currents. Its size would appear to classify it as so-called macroplankton, i.e. organisms easily visible to the naked eye. In actual fact its tissues are comprised essentially of water and only its internal organs and light effects give the animal color.

on the other hand are highly active, tenacious predators.

Small organisms of just over a centimeter in length belonging to the phylum *Chaetognatha*, they have sharp jaws which they use to catch small crustaceans, whose final destiny, thanks to the transparency of their hunters' bodies, is clearly witnessable.

The crustaceans probably make up the largest component in plankton, both in quantity and in number of species. Cladocerans or water fleas, ostracods, copepods, mysidaceans, cumaceans, amphipods (sandhoppers or beach fleas) isopods, euphausiaceans and decapods - all belong to the long list of arthropods which contribute to life in the sea.

H

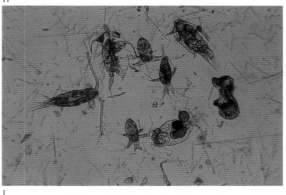

I

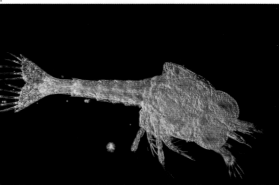

J

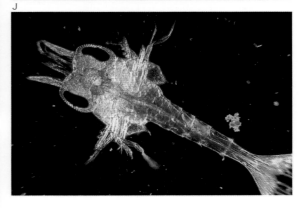

F

G

E - Divers who chance upon this ribbonlike jelly are generally unsure what to make of it. It is in fact a fairly common ctenophore known as Venus' girdle (Cestum veneris): it swims with an undulating motion, aided by the thrust of cilia along its edges.

F - Salpa maxima is one of the planktonic organisms most abundantly found in the Mediterranean. Although solitary organisms are sometimes seen, it more commonly exists in long chains formed of dozens of individuals, reproduced by budding off one individual from another.

G - This photograph, a close-up, shows a chain of planktonic tunicates (class Thaliacea) belonging to the Thalia democratica species. This species is particularly common in the winter months, and can be found mostly in the western Mediterranean.

H - A quick flick of a plankton net in sea water and up come creatures which, under a microscope, reveal the strangest of forms.

I, J - Two crustacean larvas from a catch of spring plankton. Like many other species, they will soon complete their planktonic life and continue to grow on the sea bed.

Perhaps the best illustration of the importance of this group can be found in an area known as the cetaceans' deep-sea sanctuary. This is a huge triangle of sea between Italy, France and Corsica, opposite part of what was historically called the Whaling Coast between Albenga and Ventimiglia, where there is the maximum concentration of large marine mammals in the Mediterranean. The life of the whales here depends directly on the plankton and, to an even greater extent, the sea's motion.

There are marked rises of cold, nutrient-rich water in this area during winter, partly due to the Mistral. In addition to this, westward-moving surface, intermediate and deep-water bands create cyclonic, i.e. anticlockwise, currents, which draw up more water and nutrients from the bottom and enrich the sea further. Of course, the nutrients are only the fertilizers. They give rise to the algae, after which, climbing the steps of the food pyramid, come the euphausiacean crustaceans of the species *Meganyctiphanes norvegica*. This is a mesopelagic organism which is both herbivorous and deposit feeding or carnivorous, depending on its age and the season, and is practically at the limit of the concept of plankton, due to its motility. It cannot however always combat the motion of the water and is often beached on the shoreline in great quantities. This crustacean, the Mediterranean krill, is essential not only for the whale *Balenoptera physalus*, but for the whole of the Ligurian Sea, where it is proving of fundamental importance. *Meganyctiphanes*

norvegica is hunted by many fishes, cephalopods and even other crustaceans, as well as the whales. All these predators are distributed at depths between the sea-bottom and the surface, where each exploits their own situation to take the best advantage possible of the vertical movements made by the krill, in response to the different light conditions at night and during the day. The last components of the holoplankton are a group of molluscs which have cleverly camouflaged themselves to deal with the environmental conditions. *Carinaria mediterranea* is one such case. Its body has a gelatinous appearance - although

it is solid to the touch - in which the small, whitish, oblong-conical shell almost disappears.

At first sight the mollusc is hard to recognise as such, as it has a caudal appendix and two fins, a dorsal and ventral.

As if this were not enough, the animal has been observed moving in water with its shell pointing downwards and not, and this only illustrates how little we still know about molluscs, as it appears in many traditional illustrations. Other fascinating members of the plankton are the sea butterflies *Creseis acicula*, with two thin evaginations sticking out of the shell which beat the water vigorously like wings.

A

B

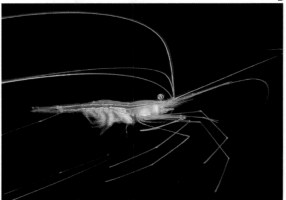

The abundance of Meganyctiphanes norvegica, *the Mediterranean equivalent of krill, in the Upper Tyrrhenian and Ligurian Seas is the main reason for the numerically notable presence of cetaceans, particularly the fin whale, in these areas. Part of a rich food chain initiated with the nutrients of the river Rhone and the meteorological and climatic conditions of the Gulf of Lions,* Meganyctiphanes *appears to be the key to what is now a pelagic sanctuary for the Mediterranean cetaceans.*

A - *This common fin whale (*Balenoptera physalus*) has been photographed just before diving, when its dorsal fin is visible.*

B - *Small crustaceans - pictured here is a* Plesionika narval - *are often nocturnal creatures. As a result of this choice of lifestyle, they* have fewer possible predators and can more effectively exploit their coloring, which makes them much less likely to be spotted in the dark.*

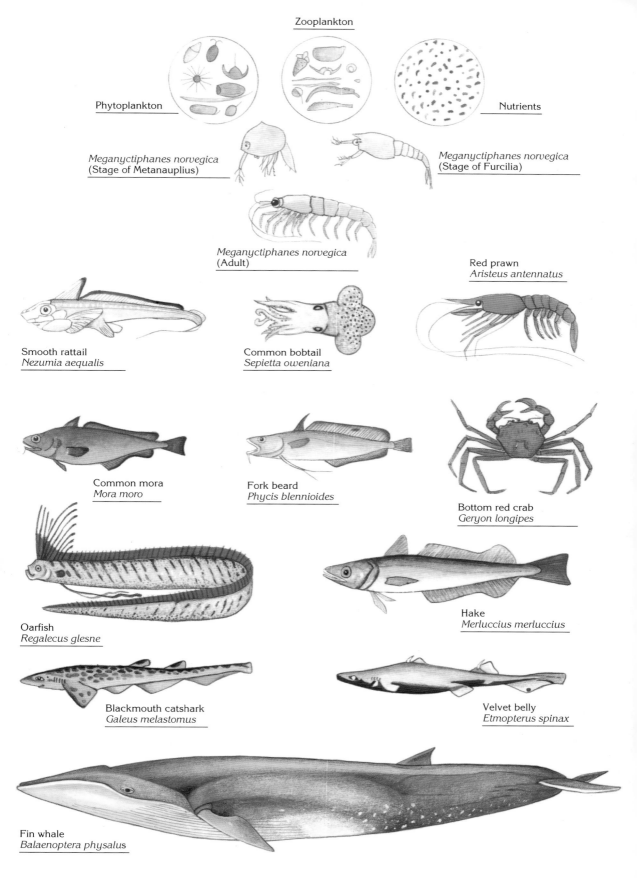

Zooplankton

Phytoplankton

Nutrients

Meganyctiphanes norvegica
(Stage of Metanauplius)

Meganyctiphanes norvegica
(Stage of Furcilia)

Meganyctiphanes norvegica
(Adult)

Red prawn
Aristeus antennatus

Smooth rattail
Nezumia aequalis

Common bobtail
Sepietta oweniana

Common mora
Mora moro

Fork beard
Phycis blennioides

Bottom red crab
Geryon longipes

Oarfish
Regalecus glesne

Hake
Merluccius merluccius

Blackmouth catshark
Galeus melastomus

Velvet belly
Etmopterus spinax

Fin whale
Balaenoptera physalus

NUMEROUS SOLUTIONS TO A SINGLE PROBLEM: HOW NOT TO SINK

Life at the mercy of the marine currents presupposes a series of adaptations seen regularly in plankton, whose components have to satisfy certain specific requirements. The principal problem for the algae is the one of staying as long as possible in the layers of water with the correct light intensity; the herbivorous animals have to stay close to the algae and the predators have to be close to their prey. In many cases these aims are only achieved thanks to the currents, but not all planktonic organisms are incapable of any form of independent movement. It is obvious from observing a jellyfish, for example, that the rhythmic pulsations of its canopy allow it to rise and fall in the water and to move round an obstacle or get back into its original position when overturned.
Other groups have visible limbs or pinnules or cilia, with which they

B

C

B - The large Rhizostoma pulmo jellyfish, known as the sea lung on account of its shape, offers plentiful evidence of adaptations that prevent it sinking to greater depths. Its umbrella-shaped body acts as a parachute and its tissue has almost the same specific weight as water.

C - Squid propel themselves through the water using the exceptionally powerful muscles in their outer layer, which force the water through their "funnel". With a specific weight only slighter greater than that of water, they can be swift swimmers.

A

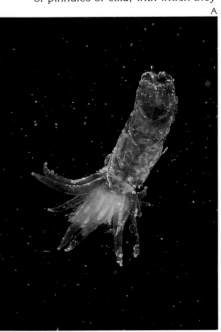

A - Siphonophores, like this Forskalia, remain suspended in the water thanks to a hollow float filled with gas while a series of zooids in the form of a bell allows the colony to swim. Like jellyfish, their tissue is comprised almost entirely of water.

can move in calm seas. However, they all have limited abilities to deal with stronger currents. Although small, planktonic animals are subject to gravity and have to use up some of their energy to stay put in the mass of water most suited to their vital requirements. The relationship between plankton and water is so close that many organisms are now considered to be excellent ecological and hydrological indicators. Nowadays experts can identify the presence in the Mediterranean of Atlantic waters or pelagic mixed with neritic, or coastal, waters, just by analysing the plankton population and can in some cases distinguish the warmest ones without thermometers. The presence of jellyfish close to the shore at the end of the summer should, for example, be interpreted as a good omen, because it indicates something new and the arrival of clean water from out at sea. Being able to identify the euphausiacean *Thysanoessa gregaria*, a shrimp with a long

pointed rostrum , or the pteropod mollusc *Spiratella lesueri* or the copepod *Acartia danae*, would make it possible to follow the flow of currents from Gibraltar without having recourse to so many chemical analyses. So the importance of remaining associated with a given mass of water is obvious and the simplest system is to stay suspended in it for as long as possible, using a broad float such as a disc or a parachute. Examples of this are the many circular-shaped diatoms, the Coccolythophora, the jellyfishes, floating hydrozoans like the *Porpita* and the pelagic molluscs without shells.
On the other hand it is easy to see that a broad, flattened, shape is an aid to flotation. Just take a polystyrene float like the ones they use for swimming lessons and try and push it under water. It would be easier to sink it vertically, than with the plane parallel to the surface of the water. Even the development of just one of a body's axes helps to hold it up, as the arrow worms, or

Chaetognatha show. The sphere is another ideal shape, and the world of plankton is filled with transparent balloons which can move in the dense aquatic universe at heights which, when measured from the bottom, compare favorably with those attained by air balloons flown by humans. The only difference is the absence of a hot-air mechanism to hold them up; instead there are physiological adaptations made to reduce specific weight, like the inclusion in the body of minute drops of oil or gas, or a liquid which is less dense than the surrounding water. Up until now we have mentioned regular shapes. Set against these are the astounding looks of many planktonic organisms furnished with filaments, spines, extremely long legs, tendrils, feathered tentacles, flattened oar-like antennae all with the same function, or more than one function really, as many appendices are used to catch food too. Some of these structures are fixed,

while others are mobile and only function, either as parachutes or delta-planes, when the animal stops and starts to sink towards the bottom. So although there is a range of shapes as vast as the types of plankton, it is easy to identify the same aim in them all: to stay afloat. Some scientists believe that it was the relative uniformity of the abiotic factors in the pelagic environment which encouraged the multiplication of the designs, as if there was a competition in which the most important thing was to take part, where the density caused by temperature and salinity seems to have had an important role in the outcome. In some species of copepod crustaceans, the specimens born in the cold season are smaller than those born in the warm season and this is simply because cold water is twice as dense as warm water and gives more support. The variations in aquatic viscosity affect the hydrostatic equilibrium of the organisms, which react with a

G - The Geryonia proboscidalis *belongs to the* Trachymedusan *class of hydrozoans and is so completely transparent it looks like a water-filled*

cellophane bag. A few contractions are sufficient to keep it afloat in the current which takes care of moving it from place to place.

F

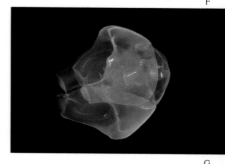

G

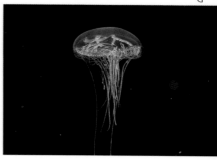

morphological or functional "adaptation complement". Another solution they have come up with to solve the problem of flotation is the appearance of gelatinous tissues, perhaps one of the most distinctive characteristics of the inhabitants of the plankton. The bodies of many of the organisms described in the previous pages have virtually no support structure, barely any muscles and extremely hydrated tissues consisting of 95% water - which makes many of these planktonic organisms akin to plastic bags floating on the water. The combination of devices such as these once again makes the animals' specific weight almost equal to that of their habitat, so that a few movements are all that are needed to keep them afloat.

D

D - The Tethys fimbria *is a large nudibranchs which usually stays on muddy sea-floors. Thanks to its long, flat cerata, however, it can also swim. When it does so it sometimes looks like a jellyfish, as this photo shows.*

E - Some hydrozoans have solely planktonic forms which shows that even creatures belonging to different classes can have the same appearance as jellyfish. The need to inhabit the same environment and abide by the same rules has made it necessary to have the same form too.

F - This strange-looking organism, is a siphonophore of the Hippopodius hippopus *species. Adaptations to planktonic life have resulted in bell-like again bodies and transparent tissue comprised over 95% of water.*

E

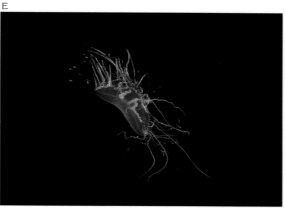

A

COLOR? THANKS, BUT NO THANKS

The consequence of the reduction in heavy structures, whether for support or for protection, is a marked tendency amongst the animals to be transparent, although this characteristic is not always associated with gelatinous bodies. Many planktonic organisms, from jellyfish to worms, from crustaceans to appendicularians to fish larvae, have diaphanous bodies which only become visible underwater in certain light conditions. Several of the

B

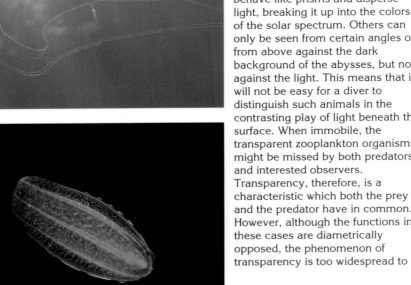

C

D

E

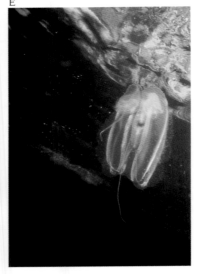

Ctenophora become iridescent only because their locomotive paddles behave like prisms and disperse light, breaking it up into the colors of the solar spectrum. Others can only be seen from certain angles or from above against the dark background of the abysses, but not against the light. This means that it will not be easy for a diver to distinguish such animals in the contrasting play of light beneath the surface. When immobile, the transparent zooplankton organisms might be missed by both predators and interested observers. Transparency, therefore, is a characteristic which both the prey and the predator have in common. However, although the functions in these cases are diametrically opposed, the phenomenon of transparency is too widespread to

A - Light from above seems to pass practically right through the body of the jellyfish, making it disappear into the glimmering surface.

B - Perhaps it is on account of the powerful weaponry of the Pelagia noctiluca *that these little jellyfish are pink with red blotches.*

C - Venus' girdle (Cestus veneris) is a transparent ctenophore. Although it is often over a meter in length and nearly 10 centimeters high, it is very hard to spot underwater.

D - The color assumed by the flattened helmed combjelly is pure simulation. If one of these individuals is placed in an acquarium with diffused light, it becomes almost transparent. In the same way as a Swarowsky cut-glass ornament, its colors depend solely on light effects.

E - The iridescent reflections on this flattened helmed combjelly's body are caused by rays of light reflected by the numerous vibratile cilia which run the length of its body.

think that it does not have an evolutionary function. The defensive effect of transparency is increased by the presence of colored structures. Eyes, digestive system, gonads and muscles are often colored and end up looking like black, red, brown, green or yellowish blotches. The eye of an observer could be distracted by these blotches, seemingly suspended in a void, and lose sight of the rest of the animal, to the latter's obvious advantage. But transparency is not the rule in plankton. Anything which lives suspended in a column of water is affected by the different light conditions between the surface and the sea-bottom and this leads to color modifications. After all, what advantage could a deep-sea jellyfish or an abyssal ctenophore derive from being transparent, in a environment distinguished by continual night? The answer is almost certainly none and in fact the plankton of the abysses and those which only rise to the surface at night are black, red or purplish, colors which stand out in the sunlight but which are invisible at night, or where the sun and the wavelengths corresponding to red never arrive. The plankton which live in the "blue layer", the stratum closest to the surface of the sea, have also adapted chromatically to the extent that they have a specific name: neuston. The neuston consists of animals specialized in living permanently in the air-water interface and they often have protruding structures such as the "sails" on the By-the-wind sailor, for example, or the gas-filled canopies of the Portuguese man o'war *(Physalia physalis)*, which can be tangibly affected by the winds, which are the rivals or allies of the currents in conditioning the movements of this type of animal. Whereas transparency is the characteristic of the plankton which inhabit the intermediate waters, and color is the characteristic of plankton which lives in the deeps, most neustonic organisms are two-colored: blue on the top and silver-white underneath. This color has a camouflage function for the fleets of neuston. The blue of the upper part, when seen from above, blends in with the color of the sea, while the light, underpart is lost in the light coming down from above. This type

F - Organisms which live in the plankton generally have few means of self-defense. This is why many try to make themselves invisible, by losing all their color.

G - Only laymen mistake siphonophores for single organisms. They are in fact colonies comprised of a series of individuals, each with its own precise role to perform: nutrition, defense, reproduction, floating. These creatures are not unlike ships under the control of an efficient, specialized crew.

H - Compared with the showy colors and markings of many other benthic species, this free-swimming nudibranchs looks decidedly drab. Pale blue is nonetheless the ideal color when the intention is to pass unnoticed in the water masses all around.

F

G

H

of camouflage coloring, and it is no coincidence that it is also found in pelagic fish, is even more effective when one thinks of the particular conditions in which neustonic organisms live. Wave movement causes the bodies of these animals to oscillate continually so that predators are never given a constant sight angle.

SURVIVAL STRATEGIES

There is no doubt that coloration and flotation are important for the survival of a planktonic organism, but they are not all. Zooplankton for example has to tackle the problem of maintaining a stable population whose members can crossbreed and reproduce and, as we saw earlier, stay close to the phytoplankton which is their source of food. For the smaller zooplankton animals, which are governed by similar rules to those of the phytoplankton, the solution of this problem has involved the development of several extremely sophisticated behavioral strategies. One of the most important of these is the formation of swarms which are promoted by the substance the animals themselves produce. The antibiotic, repellent substances

which the phytoplankton produce have the opposite effect, thereby countering the zooplankton's attempts to prey on them. The ability to reproduce rapidly permits the animals to exploit certain hydrodynamic situations which occur in certain areas effectively. The vortices formed by wind or currents create areas of convergence and divergence which cause an accumulation of water which then, respectively, descends to the abysses or wells up. In the former case there is an aggregation of plankton, which is carried to the center of the vortex; in the latter there is an increased development of phytoplankton thanks to the nutrients carried to the surface, while the zooplankton is kept to the outer margins. The effects of these vortices are comparable to those produced

by the upwelling currents of the Alboran basins and the north-western shores of the Mediterranean, especially in the winter months or during strong winds. But the effect of the currents goes much further than concentration or dispersal. Because the speed and direction of the currents vary according to a gradient which is a function of depth, it is possible for an organism to move horizontally and vertically by exploiting the different current flow, as if it had at its disposal a sophisticated system of escalators and subway lines. At this point the only problem is the evolution of techniques which allow the organisms to exploit the sea's movements to their own advantage. In order to understand this evolution, reference must be

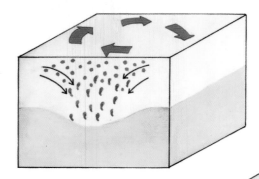

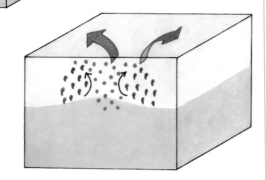

The concentration of plankton in the surface layers is often conditioned by the formation of vortices and currents. In anticyclonic vortices, i.e. those which rotate clockwise, (above), water accumulates *in the center of the vortex and then sinks to the depths, bringing about a concentration of plankton. In cyclonic vortices, which rotate counterclockwise, rising zones are formed and carry the nutrients up* *towards the surface where they increase the growth of phytoplankton. The same effect occurs in the presence of diverging currents (below) which, in addition, transport the phytoplankton into neighboring zones.*

Mysids

Coelenterates

Copepods

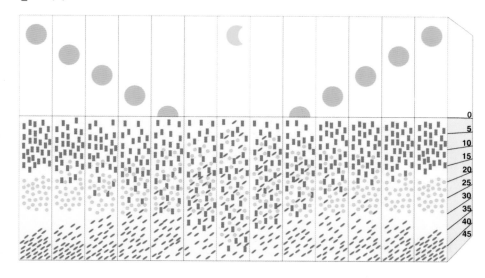

0
5
10
15
20
25
30
35
40
45

There are considerable vertical planktonic migrations throughout a day. They are also called noctidiurnal, to underline their dependence on the alternation of day and night. These migrations involve numerous species belonging to the zooplankton, whose populations move upwards during the night-time hours and back downwards during the day. This permits them to exploit different food resources or to escape predators.

made, at least in part, to the solutions developed to stay afloat which were described above. However well-perfected these are, gravity is an unavoidable and inescapable phenomenon and every organism, therefore, tends to sink. For a planktonic seaweed, incapable of any kind of movement, sinking means embarking on a voyage without return to into the darkness and, of course, no plant can live for long far from the sun.
Luckily the Mediterranean waters are transparent and it has good chances of being able to synthesize a few sugars seven at depths of 100 meters. Furthermore, there is no lack of rising currents.
A good rising current can bring the seaweed back into play and carry it upwards toward the light.
The same phenomena, more or less, affect animal plankton. Many zooplankton are extremely active herbivores. If segregated in a mass of water with the plants on which they feed, sooner or later their food reserves will run out with the result that they will find themselves without any available resources. The only, obvious, solution would be to change water, but for many of these organisms

swimming constitutes an effort which is comparable to a man moving through syrup. All they can do therefore is let themselves sink until they find a cross current and then a rising one which takes them up towards new pastures. Although highly complex in appearance, the technique is very simple and widely applied by large numbers of decidedly more mobile species, which couple transportation by currents with regular transfers timed by the succession of night and day.
These migrations were discovered by chance during the Second World War, thanks to the increased diffusion and use of sonar.
Its ultrasonic waves were reflected both by real sea bottoms and by others, which were not only non-existent but able to vary their depth, The combination of sonar, nets and photographic equipment made it possible to identify many planktonic organisms as the creators of these enigmatic reflecting bottoms and to discover the existence of this incredible underwater "traffic". The upwards migrations occur during the night and scientists believe that the aim is to find better-stocked grazing or hunting grounds, while the daytime

descent is thought to be a defense against predators. Naturally, this is only one of the possible explanations because there are animals which certainly move in this way in order to avoid excessive competition for food resources or exploit the currents in order to save energy during migrations. The wide range of applications of this underwater coming and going involves therefore a vast number of organisms, some of which, despite their size, or lack of it, actually migrate several hundred meters - some shrimps which are 4-5 centimeters long migrate 800 meters upwards and downwards - either between the surface and a certain depth, or between different levels far from the surface. In this way, over a 24-hour period, animals of different species and different stages of development move from one level to another inside the column of water, in response to factors such as variations in luminosity, pressure and temperature. The result is step-ladder migrations, where different organisms, all stimulated to move by their differing degrees of sensitivity and reaction to the stimuli listed above, alternate in the same layer of water.

MOVEMENT IN MOTION

Coastal and off-shore waters are not just inhabited by plankton, there is nekton too. This definition covers animals which always live suspended in the water and which can swim actively against the currents. However, as is always the case, the differences at the extremities of every category are so subtle as to be almost imperceptible. There are planktonic organisms whose dimensions and structure would not be out of place in the nekton and vice versa.
To cast light on the question a mathematical formula has been devised to distinguish nekton.
It takes into account the animals' hydrodynamic and morphological characteristics (e.g. length and speed) as well as the relationship between the inertial force and the viscosity of the water.
The calculation based on these parameters produces a numerical factor (Reynolds number) which, depending on whether it is greater

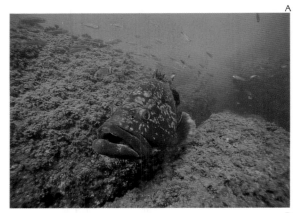

A

B

A - Moving swiftly through a dense environment like water implies a whole series of problems: one is the acquisition of physical features suited to the purpose. A grouper moves its large body thanks partly to its muscles and fins but mainly to its gas-filled bladder which makes it almost weightless in water.

B - Deep-sea sharks have tapered, powerful bodies. However, their specific weight is greater than that of seawater, which means they are forced to keep swimming to prevent themselves from sinking (their streamlined anatomical features and internal organs also help them remain afloat).

C

D

than, equal to or less than 100,000, constitutes the discriminating factor between nekton and plankton.
Nekton is made up for the most part of fishes, but other zoological groups, such as the molluscs, reptiles and mammals, include nektonic specimens. But the Mediterranean nekton does not include any birds, which are represented in the oceans by penguins. Just as with plankton, so the study of nekton ends sooner or later with the realization that there are certain recurring characteristics. For example, a blue shark *(Prionace glauca)* a swordfish *(Xiphias gladius)* and a dolphin *(Tursiops truncatus)* look very similar at first glance. But their relationship is only apparent, as they are members of quite distinct classes: *Chondrichthyes* (cartilaginous fish), *Osteichthyes* (bony fish) and mammals.
Yet the similarities do exist and they are due to the manifestation of forces which biologists group under the name of evolutionary convergence. To live in a truly three-dimensional area, where it is

possible to move in every direction, pursue a prey or search for others of the same species, presents a number of needs requiring a series of adaptations to overcome the individuality of each species.
First of all the resistance of the water has to be overcome.
A high Reynolds number transforms the viscosity of the water into an advantageous support during movement when the fluid acts on the fins of many fishes, supporting then as the air does on the wings of aircraft or birds. Obviously, every movement within this dense barrier is easier if the organism has strong muscles and a tapered body.
The bodies of those animals which can swim the fastest might have been designed in a hydrodynamic tank. Every protuberance which could constitute a brake on advancement and create an area of turbulence close to the body by increasing friction has been eliminated. In dolphins, whose skin is a masterpiece of engineering capable of modification at every point of its surface under pressure from water, the male sexual organs

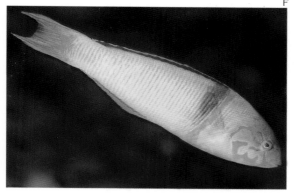

peaks of 20 times, when a prey has to be pursued or, on the contrary, escape. But it is not always necessary to swim fast. There is no lack of fish either in the midst of posidonia meadowlands or close to a reef and other factors become important, even though they make the concept of nekton less clear. Whereas a strong, hydrodynamic body will always permit a fast break, it is also true that the ability to manoeuvre can be more useful when the available space is scarce and complex. Much can be learnt from watching the behavior of a large grouper or a black wrasse or a black corb during a dive. The elegance and lightness with which a huge 20-30 kilo grouper moves in the water, withdraws into its den and turns to look at you, whilst staying perfectly still except for a few beats of a pectoral fin, are eloquent proof of how many meanings adaptation can have, even when it is applied to the shape of nektonic fishes.

E - The profile of the corb, with its compressed head and wide tail, is ideal for fast, darting, swimming close to rocky bottoms.

F - The labrids, the family to which the peacock wrasse (Thalassoma pavo) belongs, swim mainly with the pectoral fins.

C - Bottle-nosed dolphins are very well equipped to move in water. As well as perfect hydrostatic balance, they have a special type of skin which greatly reduces resistance to motion.

D - The hydrodynamic form of the bottle-nosed dolphin is highlighted in this photo, which shows the snout of one of these cetaceans. Broad at the front and tapered behind, its resemblance to a drop - considered one of the most hydrodynamic shapes - is certainly no coincidence.

and the mammary glands disappear inside special folds on the body. The eyes of tunny fish do not protrude from the head's smooth surface and the fins are folded into special cavities when the fish swim at top speed. In swordfish the ventral fins disappear while in many tuna, mackerel and similar species, small pinnules capable of reducing turbulence at high speed appear both dorsal and ventrally at the rear part of the body. Once again we see that in the pelagic domain it is possible to express the relationship between environment and movement in a series of numerical relationships: given the same shape, the bigger organisms will be faster than the smaller ones, which explains some of the classic food chains, like the one with tunny, shark and dolphin at the top, which are principally based on speed. Furthermore, where the most active fishes are concerned, we can assume a cruising speed that corresponds to around 1-2 times body length per minute, increasing to 10-12 times, with

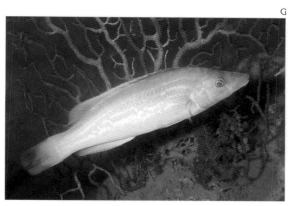

G - One of the factors which aids many fish to swim is the possession of an air bladder. This organ, which is thought to have been at the origin of the terrestrial vertebrates' lungs, acts like the buoyancy compensator jackets worn by divers: by inflating and deflating it alters the fish hydrostatic balance, enabling it to stay immobile at the desired depth, or assisting ascent or descent.

NEKTONIC COLOR AND LIGHT

The Mediterranean is blue because this is the color of the luminous radiations which reach the greatest depths. A diver can descend through this blue, passing from a planktonic phase to a nektonic and then a benthic phase.

Of course, the blue can have many shades. The coastal waters of Sardinia, for example, provide a huge range of colors which bear comparison to many tropical marine landscapes, but there is no doubt that certain intrinsic Mediterranean factors such as its size, sea-bottom geography, the transparency of its waters and its

biological characteristics, all combine to give it its characteristic blue color and this is the color of the most emblematic nektonic organisms, those that live in the surface waters.

It is virtually a compulsory choice in an environment where there is only one predominant color and where there is no shelter from it. The only hiding places here are the light, the water and the black of the bottom. The combined effect of these three simple factors becomes embodied in a single idea, although it is achieved in many versions, expressed as countershading. The back of a pelagic fish is dark blue or blue

A - The streamlined form of a shark (Prionace glauca) suggests the extent to which its "lifestyle" depends on its supremacy over the populations of the high seas.

B - A long-snouted dolphin (Stenella coeruleoalba) leaps from the water, thrust upwards by its powerful muscles. Cetaceans are among the creatures best suited to life in the boundless waters of the open sea, a world which has much in common with the sky.

C - The coloring of fish which populate the open seas tends to be fairly uniform. The silvery surface of their bodies can catch the sunlight like a mirror and create reflections which mix and mingle with the ambient light, cleverly masking the fish themselves.

D - Being part of a shoal is often an ideal solution for a fish hard-put to cope with the difficulties of survival out in the open sea.

with green shading, its intensity varying according to whether it is mainly an open sea fish or one which plies the coastal lanes. The sides and belly are white or silvery. Close observation of, for instance, a case of mackeral or anchovies, show this description to be exact, but it does not explain the term use to define it.

To understand the advantage it provides for a fish or cetacean, we must either see or imagine them in their environment, where it hard to pick out the dark

upperside of the fish against the dark sea bottom. Equally, it is hard to distinguish the outline when the animal's light-colored belly blends into the light coming from above. The color layout renders the fish a fairly uniform whole with its environment and only lengthways movements or oscillations of the body, by varying the orientation of the back and the underside compared to the light, make the fish visible, as it appears and disappears before our eyes. Silver-colored fishes are well-camouflaged too. A shoal of anchovies or smelts, which it is not uncommon to come across during a dive close to the coast, changes color according to how the sun strikes its. Thanks to the thin crystals of guanine they contain, the scales act like mirrors and reflect the lightís rays, masking the fish by making them as shiny as the water around them. A diver observing the movements of a school of pelagic fishes will see an endless series of dark blotches and flashes of light which will confuse predators. But what happens in deeper waters where the sunís light fades until it disappears totally? Thinking about life in caves may lead us to imagine that the animals which live on these dark bottoms might lose their color altogether.

This hypothesis is partly correct, in that the bright colors of the surface are lacking here and many fish are whitish or translucent. Despite this however, many others are extraordinarily silvery, like the lantern fish and the hatchett fish, or have distinctive silver or gold flashes, like the *Chauliodis sloanei* devilfish or the *Stomias boa*, with its mouth full of long, sharp teeth. Others take on a dark red or black coloring. Whereas the latter color can easily be understood in a dark environment, the red taken on by many species in deep waters requires some explanation.

This color actually only appears very bright in sunlight. Down in the deeps, where the most diffused light is from blue-green dominant marine luminescence, these animals are practically black and just as invisible as the dark fish in that shadowy realm. As an old proverb says "all cats are grey in the night".

As the water gets progressively deeper, the altered relationship with light influences the sight organs as well as the colors themselves. Moving from the surface to the darkness of the bottom and abyssal waters, (this term should be reserved for waters below 3,000 meters), many fish have enormously developed or telescopic eyes almost detached from the body, to capture the weak

light radiations which are still present at 400-500 meters and beyond, as well as the light given off by other animals. Many mesopelagic fishes which live in dark waters and prefer the dark are not, however, tied to this environment all their lives. Some species have larvae which live on the surface and many others make regular journeys upwards to the surface waters, even though this is only during the night. If these excursions take place in adverse sea conditions, they often result in these strange fishes being beached, a phenomenon which occurs often on beaches along deep-bottomed stretches of sea. It is particularly common along the coasts of the Strait of Messina, due to the particular play of currents, where scientists have been able to haul in by hand and study fish which they would otherwise have had to capture and observe either with special deep-sea nets or submarines.

No chapter on the colors of the deeps would be complete without

E - Living in a school often proves an excellent strategy for survival. When face-to-face with a larger, fast predator, the school is able to disorientate the attacker, by presenting it with several possible victims simultaneously and by transforming the school into a single, huge individual.

G

H

E

F - The tapered form of this amberjack (Seriola dumerili) and its curved caudal fin, attached by a slim peduncle, are an indication of the deep-sea habits of the species.

G - Sardines, here is depicted a small one, and anchovies, with their silvery brown coloring, are one of the fundamental links in the food chain of the Mediterranean Sea. Huge shoals of these fish turn plankton into food for predatory fish and man.

H - A picarel (Spicara maena) photographed at night when the distinctive black mark on its sides tends to fade and even disappear. The color of fish varies enormously, depending on age, sex and period of life.

F

A

B

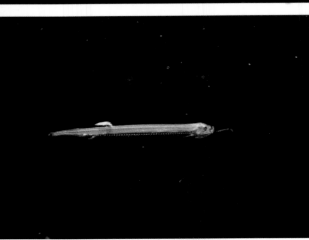

C

a mention of the fascinating subject of the living lights. This unique biological phenomenon gives a more importance and further significance to the dark or shiny colors of many families of mesopelagic and bathypelagic fishes.

Black and silver are transformed into the ideal background for showing off the photophores, bright points of whitish-green light scattered all over the body, mainly along the belly and close to the eyes, which the fish can switch on and off. The markings which appear in the sunlight as colors, blotches, stripes and bands, in the dark become a coded message in light, which is different for every species. This permits individuals of the same species to be recognised, to identify other members of the same species and form shoals. But this is not all. The silvery sides of fish which live at depths between 200 and 700 meters are effective camouflage against predators (and in this habitat where there are no algae, the only way to feed is to be a carnivore or a bottom-feeder), but not if the attack comes from below. Seen from this angle the fish tend to appear clearly as outlines against the diffused light from above. With the photophores lit up, on the other hand, the shape of the fish is evanescent and less obvious. In view of its diffusion in the dark layers, the mechanism obviously works, even though the photophores must have a precise degree of luminosity to perform their function effectively.

This requirement is brilliantly - the very word - carried out by the fish, thanks to the little luminous organs close to the eyes.

They act as light meters, determining the amount of ambient light and regulating the luminosity of the other photophores.

A - In the profound depths where darkness reigns, colors tend to vanish and only a few - black, red, silver - remain visible. The world of color is replaced by one of amazing luminous geometric forms, like that of this viperfish (Stomias boa).

B - This close-up of a devil fish (Chauliodus sp.) highlights its long sabre-like teeth and luminous spots, adaptations typically found among deep-sea fishes.

C - A rare picture of a Stomias boa, taken by surprise while out and about at night.

D - The beach of Budelli is one of the best known and most fascinating places on the coastline of Sardinia. The pink of its sands comes from the remains of tiny reddish-colored marine organisms, cast onto the shore by the waves. Man's ignorance and indifference puts even wonders like this at risk.

NEPTUNEIS TREASURE CHEST

In view of the wealth of shapes, colors and environments involved, it seems almost impossible that a single word, benthos, should be sufficient to define the entirety of the organisms which live permanently fixed to the sea bottom, or depend upon it, or are closely linked to it. Close examination of plankton and nekton shows how extraordinarily varied they are, but the benthos is stunning. Algae, plants, invertebrates and

E - A breathtaking wall of gorgonians and black coral. Faced with stunning sights like these, it is easy to understand why the Mediterranean is considered one of the loveliest seas in the world.

F - Non-uniform exposure of the substrate along a rocky spur has resulted in encrustations of different organisms. In this particular case the dim light has encouraged the growth of colonies of red coral.

G - A crack in a wall has allowed through currents which have contributed to the development of a flourishing colony of yellow gorgonians (Eunicella cavolinii). The clumps of coral have "directed" their growth to ensure the greatest possible number of ramifications face the oncoming current.

D

E

G

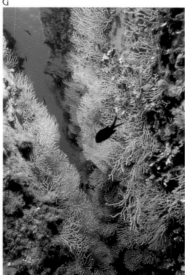

vertebrates (and these are only the widest of the systematic classes) are more than amply represented. Being faced with a meadow of Neptune grass or a wall of corals, two of the most typical of the Mediterranean ecosystems, is like finding oneself in a room piled with shining jewels. Everything seems to conspire to make it impossible to concentrate on one thing and to make variability a soon-contradicted rule. The benthos is the counterpoint to the plankton and the nekton and interacts with it, exchanging energy, resources and living organisms.

Its dominion begins above the surface of the sea and reaches right down into the abyssal plains, extending from the blinding light of the summer sun to the eternal dark. Light, pressure, currents, temperature and the nature of the substrate are the principal factors the benthos has to face. The result is the extreme diversity of this dominion, the most interesting one for humans, one which has always drawn us towards the ocean bottom in search of treasure and, why not, of knowledge too.

C

A

B

D

A - Relations between the varied organisms that populate the bottom are not always governed by predation or symbiosis. On occasions one species can become an ideal temporary resting-place for the eggs of another, as can be seen from this gorgonian holding the eggs of a lesser spotted dogfish.

B - In the calm waters which form in the midst of a meadow of posidonia a spirograph opens out the spiral crown of its branchial tuft.

C - Despite the depth, identified by the abundance of red sea-fans, powerful sunlight still filters through the transparent water.

It is difficult to find adequate words to describe the benthos.
In the plankton and the nekton it is possible to identify common rules or adaptations which permit observers to group species together, but it is all much more difficult with the benthos.
There is no common color as in nekton. There is nothing like gravity to combat, like that plankton. An alga or a plant of Posidonia or an encrustant sponge are, of course, part of the benthic realm, but immobility is a feature of only a part of the benthos.
The other half moves and does it with a variety of extraordinary methods. There are organisms which move so little as to be defined as sedentary, others are more active and slide, hobble, climb, bury themselves or swim, either always, or only when it is necessary. Even the colors are not uniform. Some act as camouflage and some are as lively and visible as advertising hoardings. In conclusion, whereas a meeting with a planktonic or nektonic organism is neither guaranteed nor necessarily noticeable, this is not the case with the benthos. Just a walk along the rocks soaked by the splashes of the waves will produce more benthic organisms than we could imagine. A snorkelling expedition, despite its limitations as a technique of exploration, opens our eyes to an entire catalogue of living things. A dive takes us right into life itself. Wherever we look, something is there and something is happening; every crevice hides a discovery or a mystery.
A scientist relies on his knowledge to give a name to what he observes, the amateur has illustrated guide books, but this does not always mean that they see. Seeing means letting emotion take hold, when you see a fragile nudibranche moving confidently through a forest of hydroids, or the egg of a catfish ready to open, or a shoal of anthias in a cave, or when you savor the discovery of being able to move to the same rhythm as the fishes, in the waves breaking against the rocks.

D - The Cuthona coerulea *is a medium-sized nudibranchs with bright yellow and blue respiratory cerata. Particularly abundant in the winter months, it lives on rocky bottoms where it finds hydroids to feed on.*

Seeing underwater, as unsighted divers know, can mean extending your sensations, letting yourself be wrapped in the aquatic world and transformed from a stranger into a guest. Of course, it is not easy and it cannot be taught in one slim volume. Our message is a difficult one, but it is well worth the effort of trying to get close to the Mediterranean in this sense, too.

G

E

F

H

*E - Sea lilies (*Antedon mediterranea*) are able to fix themselves firmly to the substrate with prehensile suckers on the underside of the central disc.*

F - Taking advantage of the variegated coloring of its carapace, a crab conceals itself among the encrusting red algae which carpet the rock.

*G - A Mediterranean cleaner shrimp (*Stenopus spinosus*) hides among the orange tentacles of the* Astroides.

H - A small red scorpionfish lies in wait, amid sponges on the sea bottom.

EXPLORING THE BENTHOS

IThe large number of factors which can simultaneously affect a limited area of the sea bed contribute towards diversifying it from the bordering zones. For example, different light exposure will drastically change plant and animal populations living at the same depth. Underwater caves are a good illustration of how the light gradient regulates and modifies the inhabitants. Going progressively further into the cave, it is immediately noticeable that the algae which are numerous on the outside tend to disappear, leaving the field to animals, such as the colonies of red coral *(Corallium rubrum)*, the soft, yellow Axinellina, the plump orange cushions of the Astroide, the harmonic architecture of the bryozoans, the transparent clavelines and the amazing colors of the sponges in general. Molluscs, both nudibranchs and gastropods, move amongst these immobile components of the benthos, along with crustaceans and fishes like the red anthias or the king of the mullet *(Apogon imberbis)* which in the light of a diver's torch create the amazing impression of being in a tropical aquarium. Close to the surface where the environmental conditions are more variable than in other places, the population is more diversified. There are the

C

A

D

B

A - Crevices in rock walls often become lairs for numerous benthic organisms like this spiny lobster (Palinurus elephas). Its long antennae serve as efficient sense organs with which the lobster detects the presence of food or enemies.

B - Red coral (Corallium rubrum) is one of the best known and most highly sought-after species in the Mediterranean, where it has led to the development of a thriving industry. Regrettably, overexploitation has made this precious resource increasingly scarse and many Mediterranean countries have now suggested that protective measures be enforced.

C - The rich variety of life-forms on this rocky bottom is evidence of the competition for space. Gorgonians, black coral, algae and a gorgon star appear to be competing in a race to emerge from the throng and occupy the places best exposed to the currents.

D - A seastar (Ophidiaster ophidianus) with smooth, cylindrical, crimson-red arms moves slowly over a wall encrusted with colonies of Astroides. Both the star and these hard corals are typical of southern regions of the Mediterrean.

E - Sandy and muddy bottoms are the typical habitat of weevers (Trachinus sp.); they bury themselves in the sand and leave only their eyes and part of their dorsal fin exposed. The dorsal fin has venomous spines which can cause very painful wounds.

F - A typical stretch of coralligenous sea-bed. The colonies which populate rocky bottoms are typically formed of gorgonians, sponges, calcareous seaweeds, cnidarians, polychaete worms and molluscs. They cover rocks with thick encrustations in which other life-forms find refuge.

G - The most prominent feature of the rock blenny (Parablennius gattorugine) is the large fringed tentacles over its eyes. It is the largest blenny found in the Mediterranean, reaching lengths of up to 30 centimeters.

H - An octopus pictured inside its hole. Its huge tentacles with rows of suckers are wrapped around its body for protection. At the same time, thanks to its very efficiently functioning eyes, the octopus can keep watch on what is happening in the vicinity.

F

G

H

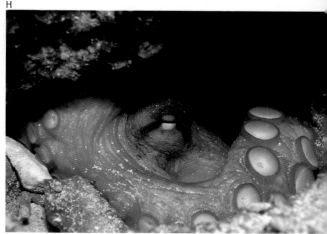

calcareous encrustant algae, which can make huge spongy platforms inhabited by myriad drilling animals. The red beadlet anemone (Actinia equina) are common in this surface zone. They have an amazing biological clock which permits them to open and close at the same rhythm as the tides, just like the white barnacles - the tiny filaments which shoot out of their cone-shape walls are actually the modified legs of these crustaceans, dramatically transformed by the need to live clamped onto a rock. Biological clocks make an appearance in more evolved animals, such as the limpets, which are surprisingly territorial in behavior and always return to their

E

"den". The shallowest, but perennially underwater, rocks are covered in dense vegetation made up of the brown light-loving algae, but the different species occupy different and hydrodynamically differentiated environments. These floating forests are easy to explore with a snorkel and are inhabited by other algae encrustant worms, molluscs and crustaceans, as well as numerous little fish like the blennies and gobies. Sea anemones, with long, pink-tipped tentacles, are common in crevices and unexposed places, especially on the border between rocks and sand or pebbles. Further on are the spiny - and for obvious reasons, unloved - urchins.

A

B

C

D

One species, the rock urchin, (Paracentrotus lividus) is covered during the day by algae or other detritus, some of human origin, used as a shield against the sun's rays. It is not uncommon to find red starfish in this zone as well as the smaller spiny starfish, (Coscinasterias tenuispina) less visible but interesting. Swimming along the sea bed and looking carefully into the gorges, there are fish, often brightly colored, to be seen in the holes dug by the mussels or urchins. The most common are the blennies and the gobies and the strange rock-sucking fish with a sucker on its belly allowing it to stick tenaciously to the rock in every position.

E

Deeper down, you might meet shoals of fish such as saddled bream or the golden-striped salema, grazing on the sea-bed algae which is their food, a not-uncommon occurrence in the Mediterranean. In late spring and summer (the seasons transform the benthos too) young damselfish can be seen sheltering under the ridges at the mouth of caves in their stunning, almost phosphorescent, electric-blue livery so different from the brown of the adults. The various labrids are common, the most numerous being the rainbow wrasse (Coris julis) and the Thalassoma pavo, which head for the northern Mediterranean waters as they

A - Although a good swimmer, the red anthias (Anthias anthias) never strays far from the bottom, which is why it is sometimes described as necto-benthic.

B - Red mullet (Mullus barbatus) are prominent among the fish that dwell on sandy and detrital bottoms. Their ventrally flattened bodies and barbels are typical adaptations to life on the sea-bed.

C - The gurnard (Trygloporus lastoviza) uses its large, colored pectoral fins to glide slowly over the bottom after suddenly darting forward.

D - A melon urchin (Echinus melo) surrounded by small ophiura. Both these echinoderms are frequently found on muddy and sandy bottoms. The urchin feeds on tiny invertebrates and vegetation.

E - Scorpionfish are in many respects emblematic of life on the sea-bed. Their stout body and wide pectoral fins do not lend themselves to swimming fast for long periods but they are ideal for a sedentary existence, spent waiting for passing prey.

warm up. The proximity of the sea bed has imposed a certain lifestyle on these fish and they have interwoven unusual relationships with their environment and developed reproductive techniques involving nest-building. During this period of the year an observant diver will be able to see some of these fish darting through the water with pieces of algae in their mouths. By following them patiently and taking care not to frighten them, it is possible to watch them building their nests. Descending even further in the water, the diver comes to the flower garden of the benthos. The light conditions here permit the growth of a large number of

spontaneously interested in divers. Sole, plaice and hake lie camouflaged beneath the sand, as does the dangerous weever with its poisonous dorsal fin. The sight of a flying gurnard with its big, blue-spotted fins is ample reward for those who go so far into the depths. There are plenty of invertebrates too - a small, newly-born cuttlefish, already able to hide itself and to prey, or a sand urchin, or hermit crabs, leaving their tracks to intersect with those left by the molluscs in their night-time sorties. Then, like a familiar note, you might see a star and, further off, a weak light, a greeting from a luminescent sea plume to an unknown visitor from afar.

F - Sea plumes are organisms typically found on muddy and sandy bottoms. They manage to remain erect and firmly anchored thanks to a special muscular peduncle which functions in much the same way as an expansion plug.

G - With its characteristic reddish color and blue hoops the squat lobster (Galatea strigosa)

does not easily escape notice. This crustacean is often sighted on rocky and gravel bottoms and can live at depths of up to 600 meters.

H - A turbot finds effective camouflage on a detrital bottom. This flatfish belongs to the Pleronettiform order comprising species which, after birth, undergo drastic changes to adapt to benthic life.

F

G

brown, green algae, from the fluorescent *Dictyota* to the green and globulous *Codium* to the bladed *Peyssonnelia*. As the light decreases and the diver has to use a torch to wake up the colors of the benthos, the sponges once again make their appearance: zoantaria, gorgonians, bryozoans, Ascidiacea and the red coral, whose kingdom this is.
No introduction to the benthos can ignore the sandy bottoms, either transformed and hidden by the meadows of posidonia, the Mediterranean's submerged "lung", or empty and desolate. But the latter is merely an impression. It is not uncommon to see mullet and striped bream and they are

H

A UNIVERSE OF MOUTHS AND COLORS

Depth - 20 meters. In front of us the wall rising to the surface becomes a little less vertical and widens out towards the open sea, creating a space in which to pause and reflect. Yellow, red and some white gorgonians lift their flowered branches pointing in the direction of the current. In the undergrowth algae and sponges share the territory together with the axinellae the ascydians, and the bryozoans. A red starfish moves slowly on its tube feet, brushing the long tube of a spirograph which is turning a cartwheel. Rayís bream swim round us and other kinds of bream dart by in a hurry, disturbing a black corb and some anthias which share the same crevice.

A scorpion fish moves suddenly and so doing, loses its invisibility. A blenny is sure to be watching us through some tiny hole . Everything looks tranquil and the calm is only broken by the noise from the cylinder and the air bubbles which rise at intervals up to the surface. But there is a bitter struggle for life going on as we watch. By stopping breathing and listening hard, we should hear that the silence is broken by a series of sounds, some clearer than others: creaks, whistles, cracks, rustles and knocks can be heard all around us, once again giving the lie to the definition of the sea as a world of silence. It is easy to image at this point that the noises we hear are made by the movements of claws, jaws and radulae, busy breaking off, gnawing or scratching a suitable

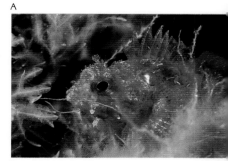

A

B

food source. The scorpion fish we have just seen is probably lying in wait again and its next victim might be one of the little peeping blennies. Amongst the sea-bed predators, the scorpion fish is a symbol of one of the most typical hunting strategies in the benthos - ambush. Hunting by ambush requires certain adaptations, such as a capacious mouth which can open fast and powerful muscles for rapid movements in a few tenths of a second to surprise the prey. All this is important but it would be useless were it not accompanied by camouflage coloring. Camouflage seems to be part of the hunting strategy. The octopus is a master at it and can change its mouldable, changeable body into a piece of rock, imitating not just the color but its texture. The elusive sole on the sandy bottom have the same ability, and so does the angler fish, whose only hope of catching a prey lies in its strangely shaped body which stays perfectly immobile except for the long filament it waves in front of its mouth. It looks like a little worm swimming with difficulty in the middle of the water and this is exactly what the other fish think it is, so that they are eaten as they eat, as it were. Not even fishing with bait was a human invention, after all.

A - A small scorpionfish stays hidden amid the algae. Given its size, mimetic skills and the spines on its body play a major part in keeping it alive.

B - The claws of crustaceanas are extremely effective weapons for attack or self-defense. Their shape varies according to the feeding habits of individual species and may take the form of knives, pincers, grinders, chisels or levers.

Diagram illustrating the different feeding habits of some fish species, representing an example of fish behavior.

Plankton eaters:
 1) Anchovy (Engraulis encrasicolus)
 4,5) Damselfish (Chromis sp.)
Omnivores:
 2) Mullet (Mugil sp.)
Fish eaters:
 3) Amberjack (Seriola dumerili)
 14) Anglerfish (Lophius piscatorius)
Benthic carnivores :

 6) Peacock wrasse (Symphodus tinca)
 7) White seabream (Diplodus sargus)
 8) Rainbow wrasse (Coris julis)
 10) Ocellated wrasse (Symphodus ocellatus)
 11) Cardinalfish (Apogon imberbis)
 12) Needlefish (Sygnathus typhle)
 13) Red mullet (Mullus surmuletus)
 15) Ray (Raya sp.)
Herbivores:
 9) Salema (Sarpa salpa)

But hunting can be active, too. There is no lack of fish which pursue their prey or look for it amongst the crevices in the rock or the sediment on the bottom. Some are specialized, but others go happily from one type of food to another, depending on supply at that moment. The benthos, although it appears to teem with life, is not over-supplied with food sources and for this reason it is dependent on the waters around it. The continuous rain of organic detritus from above is a real manna

B

A

for all the fixed or sedentary benthic animals. If they did not live in an environment rich in bacteria, plankton and organic particles, the sponges would not manage to survive, condemned as they are to immobility. It is only by incessantly filtering the water that they many to satisfy their alimentary needs and to grow. Some can draw a certain advantage from symbiosis with specialized microalgae, but these are not constant, as the sponges prefer some environments, such as caves and the deepest, poorly-lit sea-beds, which are hostile to plant life. A carnivorous sponge was recently found in one of the canyons off Marseilles (*Asbestopluma sp.*). This species was already known in deep water, but up until then it had never been found at depths accessible to humans. The fact that a sponge exists which can capture its prey

C

D

with special laces and digest it would seem to support the many scientists who maintain that the sponges are a lot less primitive and more complex than they seem. This is especially so when one thinks that they have made themselves interesting to human eyes by sublimating their immobility in a variety of colors, from yellow to red to purple to blue to yellow to white, with all the intermediate tones, it is hard to imagine, as well as an equally wide range of shapes.

The ascydians are active filterers too, close relatives of the vertebrates and therefore of humans, despite their funny barrel-shape with two openings on top. Their body should be seen as a packaging wrapped round a pump with a filter. The former sucks water and the latter filters out everything which is edible. The gorgonians and worms like the spyrographs or the white-crested fan worms are filterers too, but less active and more dependent on what the currents

A - The anglerfish (Lophius piscatorius) is an amazingly cunning predator. Carefully camouflaged on the sea-bed, it lures its prey with a long ray which looks like a tiny, defenseless worm.

B - The gaping mouth of an anglerfish is an all too obvious indication of the potential risk that this fish represents for other species.

C - The stargazer (Uranoscopus scaber) has adapted perfectly to life on the bottom, and to lying in wait for its prey. It hides amid sediment and leaves exposed only its eyes and mouth which it then snaps wide open at the opportune moment, infallibly sucking in its hapless prey.

D - This cuttlefish has captured a tiny ray's bream. Unlike the species in the pictures above, the cuttlefish is an active hunter: its success depends on speed of action and on the infallible grip of its tentacles, equipped with suckers which stop its prey escaping.

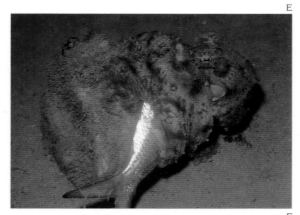

dwelling anemones with double crowns, they are distributed along the sea-bed on the basis of their favorite substrates. They stretch into the water their concentric circles of tentacles, which make them look like delicate flowers. Delicate flowers, perhaps, but not innocuous ones. Each of these tentacles is a terrible danger, ready to enter into action as soon as it comes into contact with a possible prey. The surface of these animals is scattered with stinging cells containing tiny poisoned harpoons, which hit and paralyse and animals they touch. For a small fish or a crustacean the encounter with predators such as these is generally fatal and, paralysed by the poison, they are wrapped in the tentacles and dragged to the middle and the mouth, where they are swallowed.

G - The sea cucumbers in this photo are shown in the unusual vertical position assumed during reproduction; they feed while walking on the bottom, swallowing large quantities of sediment which they then expel in long strands after removing all the nutritious substances.

H - The row of spirals on the spirographs dotted all over this long-submerged rope is in fact a huge trap for smaller planktonic organisms. Each one of these crowns is a net which catches whatever happens to pass by.

E - Fish generally manage to escape from the tentacles of an octopus but, once weakened by the struggle, they become an easy prey for this intelligent invertebrate. Its suckers maintain a firm hold on the victim and the inky substances ejected through its beak can paralyze the sensory organs of its prey, dashing any last hope of resistance.

F - Many sea anemones have retractile tentacles, controlled by special muscular fibers. The anemone usually draws in its tentacles after catching some tasty morsel. Only when the digestion process is over does it open up again, spreading its tentacles in readiness for the next victim.

carry to them or what falls around them. The gorgonians, yellow, white or black, create fan-shaped bushes and bear thousands of little polyps on their branches, each one of which is a minute mouth surrounded by eight feathered tentacles. The myriad polyps are transformed into a tight network which grasps the particles of food transported by the current and feeds on them. The sedentary worms mentioned above take their food from the water by intercepting it with their long tentacles like feather crowns or spirals, which disappear as soon as we approach, as if by magic. The sands and other sediments are home to molluscs, predators and prey at the same time and to carnivorous starfish and sea cucumbers which feed on detritus in great quantities and then expel it without much of the organic substance associated with it. Many cnidarians are predators, although they are condemned to immobility. Purple, green and red, brown or diaphanous and tube

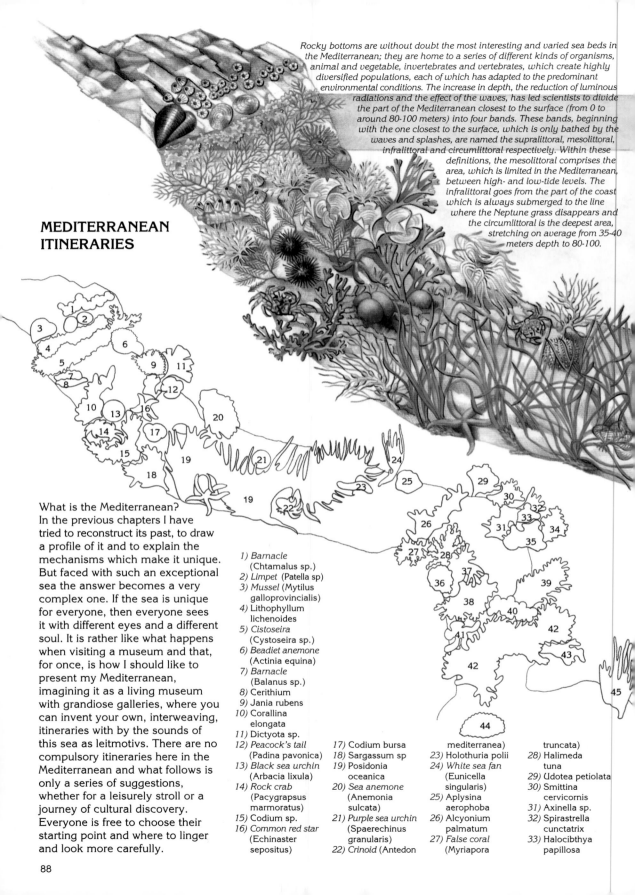

Rocky bottoms are without doubt the most interesting and varied sea beds in the Mediterranean; they are home to a series of different kinds of organisms, animal and vegetable, invertebrates and vertebrates, which create highly diversified populations, each of which has adapted to the predominant environmental conditions. The increase in depth, the reduction of luminous radiations and the effect of the waves, has led scientists to divide the part of the Mediterranean closest to the surface (from 0 to around 80-100 meters) into four bands. These bands, beginning with the one closest to the surface, are only bathed by the waves and splashes, are named the supralittoral, mesolittoral, infralittoral and circumlittoral respectively. Within these definitions, the mesolittoral comprises the area, which is limited in the Mediterranean, between high- and low-tide levels. The infralittoral goes from the part of the coast which is always submerged to the line where the Neptune grass disappears and the circumlittoral is the deepest area, stretching on average from 35-40 meters depth to 80-100.

MEDITERRANEAN ITINERARIES

What is the Mediterranean? In the previous chapters I have tried to reconstruct its past, to draw a profile of it and to explain the mechanisms which make it unique. But faced with such an exceptional sea the answer becomes a very complex one. If the sea is unique for everyone, then everyone sees it with different eyes and a different soul. It is rather like what happens when visiting a museum and that, for once, is how I should like to present my Mediterranean, imagining it as a living museum with grandiose galleries, where you can invent your own, interweaving, itineraries with by the sounds of this sea as leitmotivs. There are no compulsory itineraries here in the Mediterranean and what follows is only a series of suggestions, whether for a leisurely stroll or a journey of cultural discovery. Everyone is free to choose their starting point and where to linger and look more carefully.

1) Barnacle (Chtamalus sp.)
2) Limpet (Patella sp)
3) Mussel (Mytilus galloprovincialis)
4) Lithophyllum lichenoides
5) Cistoseira (Cystoseira sp.)
6) Beadiet anemone (Actinia equina)
7) Barnacle (Balanus sp.)
8) Cerithium
9) Jania rubens
10) Corallina elongata
11) Dictyota sp.
12) Peacock's tail (Padina pavonica)
13) Black sea urchin (Arbacia lixula)
14) Rock crab (Pacygrapsus marmoratus)
15) Codium sp.
16) Common red star (Echinaster sepositus)
17) Codium bursa
18) Sargassum sp
19) Posidonia oceanica
20) Sea anemone (Anemonia sulcata)
21) Purple sea urchin (Spaerechinus granularis)
22) Crinoid (Antedon mediterranea)
23) Holothuria polii
24) White sea fan (Eunicella singularis)
25) Aplysina aerophoba
26) Alcyonium palmatum
27) False coral (Myriapora truncata)
28) Halimeda tuna
29) Udotea petiolata
30) Smittina cervicornis
31) Axinella sp.
32) Spirastrella cunctatrix
33) Halocibthya papillosa

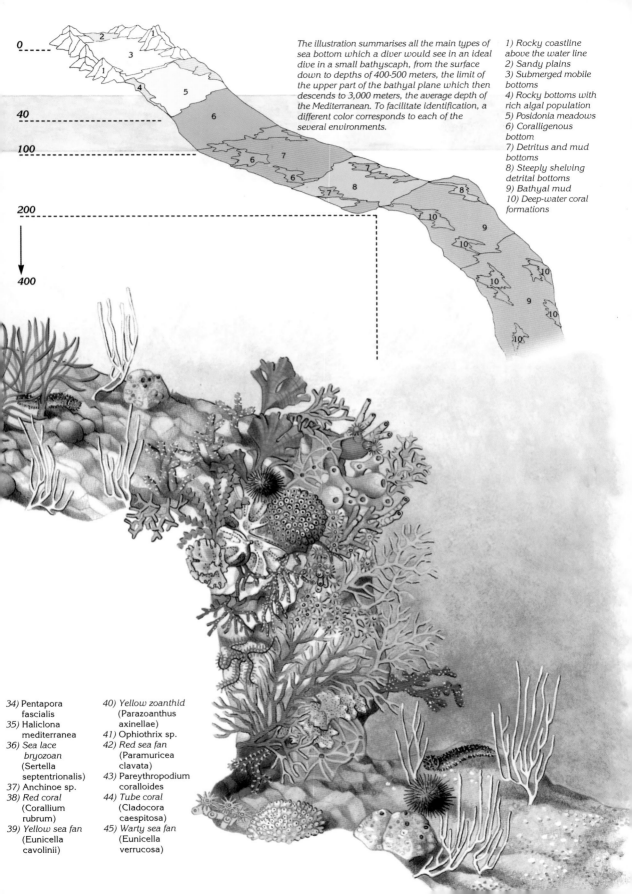

0 -----
40 -----
100 -----
200 -----
400

The illustration summarises all the main types of
sea bottom which a diver would see in an ideal
dive in a small bathyscaph, from the surface
down to depths of 400-500 meters, the limit of
the upper part of the bathyal plane which then
descends to 3,000 meters, the average depth of
the Mediterranean. To facilitate identification, a
different color corresponds to each of the
several environments.

1) Rocky coastline
above the water line
2) Sandy plains
3) Submerged mobile
bottoms
4) Rocky bottoms with
rich algal population
5) Posidonia meadows
6) Coralligenous
bottom
7) Detritus and mud
bottoms
8) Steeply shelving
detrital bottoms
9) Bathyal mud
10) Deep-water coral
formations

34) Pentapora
    fascialis
35) Haliclona
    mediterranea
36) Sea lace
    bryozoan
    (Sertella
    septentrionalis)
37) Anchinoe sp.
38) Red coral
    (Corallium
    rubrum)
39) Yellow sea fan
    (Eunicella
    cavolinii)

40) Yellow zoanthid
    (Parazoanthus
    axinellae)
41) Ophiothrix sp.
42) Red sea fan
    (Paramuricea
    clavata)
43) Pareythropodium
    coralloides
44) Tube coral
    (Cladocora
    caespitosa)
45) Warty sea fan
    (Eunicella
    verrucosa)

FIRST GALLERY: THE SANDS

At first glance this looks like an empty room, a connecting gallery. Immediately one has passed through the waves the eyes search the area quickly looking for something to fix on. At the furthest point of the horizon everything seems to be one continuous desolate land, covered with a liquid sky, but it is not so. These sea-beds look like desert, but they are not! Their dominion is in fact one of the largest and one of the richest and most exploited biologically.
Not only do most beaches extend into the sea, albeit varying from sand to very fine mud, down to depths of hundreds, if not thousands, of meters, but every rocky coast, no matter how huge, ends up in an incoherent seabed, sooner or later. But to see this world we have to adjust our viewpoint and glide over the sands or the detritus mixed with mud which make up these mobile

A

B

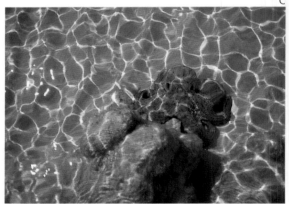

C

D

substrates. Mobile is the right name for them, because everything here is unstable and in motion. A storm at sea is enough to upset its apparent monotony rapidly. When the sea is temporarily "closed" as it were, for bad weather, waiting visitors can see how the gallery is restructured. The motion of the waves lifts the seabed, mixes and blends the sediment so that it is once again suspended in the water, altering the color of the huge tracts of the sea. When everything is calm again, the sediment settles back to its place and the gallery is open to the public once more.
The clearest sign of this relationship with the sea which lies above it are the ripple marks on the top layers of the mobile bottom. Hills and valleys of varying depths, a repeating pattern like dunes in the desert, with the first signs of life between them. Little shells which move in bursts. Unnatural behavior for molluscs, but not for the hermit crabs. Having no armor of their own like the other crustaceans, they

A - The sedimentary ripple marks formed by waves are one of the commonest features on sand bottoms.

B - These ripple marks do not make ideal habitats in shallow waters. The sea's continued stirring action prevents fixed and emergent forms of life from becoming established. Most organisms live underneath the sand.

C - The occasional rocks which break up the mobile sea bed immediately become oases of life, even attracting big predators like this perfectly camouflaged octopus.

D - The sea bed at the bottom of the reef is usually sand or detritus. Such sediments often attract burrowing organisms like this large *Cerianthus membranaceus*, its tube decorated with a colony of bryozoans.

E

F

G

H

I

are forced to seek shelter in abandoned shells and live a protected life in a rented home. Looking from one little hermit to another the eye might be drawn by a sudden movement revealing the presence of a camouflaged goby, a small sole *(Solea sp.)* or flatfish like the *Bothus podas.* On a pale sea bed with hardly any obvious shelter, camouflage is almost obligatory and taking on the color of the surrounding substrate is an art exercised by many. Even large and more easily-seen fish are not excessively colored, in the more superficial waters at least. Of course, bream and mullet stand out more than a flatfish dug into the sand, but the light playing on the sand makes them less distinct, even with their striped silhouettes. We do have an advantage here, though. Their feeding habits mean that they follow us closely to profit from the sediment swirled up by our fins, revealing organic particles and minute invertebrates. The animal and plant life on this type of sea bed is not gaudy, but there are a considerable number of organisms, even though it is often easier to see their marks and reconstruct their lives than pick out the protagonists themselves. Strange, cone-shaped and convoluted piles of sand are proof of the presence below the sea bed of polychaete worms *(Arenicola sp.)* which spend their entrenched lives incessantly sieving the sediment and expelling the detritus when it has been purged of the organic part.

E - Trumpetfish (Macroramphosus scolopax) *generally live in deep waters, close to the bottom. They have long noses and a strange way of swimming, which keeps them in a permanently angled position.*

F - Octopus are not rare on sand bottoms. Although they prefer more varied environments, they often hunt for crabs and molluscs on the sand.

G - An ocellated sole (Microchirus ocellatus). *This species is quite common in the Mediterranean, where it is found in the posidonia meadows.*

H - A butterfly blenny (Blennius ocellaris). *This nocturnal species prefers deep waters, where it hides out during the day.*

I - The emperor shrimp (Penaeus keranturus) *lives from depths of a few meters right down to over 100 meters, on sand or mud, where it digs itself a lair.*

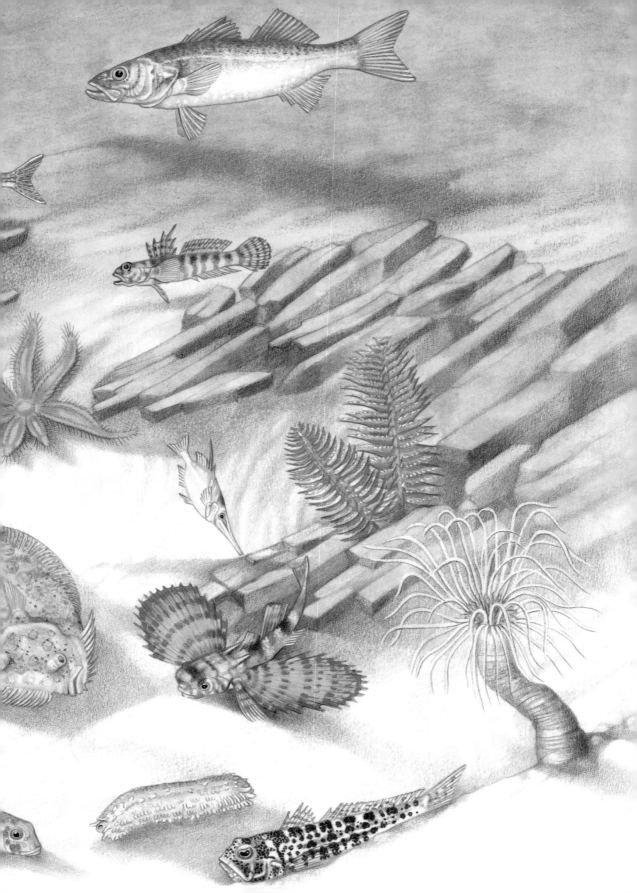

Beyond, a few perforated valves tell the tale of a *Natica hebraea*'s night-time hunt, while a small pile of shells collected at the center of a five-pointed outline tell of the predatory activity of the large comb star *(Astropecten auranciacus)* which is perhaps resting, half-buried, in the sand after its night-time raids.

A sandy bottom, and even more so one with a higher percentage of mud, transmits other messages. Diving at first light of dawn before the tidal currents erase all traces, you will be able to see not only the marks of the gastropod molluscs

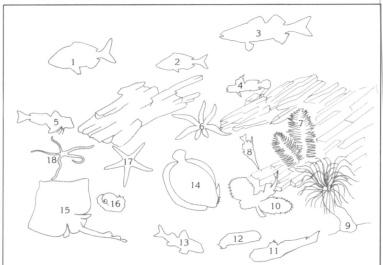

A

Mobile bottoms are so called because since the materials which make them are fine and not cohesive, they can easily be moved by waves or currents, creating the ripple marks. The kind of life found here is less varied than on rocky bottoms, but some species are found in large numbers and there is much commercial exploitation of crustaceans and molluscs typical of sandy bottoms. Although they are not very attractive, sand and mud bottoms can reserve many surprises. Here are illustrated some of the most important species found on these bottoms, starting with the ones which are visible on the surface, such as striped bream and weever, and continuing with the deeper species such as flying gurnards, trumpet fish and the sea-pen.

1) Striped bream (Lythognathus mormyrus)
2) Picarel (Spicara maena)
3) Sea bass (Dicentrarchus labrax)
4) Black goby (Gobius niger)
5) Piper gurnard (Trigla lyra)
6) Brittle star (Luidia ciliaris)
7) Sea-plume (Pennatula sp.)
8) Snipefish (Macroramphosus scolopax)
9) Cerianthus membranaceus
10) Flying gurnard (Dactylopterus volitans)
11) Weever (Trachinus araneus)
12) Royal cucumber (Stichopus regalis)
13) Red Mullet (Mullus barbatus)
14) Turbot (Bothus podas)
15) Thornback ray (Raja clavata)
16) Moon snail (Natica sp.)
17) Burrowing starfish (Astropecten aranciacus)
18) Long brittle star (Ophioderma longicaudum)

on the sea bed, but the wider pathways of the sea cucumbers or the irregular urchins (*Spatangus purpureus*, the violet heart urchin or *Echinocardium cordatum*). They are almost always buried in the sand, but their whitish shells, fragile and heart-shaped with fascinating petal-like perforations, can be found quite often.

Closer by, there are small cavities with jagged crown-like ruffs. Move the water above them and they will disappear - mysteriously it seems at first, but not really. Grab a handful of sand and you will find a bivalve mollusc. Defenseless filterers, destined almost certainly to be captured by any one of a large number of predators (including humans), the tellins (*Cerastoderma glauca*), Venus clams *(Venus verrucosa)*, razor shells *Solen sp.*) and carpet shells

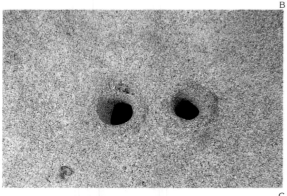

B

C

A - *Luidia ciliaris is a characteristic star found in deeper waters on sandy beds, where it buries itself under the surface. Although its size would seem to belie it, its name brittle star is well-deserved, as its seven arms break off easily.*

B - *Holes in the sand signal the presence of one of the bivalve molluscs which live buried in the sediment.*

C - *The strange "sculpture" discernible against the sand is formed of eggs deposited by the Natica, a gastropod mollusk typical of sandy beds.*

(Tapes decussates) have come up with no better defense than to live hidden, putting out elastic, telescopic siphons which are their only contact with the outside world. On the other hand, living hidden is not only useful to totally defenseless creatures who live by filtering the contents of the water, but also to much more terrifying predators. A black blotch and a pair of mobile eyes are often the only visible sign of a weever fish (Trachinus sp.) whose poisonous spines are a threat to humans too and whose wide mouth is the last leg for many small fishes and crustaceans.

E

D

F

G

D - A red sea plume (Pennatula rubra), with a trumpetfish (Macroramphosus scolopax) alongside, anchored to the sea bed by a fleshy foot. Despite its looks this is not a single animal, but a colony consisting of a main polyp and secondary lateral polyps.

E - Mediterranean alcyonium (Alcyonium palmatum) prefers to live on detritus and mud. It is commonly known as dead man's fingers.

F - Pagurus prideauxi *is a strange pink hermit crab with reddish markings, which always lives with the* Adamsia palliata *sea anemone. The symbiosis between the crustacean and the cloak anemone is so close that the two animals can only survive apart when young.*

G - A swim crab of the Portunidae *family. These crabs, with their flattened shells, have a pair of modified feet shaped like paddles which they row with.*

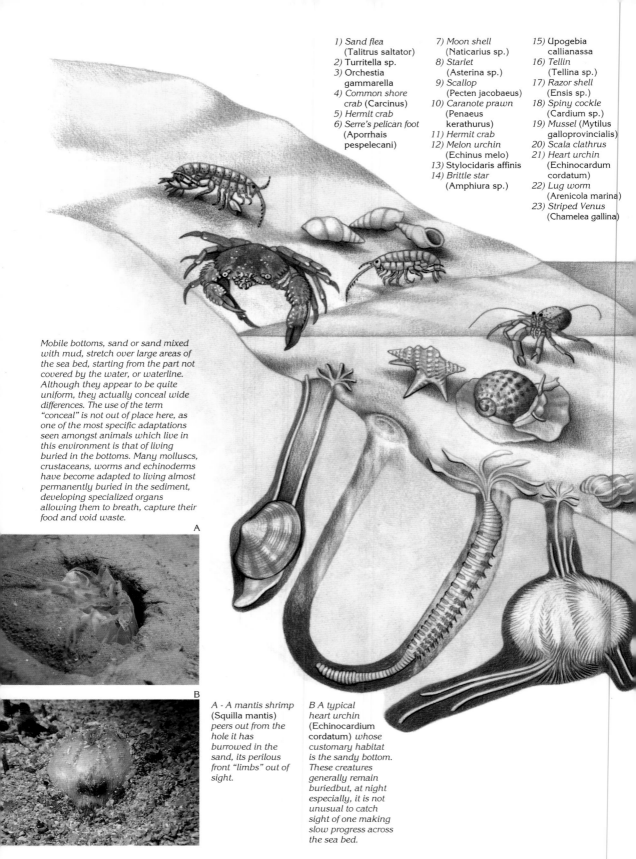

1) Sand flea
   (Talitrus saltator)
2) Turritella sp.
3) Orchestia
   gammarella
4) Common shore
   crab (Carcinus)
5) Hermit crab
6) Serre's pelican foot
   (Aporrhais
   pespelecani)
7) Moon shell
   (Naticarius sp.)
8) Starlet
   (Asterina sp.)
9) Scallop
   (Pecten jacobaeus)
10) Caranote prawn
    (Penaeus
    kerathurus)
11) Hermit crab
12) Melon urchin
    (Echinus melo)
13) Stylocidaris affinis
14) Brittle star
    (Amphiura sp.)
15) Upogebia
    callianassa
16) Tellin
    (Tellina sp.)
17) Razor shell
    (Ensis sp.)
18) Spiny cockle
    (Cardium sp.)
19) Mussel (Mytilus
    galloprovincialis)
20) Scala clathrus
21) Heart urchin
    (Echinocardum
    cordatum)
22) Lug worm
    (Arenicola marina)
23) Striped Venus
    (Chamelea gallina)

Mobile bottoms, sand or sand mixed with mud, stretch over large areas of the sea bed, starting from the part not covered by the water, or waterline. Although they appear to be quite uniform, they actually conceal wide differences. The use of the term "conceal" is not out of place here, as one of the most specific adaptations seen amongst animals which live in this environment is that of living buried in the bottoms. Many molluscs, crustaceans, worms and echinoderms have become adapted to living almost permanently buried in the sediment, developing specialized organs allowing them to breath, capture their food and void waste.

A

B

A - A mantis shrimp (Squilla mantis) peers out from the hole it has burrowed in the sand, its perilous front "limbs" out of sight.

B A typical heart urchin (Echinocardium cordatum) whose customary habitat is the sandy bottom. These creatures generally remain buriedbut, at night especially, it is not unusual to catch sight of one making slow progress across the sea bed.

The defensive mechanism of the pearly razorfish *(Xyrichthys novacula)* is equally curious. When threatened, these strange pink labrid, which are common to these sea beds, dive for the sediment and rapidly entrench most of their body, a task made easier by their pointed shape. The techniques of the angler fish *(Lophius sp.)* and the *Uranoscopus scaber* are more sophisticated.

The first of these trusts to its mimetic coloring to disappear change from normal fish into asymmetrical ones, with both eyes located on one side of the body, the top side, (right or left depending on the species) while the underside which rests on the sea bed is totally blind and almost always decolored.

Nature, in the last analysis, is economical, and what is not needed is eliminated.

Some *Echinodermata* are also flat, but they are compressed from back to belly rather than laterally; the *Peltaster placenta* or pentagon star for example, whose geometric construction makes it look artificial, as well as the smaller *Asterina gibbosa.* Proof of the wisdom of such a solution is the fact that some higher organisms have also adopted it.

Rays *(Raja sp.)*, torpedoes *(Torpedo sp.)* and the stingrays *(Dasyatis sp.)* transform the sands into immense airports where they stop over between the short flights their wings - large pectoral fins in actual fact - permit them.

A

B

C

D

from its enemy's sight and the second one buries itself. Despite the obvious differences in shape and behavior, both have developed the same hunting strategy, which requires a kind of rod and bait to trick prey and attract it close to the mouth.

So the mobile sands of the sea bed do have a determining influence on different forms of life they shelter and they impose common strategies and solutions, the most obvious of which are those developed in order not to sink. A mobile sea bed, especially if it is a muddy one, can be an obstacle to movement for all animals, so why not redistribute body weight better by enlarging the surface area?

The flat fish *(Pleuronectidae)* are the real emblems of what life on these bottoms means. In the course of their lives they

A - The lack of safe havens makes the sand a harsh habitat. Any organism which can camouflage itself has a definite advantage over the others. The photo illustrates a cuttlefish's incredible camouflage ability; not only does it bury itself, it also imitates the color of the sea bed perfectly.

B - The angler fish (Lophius sp.) *waits in ambush on the sea bed, relying on its color and its immobility to lure the prey, which it attracts with a false bait, close to its mouth.*

C - A hairy sole (Microchirus hispidus). *The fish gets its name from the roughness of its scales.*

D - A close up of a turbot's snout highlights its eyes, both located on the same side of the body.

E - A star-gazer (Uranoscopus scaber). Like the angler fish, this fish uses an imitation bait (the red peduncle) to attract prey close to its mouth.

One of the prettiest fish you are likely to meet in these waters, the flying gurnard *(Dactylopterus volitans)* also has wings. Its common name and the adjective *volitans* might almost have been coined to trick the unwary, thus perpetuating a mistake made by many people in centuries gone by.
The gurnard has very large pectoral fins, in splendid shades of blue, which actually look like real wings, although the fish will never fly with them.

F

E

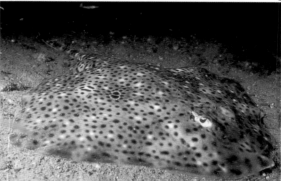

G

H

F - An ocellated ray (Torpedo torpedo) swims over a sandy bottom, showing its flattened shape and the ocellar marks from which it gets its name. This species was often illustrated in pictures by the ancient Greeks.

When disturbed it moves off the bottom with powerful beats of its tail and then planes majestically with its great fins spread, like the splendid mantle of a tranquil prince.
However, although fish do not fly, some do walk. The *Triglidae*, the family to which the gurnards belong, is distinguished by these particularly large first rays on its pectoral fins. The fish use them for walking along the sand, sometimes in the direction of the dual crown of tentacles -

white and black, or purple - of a large *Cerianthus membranaceus* growing like a lone palm tree at the foot of the reddish, brightly-colored rocks which rise from the sand to lead us into the next gallery in our underwater museum.

G - The ray has evolved into a flattened shape, as happens to most of the fish which live close to the bottom.

H - The flying gurnard (Dactylopterus volitans) has large pectoral fins, but despite its names, both common and scientific, they do not permit it to fly.

SECOND GALLERY: HIDDEN TREASURES

Unlike the previous gallery, this one appears straight away to be full of exhibits. There are those who might think that such marvels as these, which force us to keep looking in different directions as if this expanse of riches were impossible, should have been kept until last. But ours is a special museum, where all the galleries are linked to each other and there are infinite itineraries. The light in here, less than 5% of outside light, is suffused, as it should be at depths of 40-50 meters. The sun's rays lost their warmer chromatic components far from here and everything in this coralligenous area of the circumlittoral, where even the

A

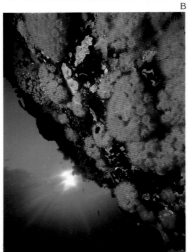

B

A - The bright yellow buttons scattered over this wall belong to Leptosammia pruvoti, *a solitary hard coral which likes poorly-illuminated bottoms.*

B - The lively orange cushions of colonies of Astroides calycularis, *a hard coral which prefers warm waters, put on a frequent show in the southern parts of the western Mediterranean.*

C - Paradoxically, it is the sea beds furthest from the light which are richest in life and color. In this photograph green and red seaweed and sponges encrust the rock with patches of color which might have been left by a careless painter. In the foreground, the black silhouettes of long-spined sea urchins, Centrostephanus longispinus.

*D - The big red sea fans (*Paramuricea clavata) *are one of the species best-known to divers in the Mediterranean, where they sometimes establish large "woods" at depths of over forty meters.*

temperature is constant and oscillates between 13 and 17 degrees centigrade, is wrapped in a dominant dark blue which turns black if we look down and light and opalescent if we look up to check the silvery wake of bubbles, bursting as they rise. Yet color is everywhere here. The flash of a camera going off, short though it is, reveals a range of colors greater than that of the rainbow and encourages us to switch a torch on. Straight away the reds leap out as the dominant colors, due in large part to

organisms like petrified leaves. This impression is more than justified, for everything here is dominated by forms of plant life. These are the calcareous red algae (Corallinaceae like *Lythophyllum*, *Mesophyllum* and *Neogoniolython* and the *Peyssonelliaceae* like *Peyssonnellia*). Their jagged shapes in all tones of red, from pink of violet, build an almost continuous covering, hiding the rock under a thick layer of algae; they in their turn are joined and held together by

E - In some parts of the Mediterranean the tips of the colonies of the red sea fans (Paramuricea clavata) *become yellow. This strange transformation is probably where the old scientific name for this species,* Paramuricea chamaleon, *originated.*

F - These acydians (Clavelina lepadiformis), *shaped like pitchers of blown glass, have established themselves on a branch of dead man's fingers, which has in turn encrusted a sea fan. It is by no means unusual to find this kind of superimposition of organisms in the marine world, where for many of them the conquest of space is a primary requirement.*

G - The coral sea beds are often colonised by large colonies of ramified sponges of the genus Axinella. *They grow for the most part close to drop-offs and ciliates, in order to exploit the currents from which they obtain oxygen and food to the best advantage.*

the skeletons of other encrustant invertebrates: sponges, bryozoans, madrepores, serpulids, to mention but a few. The poor light is by no means an obstacle to this explosion of life, in fact it is the cause of it and it is still in any case intense enough to permit the growth of small meadows of green algae such as *Halimeda tuna* and *Udotea petiolata*. These are deep waters, but it need not always be so. A different slant to the reef, or a wider rock terrace, or less transparent water, is enough to create a shaded zone where a small coral biocenosis can become established, even at 20-30 meters depth. In the midst of such plenty it is difficult to compile a list of living organisms. Rocky substrates, which are naturally richer in life,

undergo a disproportionate flowering inside this biocenosis. Every fold and every crevice is immediately contested by the sponges, which take over from one another, often at the end of silent chemical battles.
They in their turn become home to encrustant worms and hydroids, which are preyed on by crustaceans and molluscs, followed in their turn by other specialized predators.
Here and there bunches of white colonial ascidiaceans *(Diazona violacea)* and huge candelabras

of sponges break up the expanses of yellow and red gorgonians, neither of which can be found in the eastern basin, which shows what a disparate sea this is. The red gorgonians (its old name *Paramuricea chamaleon*, comes from its rare, but incredible, dual red and yellow coloring) can only be seen in all their beauty under artificial light and once again, faced with this kind of show, the same old, as-yet-unanswered question comes instinctively to mind. Why do such bright colors exist so far away from us?

H - This photograph of a few branches of a red gorgonian shows the dense covering of polyps. When they are completely open they give the whole colony a feathery look. The Paramuricea clavata is the only Mediterranean sea fan which can rival the tropical species in size.

101

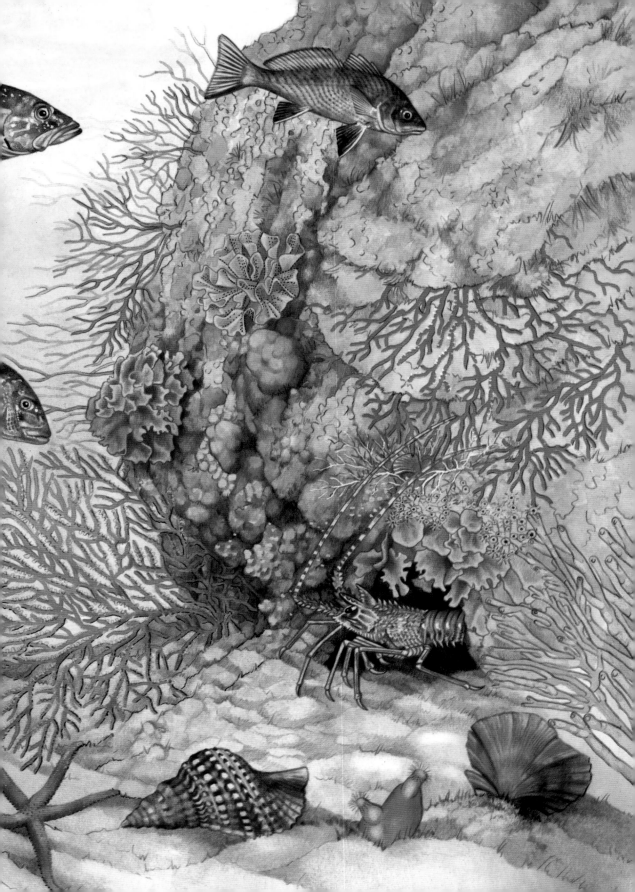

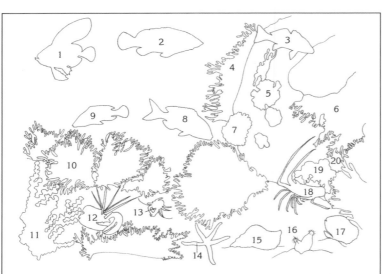

The coralligenous environment is one of the richest in life forms in the Mediterranean. Although it is characterized by lack of illumination, both the red and the encrusting algae play an essential role, covering the rock with a rigid substrate, which is enriched by the encrustations of sponges, annelids, bryozoans and molluscs. Large, highly-visible organisms, such as the sea fans, Axinellae or red coral, then become established on these rocks and it is to them that this biocenosis owes the name - mistaken from a scientific point of view - of "coralligenous".

1) John Dory (Zeus faber)
2) Grouper (Ephinephelus marginatus)
3) Corb (Sciaena umbra)

4) Yellow sea fan (Eunicella cavolinii)
5) Sea lace bryozoan (Sertella septentrionalis)
6) Red coral (Corallium rubrum)
7) Stone weed (Lithophyllum expansum)
8) Common dentex (Dentex dentex)
9) Cuckoo wrasse (Labrus bimaculatus)
10) Red sea fan (Paramuricea clavata)
11) Sea cactus (Halimeda tuna)
12) Lobster (Homarus gammarus)
13) Squat lobster (Galathea strigosa)
14) Red seastar (Echinaster sepositus)
15) Triton (Charonia tritonis)
16) Sea squirt (Halocunthya papillosa)
17) Udotea petiolata
18) Spiny lobster (Palinurus elephas)
19) Axinella sp.
20) Golden zoanthid (Parazoanthus axinellae)

Pushed by the currents which orient them in order to capture more food and thus compensate their total immobility, the fans of the gorgonians wave, rocking the eggs a dogfish has laid amongst their branches.
But the gorgonians themselves can become disputed territory too. Sometimes the guests are harmless, like the unusual feathered sea lilies, *Antedon mediterranean* or the winged oysters *(Pteria hirundo)* with their mother-of-pearl linings, or the intricate orange baskets of the elkhorn corals, or the white, crumbly *Salmacina*, strange worms which are hardly recognisable as such. But there are other cases where mortal battle is joined. Rendered almost invisible under the mimetic mantle which hides its shiny, porcelain-like shall,

C

Neosimmia spelta moves along the branches of the gorgonians hunting for polyps. It might even be partly responsible for the successful preying of *Alcyonum coralloides*, which inexorably covers the branches of the gorgonians, enveloping and transforming them; the gorgonians' downfall might likewise be engendered by their encounter with *Gerardia savaglia*, with its large, bright yellow polyps, known as the Mediterranean black coral.
Life and death are indissolubly

A - Black Mediterranean coral (Gerardia savaglia) belongs to the Zoantharia order and not the Antipatarians. The coral's name comes from its blackish, horny, skeleton.

B - A bryozoan encrusts a sea fan, in competition with an Alcyonium.

C - The rock bottom is completely covered with gorgonians and yellow zoanthids.

A

B

D - Colonies of the sea fan Leptogorgia sarmentosa, very similar to Eunicella cavolinii but with thinner and denser branches, have grown along this underwater cliff.

E - Alicia mirabilis is a large sea anemone which before the spread of underwater sport was considered rare, and thought to be present in a few areas only. However, divers have proved that this species is widespread throughout the western Mediterranean. Its rarity can probably be put down to the fact that it can hardly be seen when closed up.

F - The intricate mass of branches hides a strange Mediterranean basket starfish (Astropartus mediterraneus) belonging to the Gorgonocephalidae. As its arms grow they continue to ramify, until the animal is transformed into a gigantic net. A nocturnal animal, during the day it remains closed up close to the bottom.

G - The jewel anemone (Corynactis viridis) can cover vast sections of the sea bed or of wrecks with its brightly-colored polyps. It likes poorly-illuminated bottoms with strong currents in particular.

H - The yellow zonthids (Parazoanthus axinellae) is a colonial zoanthid which can cover large surfaces with a dense yellow carpet.

interwoven and nothing in the coralligenous system is wasted. Anything which does not become food becomes a tile in the dense coating which covers the rock, which is continually being rebuilt and destroyed, like a biological Penelope's tapestry, by the disintegrating species, principally boring sponges *(Clionidae)*, sea urchins and molluscs, which drill homes in the rock using acid secretions. *Astroides calycularis*, immediately recognisable with its hard, flowered, pads in a distinctive orange color, settles into this intricate landscape; exquisitely graceful to look at, but a terrible predator of the smaller organisms, like all the Cnidaria. Isolated yellow buttons of *Leptosammia pruvoti* grow alongside them, the same

F

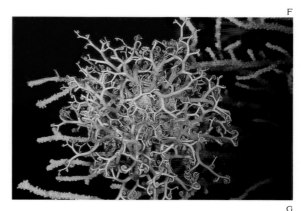

G

H

D

E

color as the yellow zoanthids of *Parazoanthus axinellae*, a colonial animal whose presence demonstrates the presence of weak currents; or there are the fuchsia-pink encrustations of the jewel anemone *(Corynactis viridis)* which decorates sections of the sea bed like rubies. The sponges include the red large spots of *Spirastrella cunctatrix* and *Crambe crambe*.

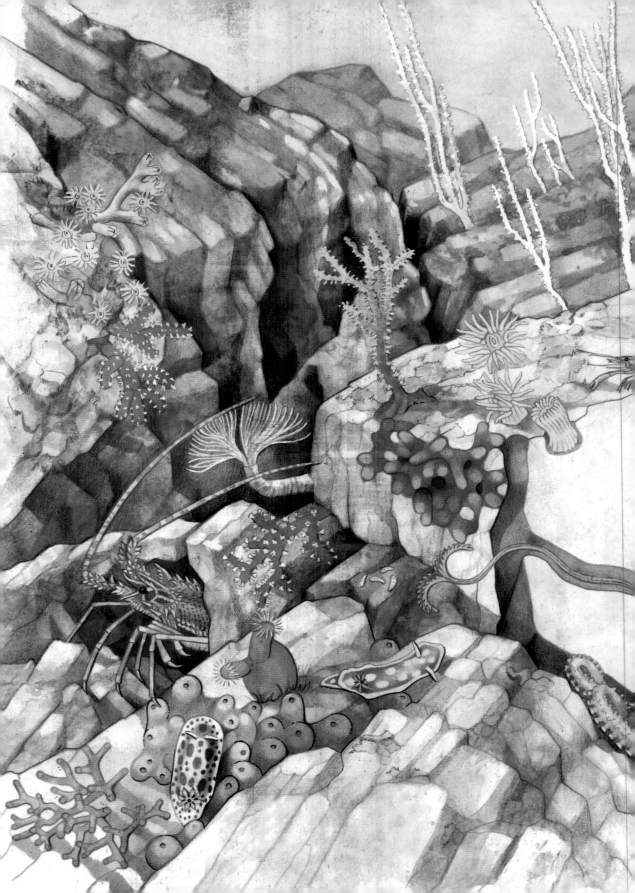

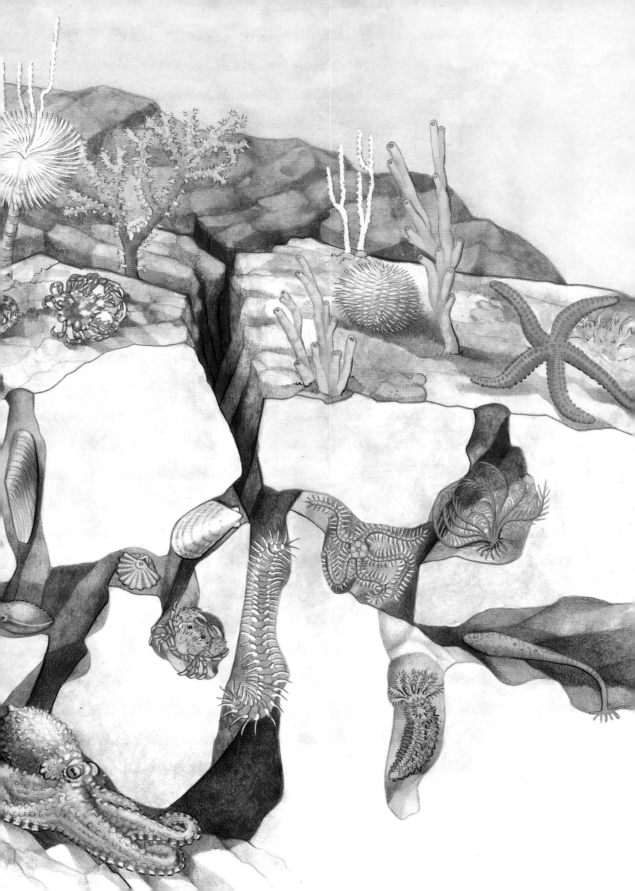

Concealed underneath are the now rare, spiny torny oysters, decimated by a rare illness, or the massed twisted tubes of the yellow *Clathrina*, not forgetting the more massive shapes of the *Aplysina cavernicola*, also yellow and the *Agelas oroides*, which is orange or the brownish *Chondrosia reniformis*. There is often a bush of false coral amongst these encrusting species, or a sedentary polychaete's white cylindrical tube, with the colored crest of its branchial corona. The race for life is run in every direction, aided by the invisible currents, which circulate everywhere and carry food both inside the coral coating, like the layers of a millefeuille cake, as well as over it and far away from it. Much of this world looks immobile and this is undoubtedly one of the reasons

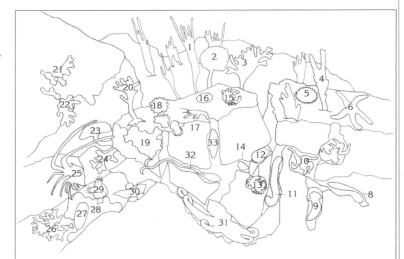

The submerged rocks of the circumlittoral and coral environments are populated by myriad organisms, many of which live hidden inside cavities in the substrate or underneath the accumulating encrustations, forming an extremely intricate environment. The drawing illustrates what one of these sections of the sea bed might look like.

1) *White sea fan* (Eunicella singularis)
2) *Seaworm* (Sabella spallanzani)
3) *Red sea fan* (paramuricea clavata)
4) Axinella sp.
5) *Meadow sea urchin* (Sphaerechinus granularis)
6) Hacelia attenuata
7) *Crinoid* (Antedon mediterranea)
8) Holothurian
9) Cucumaria planci
10) *Brittle star* (Ophiothrix sp.)
11) Eunice sp.
12) Lima sp.

13) *Bristly crab* (Pilumnus hirtellus)
14) Chama griphoides
15) Herbstia condyliata
16) Chiton sp.
17) *Cleaning shrimp* (Lysmata seticauda)
18) Leptosammia pruvoti
19) Oscarella lobularis
20) *Red sea fan* (Paramuricea clavata)
21) Dendrophyllia sp.
22) Alcyonium palmatum
23) Protula tubularis
24) *Red coral* (Corallium rubrum)
25) *Spiny lobster* (Palinurus elephas)
26) *False coral* (Myriapora truncata)
27) Discodoris atromaculata
28) Petrosia ficiformis
29) Halocinthya papillosa
30) Chromodoris luteorosa
31) Octopus vulgaris
32) Bonellia viridis
33) *Date mussel* (Lithopaga lithopaga)

A - *The feathery white tentacles of the coral polyps spread out in the water, ready to capture the minuscule planktonic organisms borne by currents.*

B - *The crinoids or sea lilies* (Antedon mediterranea) *are strange echinoderms with long, colored, feathery arms, which they use to swim as well as to capture the organic particles they feed on.*

why, alongside species which actively filter the water such as the sponges and the ascidians, including the red ones *(Halocintha papillosa)* and the mimetic but comestible ones *(Microcosmus sp.)*, there is a predominance of symmetrical forms with rays, seen on groups which are a long way apart in evolutionary terms. The gorgonians, for instance, which are virtually two-dimensional in terms of overall structure, are actually made up of thousands of small polyps, which are the same shape as the longer tentacles of the sea anemones and the fearful *Alicia mirabilis*, which rises threateningly during the night and then retires and disappears into its full daytime dress; or the feathery crests of the *Serpulidae* worms intent on capturing food from whatever direction it comes.

The real star of this gallery has elegant tentacles with white feathers: the red Mediterranean coral *(Corallium rubrum)* from which the term "coralligenous" (generator of coral) applied to the surrounding system is improperly derived. This red coral (but there are some, extremely rare, colonies of albino coral) grows anywhere it finds the necessary conditions for growth: well-oxygenated water, hardly any turbulence, little light and constant salinity, which is why divers will sometimes find colonies inside caves or crevices close to the surface.
The immobility described up until this point, which is ideal for anyone taking underwater photographs, is broken up by a series of other organisms which slither, climb or swim in and out of the coralligenous maze.

Thanks to their tube feet *Ophidiaster ophidianus* and *Marthasterias glacialis* climb even the steepest walls, slithering over the slim arms of the sand stars and crossing the pathways of colorful nudibranches such as *Flabellina affinis, Hypselodoris valenciennesi, Discodoris atromaculata* and *Chromodoris luteorosa*. The long antennae of spiny lobsters and threatening claws of lobsters, capable of cracking a mollusc's shell at first attempt, protrude from the biggest of the crevices. Other niches may conceal morays and congers,

or small, fluorescent blue fish, more suited to a coral sea bed and apparently nothing to do with the clouds of dameselfish *Chromis chromis* swimming alongside submerged cliffs. They are actually adult and young of the same species. The red *Anthias anthias*, the nosy rainbow wrasses, constantly on the move, and other labrids such as the cuckoo wrasse, *(Labrus bimaculatus)* the males easily recognised by their blue-bordered caudal fin and the blue stripes on the head and sides. You might see a rock move as you follow these fish.

This is no hallucination, just a large specimen of the red scorpionfish *(Scorpaena scrofa)*, leaving one stakeout and looking for a new position. Bream, saddle bream, blotched picarels and *Pagellus*, another kind of sea bream, are a lot easier to see. In more distant waters divers may see the odd John Dory *(Zeus faber)* and, deeper down, on the outer edge of the reef where we started our visit, a few big dentex in no mood to provide a close-up of their large teeth. Red coral is the king of this gallery, but the grouper is queen. It is becoming more uncommon now, which means that its sighting is usually a question of chance. Only those who make a habit of visiting certain parts of this particular museum will be able to

C - This nudibranch **Flabellina affinis** *moves along a colony of hydroids, feeding on its polyps, totally indifferent to their stinging cells.*

D - A large grouper (Epinephelus marginatus) *waits immobile above a sea bed dominated by red sea fans. It is only at depths such as these that encounters with groupers of this size are still possible.*

E - Plesionika narval, *a small Mediterranean shrimp; during the day it is usually found inside caves, hidden in the sediment on the bottom.*

F - A John Dory (Zeus faber), *with characteristic dark marks on the sides and long dorsal rays, which give rise in some places to its alternative name, the cockfish.*

C

D

E

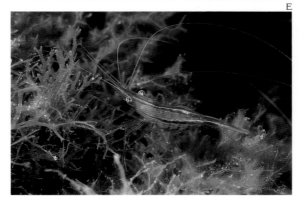

F

identify its dens and make regular visits. In any other instance it will be up to luck and her majesty's attitude towards showing herself. There are several ways of bumping into a grouper: it may be perfectly immobile, suspended in the water, or hanging around by the reef wall, or at the entrance to a cave, or it could have left its "footprint" behind in the shape of a cloud of suspended sediment, caused by the beat of its tail as it moved on inside, which leads us to follow it, into the third gallery.

THIRD GALLERY: THE DARK

The theme of this new gallery could be the allure of the unknown; it can take on the grandeur and solemnity of a cathedral, or the intimacy of a cloister, or the disturbing mystery of a maze, depending on the circumstances. When faced with the opening to a cave every diver feels a ìgutî attraction to it, but this attraction has to be carefully assessed, because an immersion into these dark environments is rather like going down into the deepest of abysses. The comparison is a perfectly valid one.

A - The shape and history of the Mediterranean coastline have formed the many caves scattered along it, producing fascinating and evocative landscapes.

C

B - A diver silhouetted against the mouth of a cave. The light gradient decreases at varying speeds, depending on the depth and shape of the cave, creating population bands. In the deepest parts of the cave there are often organisms with characteristic nocturnal habits.

C - The continuous action of the waves and the currents has eroded the rock and made tunnels. The walls are covered with encrusting organisms, mainly sponges, cnidarians, bryozoans and serpulids. Algae, even the red species which are less fussy about light, are segregated in the areas closest to the entrance.

A

D

D - A great deal of care and preparation is required when undertaking cave exploration. Underwater caves are not always huge grottoes which make fascinating, safe, diving. In fact, caves have hidden dangers and not all divers know how to evaluate them.

E - Sponges and yellow zoanthids (Parazoanthus axinellae) cover the rocky bottom at the mouth of a cave. The presence of the yellow zoanthids, lovers of half-light and strong currents, often marks a cave's entrance and the beginning of biological zoning towards increasingly dark areas.

B

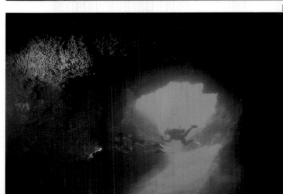

The gradual disappearance of the light can recreate ecological conditions which are found at much greater depths and, even in areas close to the surface, produce organisms which are generally found in deeper water, such as red coral, for example. But this is only one of the possible surprises to be encountered on a visit to a cave, as long as it is carried out in conditions of safety and with respect for rules which are the result of direct, and not second-hand, experience. The most important factor underwater is luminosity, as it strongly conditions the population distribution, of plants in the first place and animals in the second.

E

reflecting so fiercely on the sand that fish are tricked into swimming upside down, the beam of the torch is needed to wake the hidden colors up.

On the roof of the cave are the branches of the red bush coral, mixed with yellow *Aplysina cavernicola* and the red tufts of the fan worms which in the calm water of the caves are usually more open than in other places. A little further in, especially in springtime, some parts of the roof might host the long white festoons of squid eggs, waving slowly in the weak currents.

H - The Mediterranean grouper (Ephinephelus marginatus) is not only one of the best known of the Mediterranean species, but also one most closely associated with caves. Despite its increasing rarity, divers still sometimes see the massive outline of a grouper at the back of the cave it has chosen for its lair.

F - The presence of red coral (Corallium rubrum) shows that the environmental conditions created inside a cave are similar to those found at much greater depths.

G - Cave populations also include vagile species like octopus (Octopus vulgaris). Although they are not found exclusively in these environments, octopus find they provide handy shelter.

The latter also have precise luminosity requirements and, like the algae, can be divided into light (photophyles) and shade (sciophyles) lovers, with every possible intermediate degree. The influence of this parameter is to some extent the recurring theme in any cave dive, where there are generally two population types: one which has adapted to conditions of semi-light and one to absolute darkness.

Seen from the outside a cave looks like a dark entrance hall, but the first few meters are not much different, as far as the flora and fauna are concerned, than what can be found on the surrounding sea bed, although it does depend to a large extent on the depth of the cave entrance. Very often the entrance arch is festooned with golden zoanthids (*Parazoanthus axinellae*) mixed with green algae making the most of the still-available light and, especially, with red encrusting algae such as the *Peyssonnelliae*. Despite the light still penetrating into the cave, sometimes

F

G

H

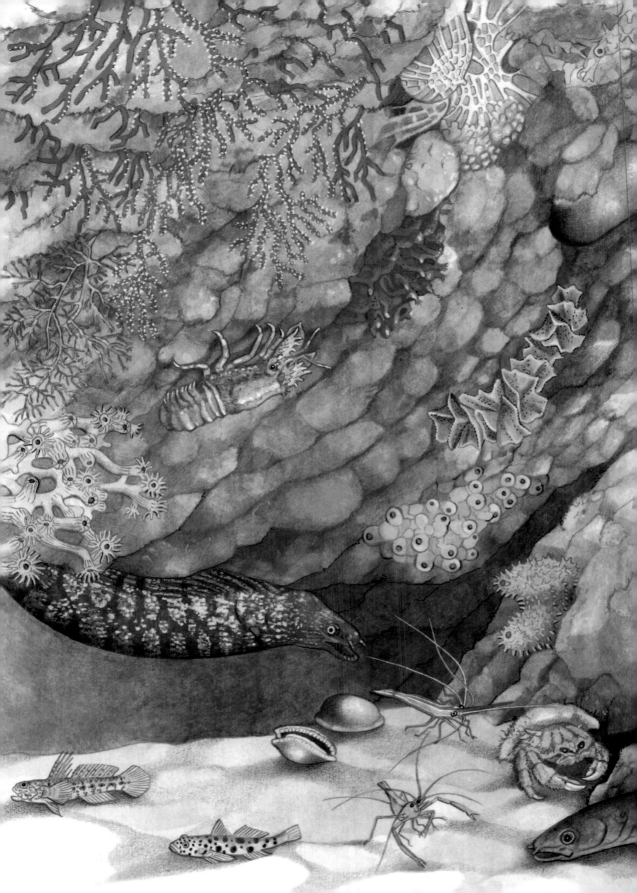

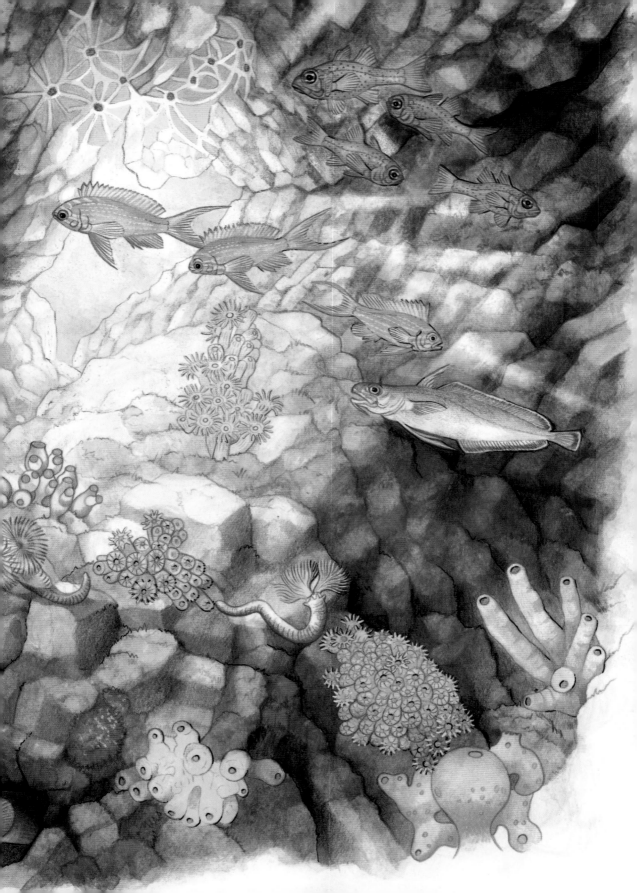

A - The moray (Muraena helena) is one of the commonest species found where the bottom has plenty of crevices and small caves. The photograph shows a particular part of underwater life which many are used to associating with the coral barrier reef. In fact, the association between cleaner shrimp (in this case, Lysmata seticauda) and morays is found in the Mediterranean too.

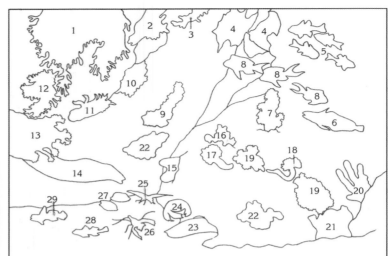

A

B

The cave environment is populated by many species, who find that the stable ecological conditions provide the ideal habitat for them to become established and develop. In other cases they provide shelter during the day for nocturnal species. The drawing shows a cross section of a cave, as it would appear to a diver able to see the whole of the inside and the forms of life it contains at the same time:

1) Red coral (Corallium rubrum)
2) Petrobiona massiliana
3) Aplysina cavenicola
4) Spirastrella cunctatrix
5) Cardinalfish (Apogon imberbis)
6) Forkbeard (Phycis phycis)
7) Golden zoanthid (Parazoanthus axinellae)
8) Swallowtail seaperch (Anthias anthias)
9) Sea lace bryozoan (Sertella septentrionalis)

10) Oscarella lobularis
11) Small locust lobster (Scyllarus arctus)
12) Eudendrium sp.
13) Leptosammia pruvoti
14) Moray eel (Muraena helena)
15) Dysidea avara
16) Clavelina lepadiformis
17) Serpula vermicularis
18) Protula sp.
19) Astroides calycularis
20) Haliclona mediterranea
21) Petrosia ficiformis
22) Agelas oroides
23) Conger eel (Conger conger)
24) Sponge crab (Dromia personata)
25) Narval shrimp (Plesionika narval)
26) Red banded shrimp (Stenopus spinosus)
27) Cowry (Luria lurida)
28) Leopard goby (Thorogobius ephippiatus)
29) Goby (Gobius sp.)

C

B - The long snout of a big conger eel (Conger conger) peeps out of its lair in the coral. This fish, which can reach a weight of 60 kilos and a length of 2 meters is often found inside wrecks. Although it is well known, many aspects of its biology, which is similar to that of eels, are still unknown. During the spawning season, mature adults gather at depths of hundreds of meters.

Elsewhere there are the conical chimneys of the orange *Agelas oroides* sponge, a red *Trypterigion sp.* flickering in its depressions and the yellow buttons of *Leptosamnia*, surrounded on the walls by the dark orange plates of another sponge, *Reniera fulva*, and *Reniera viscosa*, which owes its unusual name to the gluelike consistency of its colonies. Two white sponges joined by a long filament make their appearance in a sheltered corner. They look like a rocky concretion, a stalagtite and a stalagmite joined together, but this is actually an even more unusual phenomenon i.e. the reproduction of a sponge *(Chodrosia reniformis)*. To complete this panorama of cave-dwelling sessile organisms, there are the tufts of glassy *Clavelina lepadiformis*, like transparent paper weights, the starched lace of the bryozoan *Sertella septentrionalis* and, next to it, false coral with its regular forked branches.

All these organisms stand out for their size, in the low carpet with which cave walls and roofs are generally covered and which generally diminishes, along with the colors, the further towards the pitch black you go, until there is nothing but bare rock.

The torch beam picks up mobile organisms too. There could be a grouper or a dentex or a corb just past the entrance, but such encounters are rare, or a moray or even a blind fish such as *Grammonus ater*.

Much more common, but no less satisfying, is an encounter with a group of *Anthias*, consisting of a male, recognisable by its long dorsal ray and its harem of females reflecting the beams of our lights to great effect, as if they were suspended in an amazing aquarium.

They may be white bream and black corb and the small clouds of sediment being raised on the cave floor indicate the presence of a small goby or two, such as *Thorogobius ephippiatus* or a shy rockling with its strange bearded fins.

The crustaceans, represented by various groups, are common in caves, the darkness attracts them. They range from the tapering, big-eyed mysidaceans, which form up into dense swarms as soon as the light of the torches touches and shines through their transparent bodies, to the translucent prawns *(Palaemon sp.)*, to *Stenopus hispidus*, *Lysmata seticauda*, *Gnathophyllum elegans* and *Plesionika narval*, whose lively colors are a reminder of the Mediterranean's tropical past. There are a lot of crabs too, *Herbstya condiliata* and *Dromia personata* are concealed beneath the sponges and there is *Galathea strigosa*, a kind of crustacean which is a transition between hermits and the real crabs. There is no lack of molluscs either, but one species is the emblem of these isolated environments: the cowrie *Luria lurida*, whose shiny shell justifies the common name of porcelain, often attributed to these animals. The visit might almost be over, although our presence has certainly been picked up by the widely-differing sense organs of many more organisms than we have seen and recognised. The darkness awaits further discovery, but it does not matter when. Caves are not in a hurry and some are practically unchanging, witness the presence in some of them of the white sponge *Petrobiona massiliana*, which scientists consider to be "a living fossil, as venerable as the better-known coelacanth". Before leaving this gallery, try this: turn off the lights and wait for your eyes to become accustomed to the darkness. The water around you will slowly get less dark and a slight, increasingly distinct glimmer, as you fin towards the exit, will show you the way out and into the next gallery.

C - The spiny lobster (Palinurus elephas) is one of the best known of Mediterranean crustaceans, where it has been fished and eaten since antiquity. Less common now than it once was, due both to over fishing and the partial modification of many sections of coastline, it lives on vertical rocky walls of the infralittoral and the circumlittoral zones. It sometimes establishes lobster cities, distinguished by tens of long, waving, antennae sticking out of the rock picking up invisible signals carried by the currents.

D

E

F

D - This Galathea strigosa peeps timidly out of its lair, overlooked by a branch of coral with opened polyps. Despite its threatening appearance, due to its spiny shell and long pincers, this crustacean is not particularly aggressive. In addition to its reddish coloring with blue nuances, it has a half-folded abdomen, which marks it as a transitionary crustacean, between lobsters and crabs.

E - Caves are the ideal place to observe large numbers of the shy Plesionika narval shrimp. In the dark these nocturnal crustaceans lose their instinct to flee and stay in their groups for a few instants before splitting up under the influence of the divers' torches and searching for shelter on the bottom. Numerous other species belong to the same family (Pandalidae), mostly found in deep water and often fished.

F - The bright coloring of this small scorpion fish is illuminated by the flash. In a world where the color red is practically invisible at depths of over a few meters, this colorful livery is ideal for fading into the environment and laying successful ambushes.

FOURTH GALLERY: A MARINE OASIS

Where the extraordinary is the norm, it is difficult to prepare a classified list, but this new series of show cases, despite the apparent monotony of the dominant subject, *Posidonia oceanica,* is so important as to be one of the focal points of this hypothetical underwater museum of the Mediterranean. Unlike the other galleries, a visit

C

D

A

B

to this one can start with an excursion along the seashore. There are strange balls of brownish fiber littered amongst the detritus piled up by the waves. Many people are puzzled by them and come up with a wide range of explanations for these unusual formations, but few manage to make the connection with posidonia, the remains of whose tough eroded fibers are compacted by the slow, unceasing, movement of the waves and transformed into these curious ball shapes with the even more curious name - phytobezoars or pelotes de mer. This is the first clue to the presence of Neptune grass and the next one comes in the shape of the layers of leaves piled in banks over a meter high and giving off a characteristic odor of iodine. These leaves, a symbol of autumn in the underwater world, are unequivocal proof that there is a "meadow" somewhere near that anyone who can interpret the colors of the sea will be able to identify from above, by the sudden dark patches in areas where the sea bed is not very deep.

After this introduction in the first few showcases, we can visit the heart of the gallery. There appears beneath us a vast green expanse, a meadowland of long leaves which wave to the same rhythm as the waves in the parts closest to the surface. It looks monotonous compared with the other galleries we have seen, but it is only an impression. Gliding slowly down to the sea bed differences which are the result of the stages of development of the leaves begin to appear, mainly with differing tones of green. By overcoming a slight sense of reluctance, we can go further down, into the embrace of this green expanse, even, if we are lucky, passing through the belt of leaves and disappearing into great holes. These are similar to the giants' cauldrons found on mountains and have been created by the currents which get into the bottom layer of Neptune grass, often thanks to a break caused by a dragging anchor or a fishing net, where they erode the sediment accumulated between the roots.

E

F

G

By reaching the bottom of one of these holes, it is possible to observe the posidonia meadows in detail from an unusual vantage point and to understand how they grow. On the sides of the depression there is a dense fabric of interwoven roots and rhizomes, superimposed upon and mixed with sediment, called matte. Thanks to these rhizomes, a meadow grows vertically as well as horizontally, so that it is not buried by the progressive accumulation of sediment. This vertical growth is slow, however, estimated at about half a meter a century. This leads scientists to suppose, on the basis of measurements taken, that there are posidonia meadows in the Mediterranean which are hundreds of years old, some having engulfed even older remains.

The age of the ecosystem is one of the reasons to study the meadowland environment with more attention, but it is by no means the only one. The presence of roots differentiates these plants from the algae mentioned in previous chapters, identifying them as real plants. Neptune grass is the final stage of a long evolutionary trail which led them first to conquer the terrestrial environment and then to return to the sea, where they are only found in the Mediterranean and a great distance away in Australia, proof of the common origin of the Mediterranean and the Pacific. Posidonia has also preserved all the properties of land plants i.e. roots, stalk, leaves, flowers and fruits and has been imitated, in a miniature form, by other similar plants *(Cymodocea nodosa* and *Zostera marina).*

E- Posidonia meadows become established on mobile substrates consisting of sand of varying degrees of coarseness, mixed with mud. Here the rhizomes

and the roots anchor the plant to the sea bed and contribute to the meadow's diffusion and its upwards elevation. The latter kind of growth is very important

as the meadow tends naturally to become buried in the sand as a result of the continued deposit of sediments by (amongst other things) the leaves.

F - A ray (Torpedo marmorata) swims above a posidonia meadow. This fish is common to sand and mud bottoms and the meadowland and its edges suit its bottom-dwelling life.

G - An octopus camouflaged at the bottom of the leaves. Although the posidonia meadow constitutes a homogeneous ecosystem, there is

considerable variation within it, as is demonstrated by the richness of the life forms.

Few would expect to find a flower meadow on the bottom of the sea but with *Posidonia oceanica* this is quite possible (between August and November), especially in the more southerly waters where the higher temperatures seem more conducive to reproduction by flowering. The flowers are greenish and grow in clusters which after pollination develop fruits commonly known as sea olives. When ripe they become detached and float to the surface until, pushed by waves and currents, they reach the shore or to places suitable for germination and the development of another meadow.
Posidonia grows on the sea bed where sand and mud are mixed, from the surface to depths of 35-40 meters depending on the transparency of the water and it is not uncommon for its roots to successfully establish themselves in pockets of accumulated sediment in reefs. Sometimes the result is a uniform mantle, rich in green and brownish tones. Other times, it is irregular,

with a series of consecutive terraces, or it develops as small hills separated by expanses of sand, or else long, thin barriers parallel to the coast, or it can be a ring, typically forming an internal lagoon. However it develops, posidonia has a direct effect on the coasts behind it. The long leaves constitute an elastic barrier which can dampen the strength of the waves and the force of the currents. As a result the suspended particles are deposited and rarely taken away, thus protecting the coast.
It has been calculated that the destruction of a large enough band of meadowland could lead to shore being eroded to a distance of almost 20 meters. These oases in the Mediterranean desert only occupy 2% of the sea bottom (and this expanse is continually declining as a result of pollution and changes to the sea bed) but they are of fundamental importance to our sea. It is difficult to realize quite how important, unless one looks at figures summarising a series of studies

A, B - Posidonia flowers are borne on a stalk in clusters.

C - The base of the posidonia highlights

the dense interweaving of the roots and rhizomes thanks to which the meadow grows in height.

A

B

C

Thanks to its structure and subdivision into roots, rhizones and leaves, Posidonia oceanica creates a large variety of environments, organised along a vertical gradient (leaf layer, rhizome layer, sediment layer) which provide habitats for specialized communities. Each of these includes organisms of its own and others which can move from one layer to another, in migrations which are often regulated by the hours of light and darkness. The illustration shows an ideal section of meadowland with several species which are typically found in the leaves and the substrate.

1) Dexamine spinosa
2) Neptune grass flowers
3) Idotea sp.
4) Caprella sp.
5) Elysia viridis

6) Purple sea urchin (Sphaerechinus granularis)
7) Prawn (Palaemon sp.)
8) Purple dye murex (Bolinus brandaris).

119

A - The strange white buttons carpeting the surface of the leaves are colonies of small compound ascidians, belonging to the genus Botryllus. Each individual is arranged in star-like groups around a common center.

B - The red interlaced filament is made out of long ropes of sea hare (Aplysia sp.) eggs. These large molluscs, which are common in posidonia meadows, form groups for reproduction and lay these eggs, known as "sea spaghetti" because of their appearance.

C - Despite their apparent fragility, posidonia leaves can support the weight of even bigger organisms than this little crab with the sinister name of "death's head" (Ilia nucleus).

D - A comber (Serranus cabrilla) swims amongst the meadow looking for its prey, consisting mainly of small crustaceans and molluscs. This species usually lives close to the bottom, migrating short distances either upwards or horizontally.

carried out over the last ten years in the Mediterranean on this precious ecosystem, which is increasingly the subject of conservation and protective legislation. Every square meter of meadowland can contain over 1,000 tufts, each of which consists of 5-6 leaves. Placed beside each other, these would cover a surface area of more than 40 square meters. Leaves and rhizomes provide an ideal surface for the establishment and development of a multitude of plant and sessile animal organisms which attract other species in their tun. Furthermore, the complex structure of the posidonia system is conducive to the formation of microhabitats representing many biotic communities, from the coralligenous one to the mobile bottoms, which explains how a hectare of meadowland produces almost 30 tonnes of organic material annually and is home to an animal biomasse of over 10 tonnes, comprising 500 different species belonging to all the fauna groups, from the sponges to the fish.

This is without counting the algae, of which no less than 400 species have been identified.

A single square meter of meadowland can produce 14 litres of oxygen a day by photosynthesis. In additional to these figures, the meadowlands are the virtually exclusive reproduction areas for very many species, not only for those which live there permanently but for many others which go there specially to perpetuate their species.

Their annual cycle means that the population of the posidonia is renewed every year, with a succession of species whose order is well known as far as the leaves are concerned. The first to establish themselves on the new leaves are the bacteria, forming a patina which partly inhibits the defensive substances produced by the leaf itself. In this way they encourage the establishment of microalgae, especially on the side more exposed to the light, which changes color more rapidly giving the waving meadows a flickering effect. The first organisms are followed by other algae, macroscopic ones this time, which form a carpet of color varying from brownish to pick, depending on the species involved. The dimension of the encrustations produced by the algae are such that they can be seen with the naked eye, giving us an insight right into the heart of life in the posidonia colony. The observation of one leaf leads

F - A small red starfish (Echinaster sepositus) has climbed onto a posidonia leaf in search of food and protection.

F

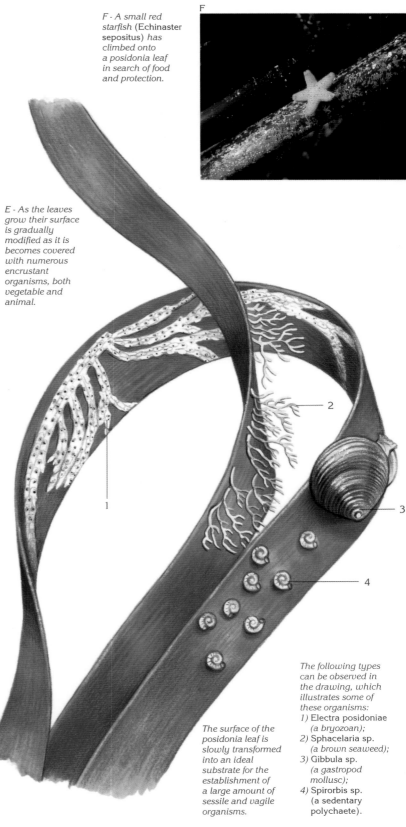

E

E - As the leaves grow their surface is gradually modified as it is becomes covered with numerous encrustant organisms, both vegetable and animal.

straightaway to the identification of certain distinctively regular shapes, such as the white lace tunnels of the bryozoan *Electra posidoniae* or the tufts of the hydroid *Aglaophenia*. Alongside these, a small pointed, pink formation, the foraminifer *Miniacina miniacea* whose remains, when carried to shore by the waves, are responsible for the characteristic "pink" color of the famous Sardinian beach of the same name. An examination of the edges of the leaves also reveals traces of some of the direct consumers of posidonia. *Sarpa salpa* leaves semi-circular cuts, while the crustaceans of the genus *Idothea* snap off the points and the sea urchins eat the margins. Small, but important, signs underlining the symbiosis between posidonia and animals, which although wide-reaching, is not always easily visible.

The surface of the posidonia leaf is slowly transformed into an ideal substrate for the establishment of a large amount of sessile and vagile organisms.

The following types can be observed in the drawing, which illustrates some of these organisms:
1) Electra posidoniae (a bryozoan);
2) Sphacelaria sp. (a brown seaweed);
3) Gibbula sp. (a gastropod mollusc);
4) Spirorbis sp. (a sedentary polychaete).

121

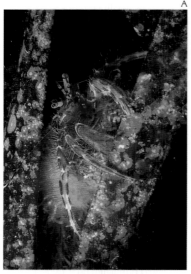

A

B

The fishes disappear between the fronds at our approach, but just by moving around the edges of the meadow or following the sand channels which criss-cross it, or moving into the center into the open expanse of sandy bed, to see salemas, blotches picarels, rainbow wrasse, scorpion fishes, mullet and myriad labrids, from the best-camouflaged, *Labrus viridis* and the biggest and darkest *(Labrus merula)* to the more colorful ones such as the red *Symphodus mediterraneus* and *Symphodus rostratus,* recognisable by its long nose, for whom the meadow represents the perfect place to build their nests. The pipefish *(Syngnathus sp.)* are able to transform themselves into perfect leaves and the sea-horses *(Hippocampus sp.),* for whom the meadow represents one of its last havens, are much harder to spot thanks to their mimetic coloring. Prawn, crab, mantis shrimp, small spiny lobster, octopus, cuttlefish, sea urchin, starfish and sea cucumber, nudibranch, all hide safely or lie in ambush, according to their habits, amongst the leaves or at the edges of the meadow, which changes appearance from day to night. When the sun goes down, for example, the labrids disappear into their holes and other predators like the morays and the scorpion fish become

A - The leafy layer of the posidonia meadow is covered with a large number of encrustant or erect organisms which attract several different predators. One of these is the "devil's hand shrimp" (Clibanarius erytropus) which is less than 2 centimeters long. It is common on the upper infralittoral zone and surface meadows.

B - Plesionika narval is a classic shrimp inhabitant of dark places. It is usually found inside caves, but the dense fronds of the posidonia groves appear in this case to have supplied the right amount of light for its needs.

The meadows of Posidonia oceanica *are one of the richest life systems in the whole of the Mediterranean Sea. The mass of leaves supplies an enormous quantity of oxygen to the surrounding water, at the same time becoming a substrate and shelter for numerous organisms. The roots and the rhizomes, which compact the bottom, also create an extraordinary environment where several different habitats can be found mixed together, from sediment to rock and even caves. The drawing illustrates diagramatically the complex organization of a meadow, from the species which inhabit the waters above it to those which live amongst the leaves, right down to the ones which live in the lowest layer, in contact with the sea bed.*

1) Gilthead bream (Sparus aurata)
2) Damselfish (Chromis chromis)
3) Rainbow wrasse (Coris julis)
4) Ocellated wrasse (Symphodus ocellatus)
5) Fan worm (Sabella spallanzani)
6) Peacock wrasse (Symphodus tinca)
7) Common cuttlefish (Sepia officinalis)
8) White spotted octopus (Octopus macropus)
9) Sea horse (Hippocampus sp.)
10) Common red star (Echinaster sepositus)
11) Pipefish (Syngnathus sp.)
12) Sea hare (Aplysia depilans)
13) Fan mussel (Pinna nobilis)
14) Antedon mediterranea
15) Holothuria polii
16) Slender goby (Gobius geniporus)
17) Posidonia roots
18) Rhizome
19) Leaves
20) Flowers

C

D

C - The Mediterranean red star (Echinaster sepositus) moves slowly on the posidonia leaves, looking for sponges and detritus to eat.

D - The presence of an eye is the only thing which distinguishes this needle fish (Syngnathus typhle) amongst the leaves, where it is perfectly camouflaged in its favorite environment.

E - A small sea anemone, probably a Parastephanauge paxi, not uncommon on posidonia leaves.

E

F

F - The leafy layer of the posidonia meadow is the perfect habitat for sea horses (Hippocampus guttalatus). Thanks to their prehensile tails they can attach themselves to various different kinds of substrates (the one in the photo is a spirograph) and be rocked by the currents to the same rhythm as the posidonia. This means that they are out of sight from predators and can capture their prey without any difficulty.

more active, as do the cuttlefish and the octopus. Even the leaves, which are almost unpopulated during the day, are the stage for nocturnal "walks" for the myriad light-hating molluscs, which take advantage of the dark to leave their shelters amongst the roots and to climb up the green ribbons in search of food, encountering as they do *Antedon mediterranea*, the sea lily, as it attaches itself temporarily to the leaves, fanning out its feathered arms to catch plankton. Sometimes you might be lucky enough to catch sight of one of these strange echinoderms attached to the edge of a big *Pinna nobilis*, perhaps one of the most characteristic inhabitants of the posidonia system and one of the most threatened in the Mediterranean, for the beauty of its shell and for its considerable size, which can exceed 90 centimeters, making it one of the largest molluscs in the world.

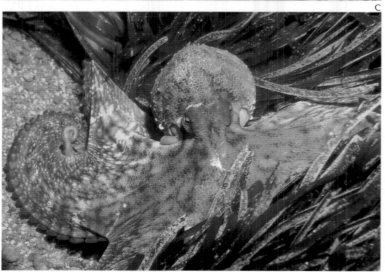

A - A red scorpionfish (Scorpaena scrofa) pictured on the sea bottom in the midst of posidonia. When the sun goes down this formidable predator becomes more active, hunting the many kinds of prey to be found in the meadow.

B - A pair of male axillary wrasse (Symphodus mediterraneus) size each other up. With the approach of the mating season the males fight to conquer and defend their territory, where they build nests out of seaweed, for the females to lay their eggs.

C - The posidonia meadows are the perfect habitat for octopus. The holes which form at the base of the leaves become perfect, well-hidden lairs. The interwoven leaves allow the agile octopus to hide itself and escape from its predators, which, unlike their intended prey, find it hard to move amongst the leaves.

D

D - The spirograph's characteristic spiral tuft turns slowly in the calm waters of the meadow. The spirograph feeds on suspended particles and micro-organisms, through the network of feathered tentacles of its branchial tuft. It is quite at ease amongst the Neptune grass, which encourages the settling of sediment by preventing the flow of the currents.

E - This transparent shrimp (Pontonia pinnophylax) usually passes unobserved, as it lives perennially hidden inside the shell of the big bivalve fan mussel.

E

G

F

F - The crinoids, or sea lilies (Antedon mediterranea) are strange echinoderms with numerous arms. These are extremely mobile and where necessary they allow the animal to swim for short distances. Using the prehensile tendrils at the base of the body, crinoids can attach themselves to the extremities of leaves, where they can better exploit the flow of the current to sieve the microplankton on which they feed with their feathered arms.

G - The fan mussel is the largest Mediterranean bivalve, with a maximum size of 90 centimeters. Its size and beauty have made it a desirable object for divers, who have in many cases been the main cause of its disappearance. It is now one of the most threatened species in our sea.

FIFTH GALLERY:
THE REIGN OF LIGHT

We could view a wave breaking against a rock, creating a waterfall of white foam and a vortex of sparkling splashes as the last exhibit in this Mediterranean museum, but it is only a junction, opening up other roads than those mapped by the sea's surface. The road upwards is eternally balanced between two conflicting environments: air and water. Above the high-tide marks lies the superlittoral, a unique environment where there are few established marine organisms and those there are not immediately recognisable as such. In fact they are often mistaken for

neritoides) small, dark, molluscs, which can stay out of water for several weeks, drawn up into their shells, without suffering any harm. *Ligia italica* is much more mobile. These small crustaceans tend to stay in the shade and flee rapidly at a approach of a human, who is generally rather disturbed by them, for although they are quite innocuous, they are quite unknown. This short external is soon over and a few blotches of color on the water's surface draw our attention. A little reddish globe appears and disappears amongst the waves which ruffle its tentacles. It is a sea anemone *(Actinia equina)*, surrounded as it often is in this environment by the numerous white plates in

A - The increased brightness is the main signal that the surface is drawing nearer. The liquid mass is not only a barrier dividing two different but complementary worlds, it is also a filter which gradually causes all signs of the outside world to disappear.

B - Sea beds closest to the surface are intensely influenced by hydrodynamism and solar radiation. Depending on the substrate, this influence translates into widely differentiated and typical animal and plant populations.

A

B

C

something quite different, as in the case of *Verrucaria amphibia*, black halophilous lichens, which untrained eyes may mistake for oil washed ashore. Next to the lichens, concentrated inside the fissures created the blue-green algae which break up the rock and by the action of the waves, are the periwinkles *(Melaraphe*

the shape truncated white cones of the sub-class *Cirripedia* (barnacles). These are anomalous crustaceans which have become radically modified in appearance as a result of the sedentary life which concludes short ambulatory periods in the larval stage. When the sea is calm, if the barnacles are observed closely

C - In general, marine organisms do not like over illumination and this is responsible for a certain thinning out of life forms in shallower, clearer water.

it is possible to see the darting movements of the feathery appendices which are the modified limbs with which these crustaceans, imprisoned in their ivory tower, capture their food. The limpets are much more mobile and numerous (there are six known species in the Mediterranean) and they have an infallible instinct which guides them back to the center of their territory. At high tide they start to graze on the rocky walls, revealing their broad foot and the little tentacles which are draw back into the shell as soon as they are touched.

This environment, alternately submerged and uncovered by the flow of the tides, is called the mesolittoral. Although it is of limited importance in the Mediterranean, by no means comparable to the vast expanses left uncovered by the Atlantic tides, it is well populated despite the inherent difficulties of life in this highly variable zone.

Some organisms such as those just mentioned withdraw into their shells where they keep a water reserve to maintain constant humidity until the next high tide. Others, such as the crab *Pachygraphus marmoratus*, have opposite behavior from divers, making rapid excursions into the aerial world taking a large enough water reserve to keep its gills damp enough to function.

Bands of mussels of varying depth build up on the most exposed areas. The molluscs are usually small where the water is not enriched, but algae and other encrusting organisms become established on top of them and increase their capacity to conserve humidity in the small community which contains numerous crustaceans, polychaete worms, molluscs and other animals which are preyed on by small fishes like blennies *(Lipophrys pavo)* which can push themselves out of the water and survive even if only wet by the waves.

This ambient, which is ideal for snorkelling, boasts an amazing formation called a trottoir which is characteristic of the western Mediterranean.

A series of pavements are formed which are wide enough and strong enough in some places, such as Punta Palazzu in the Corsican Regional Park, to take the weight of a human. Such formations, which are similar in appearance to certain parts of coral barrier reef, are actually pads of the red calcareous alga *Lithophyllum lichenoides* cemented together. Its continuously eroded surface has perforations and crevices where numerous boring (sponges, bivalves, urchins) and encrustant (coralline algae, calcareous sponges, bryozoans) organisms live.

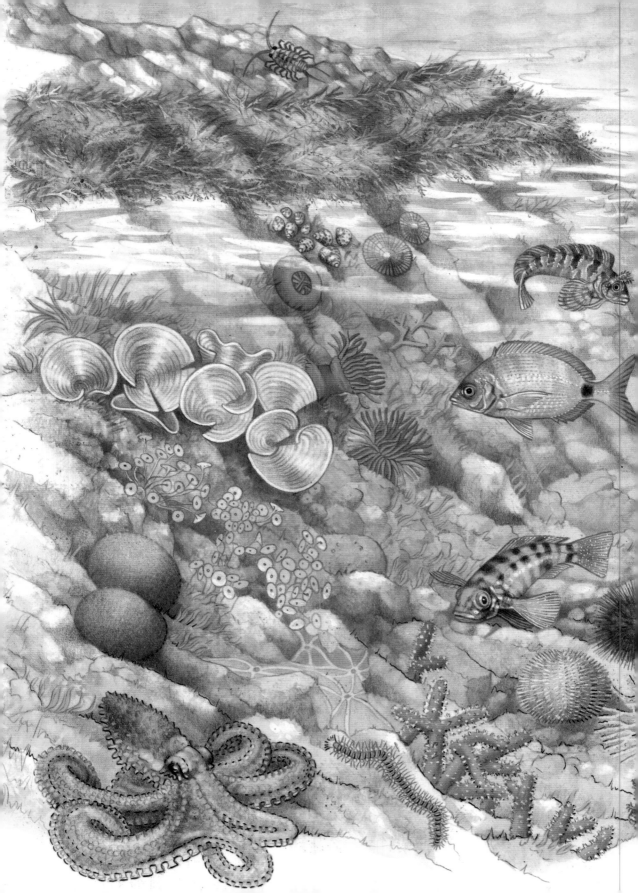

At the beginning of the infralittoral we find its herald, the gardens of *Cystoseira*, brown light-loving algae which form dense and complex belts of vegetation close to the surface, colonising the rocky sea bed with typical species for each ambient. *Cystoseira mediterranea* and *Cystoseira stricta*, for example, which grows up to 40 centimeters, will be predominant along the more horizontal infralittoral margins, which are well lit and exposed to the movement of the waves, while *Cystoseira crinita*, blackish in color, prefers more sheltered areas, although also well lit.
In areas where these brownish algae are not present, their place is filled, in areas of varying size, by the rounded peacocks tails

(Padina pavonica), fluorescent *Dyctiota dichotoma* with its flat, forked, fronds, the characteristic umbrella shapes of *Acetabularia acetabulum*, the lithophyllid and the coralline encrustants and *Jania rubens* with its branched thallus. In deeper areas where less light penetrates, it will be the less-demanding species such as *Codium bursa*, *Halimeda tuna*, *Peyssonnellia* and *Rhodymenia* which cover the sea bed.
The different ecological conditions and different kinds of substrate (rocky, detritus, from blocks resulting from landslides to pebbles or sand) which are found not only change in short distances, sometimes actually along the perimeter of a single plant mass, but provide animals with a wide

choice. Herbivores like the salemas and the purple or black sea urchins *(Paracentrus lividus* and *Arbaria lixula)*, the chitons and the iridescent *Haliotis lamellosa* move over the bottom in search of algae, whose development they strongly condition. Banks of fish (grey mullet and bogues) swim at different levels in open water, while smaller groups of other species pay closer attention to the sea bottom. *Diplodus sp.* and rainbow wrasse *(Coris julis, Thalassoma pavo)* are usually dominant, along with several species of serranids and labrids, the most interesting of which might be the little *Symphodus melanocercus* which hangs immobile in the water to attract

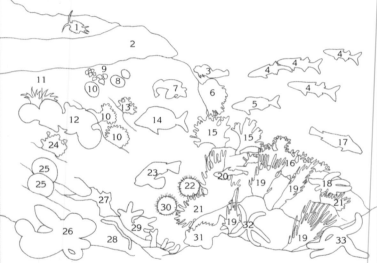

A - The strange, greenish-colored shape on the bottom is the long proboscis of *Bonellia viridis*. Extremely long (over 1 meter) and forked, it is the most visible part of the whole animal, the best known of the echiuroids.

B - *Bonellia's* body is similar to a large walnut and is usually hidden amongst the rocks. The species is characterized by considerable sexual dimorphism: the females are bigger, while the males are microscopic and live attached directly to the body of the females.

Rocky bottoms, well-lit and close to the surface, (super-, meso- and infralittoral) have a rich variety of environments and ecological conditions. They vary according to different exposure to light, waves and substrate. This provides living conditions for a rich variety of organisms. The drawing illustrates an ideal section.

1) Ligia italica
2) Cystoseira sp.
3) Peacock blenny (Lipophrys pavo)
4) Grey mullet (Mugil cephalus)
5) Bogue (Boops boops)
6) Snakelocks anemone (Anemone sulcata)
7) Tompot blenny (Parablennius gattoruggine)
8) Limpet (Patella sp.)
9) Turbinata monodont (Monodonta turbinata)
10) Beadlet anemone (Actinia equina)
11) Leafy caulerpa (Caulerpa prolifera)
12) Peacock's tail (Padina pavonica)
13) False coral (Myriapora truncata)
14) White seabream (Diplodus sargus)
15) Dyctio dichotoma
16) False coral (Myriapora truncata)
17) Rainbow wrasse (Coris julis)
18) Coscinasterias tenuispina
19) White sea fan (Eunicella singularis)
20) Black blenny (Trypterigion tripteronotus)
21) Yellow sea fan (Eunicella cavolini)
22) Balck sea urchin (Arbacia lixula)
23) Buchicchi's goby (Gobius bucchichi)
24) Mermaid cup (Acetabularia mediterranea)
25) Purse codium (Codium bursa)
26) Octopus (Octopus vulgaris)
27) Spirastrella cunctatrix
28) Fireworm (Hermodice carunculata)
29) Dead man's finger (Alcyonium palmatum)
30) Purple sea urchin (Spaerechinus granularis)
31) Red scorpionfish (Scorpaena scrofa)
32) Echinaster sepositus
33) Marthasterias glacialis

C - The horned blenny (Parablennius tentacularis) gets its name from the long tentacles above its eyes. This quite rare species lives to depths of about 30 meters, on detritus or mixed sand and gravel bottoms.

D - The salemas (Sarpa salpa) are easy to recognise, with their characteristic blue and gold stripes. They are relatively common in surface waters and over posidonia meadows. The fish find plenty of the seaweed on which they feed on these well-illuminated bottoms.

E - This long-spined urchin (Centrostephanus longispinus) belongs to the Diadematidae family which groups together certain very well-known tropical urchins. Its greater frequency in the sea's southern basins demonstrate its tropical affinities. It is found on coral and pre-coral bottoms where it stays hidden all day long.

F - The Alicia mirabilis is a sea anenome feared for its very powerful sting. In the daytime it remains retracted and passes almost unnoticed. At night it instead expands, fully extending both its cylindrical body, embellished with gold-tinged tubercles, and - especially - its long tentacles.

G - A shore clingfish (Lepadogaster lepadogaster) with its bright blue dorsal markings. The shore clingfish (family Gobidae) are called even "sucker" and get their name from the ventral sucker by which they attach themselves to rocks.

clients for its cleaning service, behavior which is usually associated only with tropical species. But this level of the Mediterranean does sometimes prove worthy of more exotic sea beds and plays host, albeit in limited areas, (the Sicilian Channel and the eastern basins) to unexpected parrot fish or *Sparisoma cretense*. In direct contact with the sea bed itself, there is another connection with the tropics, this time an association, not a compulsory one however, between the stinging anemone *Anemonia sulcata* and the mimetic rasping goby *(Gobius bucchichi)* which in the event of danger hides between the purple tentacles of this big actiniaria, an inhabitant of well-lit sea beds

C

conducive to the development of the symbiotic microalgae disseminated in its tissues.
We have seen that every place can be a showcase in this gallery, and that subject by subject, it could become infinite, proving once more that the Mediterranean is one of the regions on this planet best-adapted to life and closest to the humans to whom it has been entrusted and who hold the keys to this museum. To know it and to conserve or destroy it are both alternatives within our reach. It is our hope that these pages can make a contribution towards to the right choice.

D

E

F

G

THE MOST COMMON FISH AND INVERTEBRATES OF THE MEDITERRANEAN

To those who know the Mediterranean coastline and dive its waters, the sea bottoms appear to be rich in life and in color. But this is not born out by the facts regarding the species which live there. As was mentioned at the beginning of this book, this sea is poor in resources compared with the nearby ocean and with other, more distant, seas. But this does not prevent thousands of animal and plant species from living in it. Those counted up until now are only a little more than 5% of the world's species, but there is still room, especially in the deep waters, for new discoveries. However, what is known so far is enough to make the Mediterranean an extraordinary sea and justify those who think that it has no equal, even when compared with tropical seas. On the other hand, this basin, hemmed in by the land masses of three continents, did itself once have a tropical past and it is a past which seems to be intent on returning. Since the excavation of the Suez Canal, an increasing number of fish from the Red Sea have reached and colonised the waters in part of the Mediterranean. Whereas the foregoing pages were intended to unveil some of the mysteries in which the history of the Mediterranean is swathed and the laws which regulate its life, those which follow are intended as a guide to knowing it.

Any contribution a few hundred drawings could make, when faced with the many threats hanging over this sea and our lack of knowledge about it, may seem a vey small thing indeed. Yet it would be enough simply to be able to distinguish a healthy stretch of sea from a modified one. All too often we base out judgements about the Mediterranean on fleeting impressions of a summer's sea. But what do these millions of people who head for its coastline in search of sun and transparent waters take away with them? There is no single answer. As always the Mediterranean escapes all attempts to classify it: many believe they have understood it, few really succeed. Perhaps this introduction to the classified entries has become a sort of preface, or rather a postscript, to the entire volume; every page of which is an invitation to discover, or rediscover, this sea and, knowing its resources, keep them intact.

Bullettin of the Monaco Oceanographic Institute, special no. 9 (1992)

Group	Habitat	Species in the world	Mediterranean species (estimation)	Mediterranean species (census)	% Med/World
07 Porifera	be	5000	593	593	1,9
08 Cnidaria	be/pe	9500	420	352	4,4
09 Ctenophora	pe	100	20	0	20
10 Echinodermata	be	6500	143	143	2,2
11 Plathyhelminthes	be/pe/pa	6000	*	0	
12 Mesozoa	pa	50	*	0	
13 Nemertinea	be/pe	900	94	0	10,4
14 Nematoda	be/pa	5000	*150	0	3
15 Acanthocephala	pa	*	*	0	
16 Rotifera	be/pe	>150	>35	0	123,5
17 Gastrotricha	be	250	116	0	46,4
18 Kinorhyncha	be	107	23	23	21,5
19 Nematomorpha	pe	3	1	0	33,3
20 Gnathostomulida	be	120	>10	0	8,3
21 Chaetognatha	pe/be	102	21	0	20,6
22 Priapulida	be	9	3	3	33,3
23 Annelida	be/pe	8000	776	709	9,7
24 Myzostomida	pa	150	5	0	3,3
25 Echiurida	be	129	6	6	4,7
26 Sipuncula	be	321	22	22	6,9
27 Brachiopoda	be	335	15	15	4,5
28 Ectoprocta	be	5000	491	191	9,8
29 Entoprocta	be/pa	150	19	19	12,7
30 Mollusca	be/pe/pa	32000	1376	807	4,3
31 Tardigrada	be	60	18	0	30
34 Arthropoda	be/pe/pa	36000	1935	648	5,4
35 Pogonophora	be	100	1	1	1
36 Phoronidea	be	10	5	4	50
37 Hemichordata	be	90	5	5	5,6
38 Chordata	be/pe	1322	243	185	18,4
39 Loricifera	be	10	1	0	10
40 Vertebrata	be/pe	13494	694	694	5,1

be= bentonic
pe= pelagic
pa= parasitic
* = unknown number

The table shows, in summary form, the estimated marine fauna of the entire world and of the Mediterranean, excluding unicellular organisms. The data are the findings of the so-called medifauna research project, set up to conduct a census of all the animal species living in the Mediterranean. The abbreviations in the habitat column refer to the way of life of the species considered.

ALGAE AND PLANTS
Mermaid's cup
Acetabularia acetabulum

▶

Unmistakable, umbrella-shaped, green seaweed. Thallus consists of an expanded part with rays, hardened by the encrustant limestone and supported by a short peduncle fixed to the substrate. Found from the surface down to 30 meters on rocky bottoms. Diameter of the umbrella is 10-12 millimitres.

Sea lettuce
Ulva rigida

▶

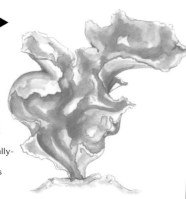

Green alga, thin-bladed and slightly frilly at the edges. The base fixed to the sea-bed is thick and stiff. Color varies from bright to pale green. Common on rocky bottoms down to 8-12 meters depth, it is also found on sandy bottoms and in organically-enriched waters. Grows up to 30-40 centimeters width and almost the same in height.

▼ **Sea fan**
Udotea petiolata

Green, fan-shaped alga with rounded edges, supported by a short peduncle fixed to the rock. During reproduction the edges lose their color and become white. Photophobic, this alga is found from 5-10 meters to below 40. Grows up to 10 centimeters in height.

◀ **Leafy caulerpa**
Caulerpa prolifera

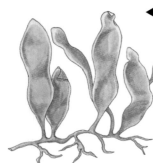

Green alga with a characteristic thallus, consisting of a thin bottom-creeping stolon from which fronds similar to lanceolate leaves grow. It forms small meadows close to Neptune grass on sandy and muddy bottoms down to 20 meters. Prefers warm water and is therefore more frequently found in the southern Mediterranean. Its "leaves" grow up to 15-20 centimeters long.

Caulerpa taxifolia ▼

Known by the picturesque name of "killer seaweed", in recent years it has begun to colonise vast areas of the western Mediterranean in increasing amounts, and has in some places replaced the Neptune seagrass. Introduced into the water by mistake at Montecarlo, it has spread rapidly and appears to be creating some problems to the underwater eco-system. Its fronds have small, frilly, paired leaves and can grow to 40-50 centimeters long. It grows down to 50-60 meters depth and perhaps deeper.

Purse codium
Codium bursa

▼

Green alga found in several different shades of dark green; unmistakable regular shape. The young plant is an almost spherical ball, but as it grows the structure changes, becoming flat and concave in the center. Grows on rocky bottoms, from the surface down to 80-90 meters. It is not uncommon to find it washed up on the beach after storms at sea. Grows up to 40 centimeters diameter.

Sea cactus
Halimeda tuna

Alga made up of a series of discoid articles, connected together and looking like a miniature prickly pear. Green or yellowy-green, with white stripes caused by limestone encrustations. Grows on rocky substrates, from the surface to a depth of 75 meters. ◀ Grows to 10-20 centimeters.

Peacock's tail
Padina pavonica

Brown alga, light-brown and whitish, with darker horizontal stripes. Shaped rather like a peacock's tail or an open fan. Grows on rocky bottoms in sheltered, well-illuminated areas down to 20 meters. ◀ Maximum size 15 centimeters.

Forked ribbons
Dictyota dichotoma

Alga with thin, flattened fronds with characteristic dichotomous branching at the tips. Color varies from brown to green, but during vegetative growth it is iridescent when observed underwater. Grows on rocky bottoms from the surface to 20-25 meters. Maximum size 20-25 centimeters.

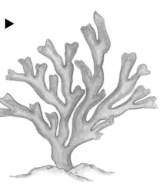

Cystoseira
Cystoseira sp.

Common in surface waters where it forms extensive populations along parts of rocky coastlines most exposed to the waves and well-illuminated. Color varies according to species from almost black through brown through yellow to golden. Some species grow to a meter in length.

Sargassum
Sargassum sp.

Brown seaweed genus consisting of a stalk with numerous primary branches whose "leaves" have a central nerve and spherical gas-filled bladders at the base, which help the seaweed to stay upright. Grows on rocky or detrital sea-beds from 30-50 meters deep. Maximum size 70 centimeters.

Sea rose
Peyssonnelia squamaria

Red seaweed with a small fan of partially superimposed horizontal laminae. The underneath part of the lamina grips the substrate with small rhizoid similar to roots. Grows on rocky, poorly-illuminated rocky bottoms, from the surface down to 50-60 meters. Maximum 10 centimeters diameter.

Stone weed
Lithophyllum lichenoides

Strongly calcified red seaweed, common in surface waters where it forms encrustant cornices up to 2 meters wide, called trottoirs. Grows on rocky bottoms in areas with an undertow. The trottoir consists of individual formations of 5-10 centimeters diameter which amalgamate with each other.

Pseudolithophyllum expansum

Completely calcified red seaweed, purplish-pink in color, which encrusts hard, poorly-illuminated substrates from 3-5 meters to over 60 meters deep. This seaweed are some of the main constituents of the coral environment, where it cements detritus, pieces of rock and algae together. Maximum size 25-30 centimeters diameter.

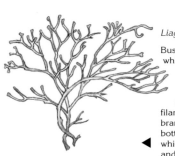

Liagora viscida

Bushy red seaweed with whitish coloring caused by calcareous encrustations. The thallus is made up of thin cylindrical filaments, dichotomously branched. Grows on rocky bottoms in surface waters which are well-illuminated and calm.

Rough coral moss
Corallina elongata

Red seaweed, made up of pink calcified feather-shaped articles. Highly tolerant of variations in environment, it can form dense carpets in surface waters. Grows on rocky bottoms. Maximum size 12 centimeters.

137

Fine coral moss
Jania rubens ▶

Red seaweed with a series
of erect, dichotomously
branched, tufts. Generally
pinkish, tends towards
yellow in strongly
illuminated waters.
Grows on hard bottoms
and other surface algae
to depths of 10.15 meters.
Maximum size 2.3
centimeters.

Cymodocea
Cymodocea nodosa ▶

Water plant with roots, stalk
and leaves. These are joined
in tufts and grow from a thin
rhizome buried in the sand.
The leaves have lacy edges.
Grows in warm, calm, waters
on fine surface sediment.
Leaves grow to maximum
50 centimeter length.

◀ ## Neptune grass
Posidonia oceanica

The most characteristic of all
marine plants, the true
symbol of the mediterranean.
Grows on sandy and detrital
bottoms, from the surface to
30-35 meters depth. Has true
roots, stem, leaves, flowers
and fruits. The flowers are
yellow and the fruits are
similar to small olives.
The leaves are around one
centimeter wide and up to
100 centimeters long.

INVERTEBRATES
▼ **PORIFERA**
Clathrina clathrus

Calcareous sponge made
up of many thin spongy
tubules which
interweave and merge
to form raised pads.
The oscula (the biggest
holes) are at the end of the
tubules. Bright yellow.
Grows on hard, poorly-lit
bottoms up to 20.25 meters
deep. Maximum size 10
centimeters.

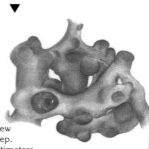

Hemimycale columella ▼

Encrusting sponge similar in
aspect to a colander. Forms
soft, fleshy plaques with
highly visible crater-like
oscula. Grows on rocky or
detritus bottoms from the
surface to 30 meters deep.
When exposed to the air it
gives off a smell of chlorine.
Maximum size 15 centimeters.

Oscarella lobularis ▼

Encrusting sponge makes
covers of lobes which are
rounded and fleshy but
smooth, as there is no
calcareous skeleton.
The oscula are at the
apex of the lobes.
Color is variable, but
in most cases it is blue.
Grows in areas with little
light and in caves, from a few
meters to 20-25 meters deep.
Maximum diameter 10 centimeters.

▼ *Chondrilla nucula*

Sponge which forms small
pads, either elongated or
rounded, but always joined
together. Color varies from
dark brown to
brownish. Grows on
rocky, illuminated
bottoms from
1-5 meters deep.
Maximum size 2
centimeters.

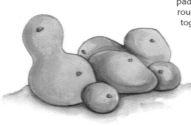

◀ *Axinella cannabina*

Columnar sponge with
axes from which grow
protuberance-like branches
having the oscula at the
tips. Yellow or orange.
Grows on rocky bottoms
from 20 to 100 meters
deep. Maximum size
50-60 centimeters.

Axinella polypoides

This sponge's colonies look like a small tree with cylindrical branches. Yellow. Often found in the mud pockets which form on the ledges of walls. Maximum size over 1 meter. ▶

Haliclona mediterranea ▼

Sponge with large fleshy tubules which have wide oscula at the extremities. Pink. Grows by forming plaques on poorly-illuminated, coralligenous, rocky walls. Maximum size 8 centimeters.

▼ *Alysina aerophoba*

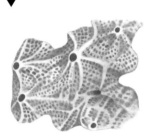

Sponge which forms fleshy, tenacious pads superimposed with big, fingerlike ramifications. The smooth, shiny surface is yellow. If expose to the air it becomes brownish due to the blue algae associated with it. Grows on rocky bottoms between 5-25 meters. Measures up to 10 centimeters.

◀ *Crambe crambe*

Encrusting red sponge often found associated with bivalve molluscs such as the Thorny oister and the Noah's ark. The oscula are in the center of raised exhaling channels on the surface. Grows on hard substrates between 5 and 30 meters. The colonies grow to 10-20 centimeters.

Phorbas tenacior ▼

Encrusting sponge which forms fleshy plaques with a soft, shiny surface. The oscula are similar to small craters and always raised. Bluish or grey-blue in color. Grows on rocky bottoms and in caves near the surface. Maximum size 5 centimeters.

Petrosia ficiformis ▼

Rigid sponge, similar to stone. Variable form, but the surface is raised with numerous, highly visible oscula. Color varies from dark brown to violet to white. Grows on hard bottoms up to 70 meters. Maximum size 50 centimeters diameter.

◀ **Elephant ear**
Spongia agaricina

Cup- or fan-shaped sponge with oscula on the inside or outside only. Generally greyish. Grows on rocky or detritus bottoms from depths of a few meters to over 50 meters. Measures up to 100 centimeters diameter and used to be commercially exploited.

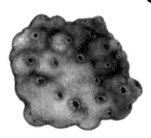

◀ **Greek bating sponge**
Spongia officinalis

This is the sponge which has been fished for centuries in the Mediterranean. Solid, rounded shape with irregular lobes. Whitish or black. Grows on rocky bottoms up to 40 meters deep. Measures up to 35-40 centimeters diameter.

CNIDARIA
Luminous jellyfish
Pelagia noctiluca

Jellyfish with a dome-shaped, wavy-edged float. The long, thin tentacles have powerful stinging cells. Pink or pinkish-yellow with numerous blotches. If blown in by the wind it sometimes concentrates around shorelines. Maximum size 15 centimeters diameter.

Cassiopeia
Cothyloriza tubercolata

This jellyfish is easily recognised by its discoid float which is raised in the center, and for the numerous short tentacles ending in small bluey-purple discs. The float is yellowish-white. Not uncommon along the shoreline during the summer months. Maximum size 30 centimeters diameter.

By the wind sailor
Velella velella

Colonial hydrozoan which floats on the surface of the sea. Made up of a basal lamina surrounded by short tentacles and a laminal expansion which emerges from the water rather like a sail. It forms huge banks which can be pushed to shore by the wind. Bluish-white, measures up to 7 centimeters.

Common jellyfish
Aurelia aurita

Jellyfish with soft, gelatinous, cup-shaped float. The tentacles around the edge make it look fringed. Pink. The four horseshoe-shaped sexual organs are highly visible in their transparent surroundings. Maximum size 40 centimeters.

Rhizostoma pulmo

This is the biggest of the Mediterranean jellyfishes and is easily identified by its big, purple-edged, translucent float. The arms are quite large and jagged. Not uncommon close to the shore during the summer months. Weak sting. Maximum size 60 centimeters diameter.

Yellow sea fan
Eunicella cavolinii

Gorgonian with fan-shaped colonies which are highly ramified, often dichotomically. The branches are flexible and rough in correspondence with the polyps. Yellow. Grows on rocky bottoms from 10 to 150 meters deep. Maximum size 30-40 centimeters.

Red coral
Corallium rubrum

Typical Mediterranean antozoan, shaped like a branched tree. Recognised by its color, which is generally red, and for the white polyps with 8 feathered tentacles. Grows on rocky bottoms with little light or inside caves and crevices from 5-10 meters to over 100 meters deep. This is a protected species and can grow to over 20-30 centimeters in height.

Red sea fan
Paramuricea clavata

Red gorgonian with huge fans made up of dense irregular ramifications, often merged into each other. The branches are thin and flexible and the presence of defensive spicules give them their rough surface. Although it is dark red in color there are specimens with yellow tipped branches. Grows on rocky bottoms below depths of 30-35 meters. Maximum height 1 meter.

Hermit anemone
Calliactis parasitica

Actinia which is rarely seen alone, as it is always associated with large hermit crabs with which it forms close symbiotic relationships. Consists of a robust column with around 700 retractile tentacles at the top end. Brownish color with yellowish-white tentacles. Lives on hermit-crab shells. Maximum size up to 8 centimeters diameter.

Beadtlet anemone
Actinia equina

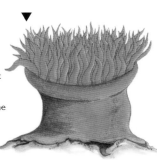

Actinia with wide adhesive base from which emerges a column whose tip is surrounded by 200 short tentacles set in concentric rows. Easily identified by its bright red coloring. Lives in the tidal area and when the tide goes out it contracts into a kind of compact ball. Grows up to 7 centimeters diameter.

White sea fan
Eunicella singularis

Gorgonian with less ramifications than the previous species, most of which are in parallel bands. The branches are covered with small, not very prominent warts, into which the brownish polyps retract. The gorgonian is whitish in color. Grows on subhorizontal rocky bottoms with plenty of light from 10 to 50-60 meters. Maximum size 40-50 centimeters high.

Golden anemone
Condylactis aurantiaca

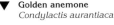

Most of the body of this actinia is concealed by sediment, but the retractile tentacles (around 100) are clearly visible - stubby and digiform, they are set out in four concentric rows. The body is whitish and the tentacles browny-green, with deep purple tips. Lives on sandy and detritus bottoms down to depths of 10 meters and perhaps further. Grows to 10 centimeters in diameter.

Snakelocks anemone
Anemonia sulcata

Actinia with wide adhesive base easily identified by its long tentacles, which are only partly retractable. Large numbers grow close together locally. Lives on hard substrates from the surface to depths of 20-25 meters. Measures up to 30 centimeters diameter.

Warty sea fan
Eunicella verrucosa

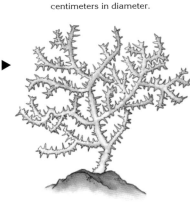

Fan-shape gorgonian with very accentuated ramifications and rough branches, caused by the closely-set, prominent, polyps. Color varies from white to pale pink. Grows on rocky sea-beds including sedimentary ones, from 20-30 meters to 200 meters deep. Maximum size 40-50 centimeters high.

Berried anemone
Alicia mirabilis

Actinia with a powerful sting which changes its appearance considerably between the daytime, when it is retracted and the night when it spreads out completely and transforms itself into a disseminated colony of tubercles with a crown of translucid tentacles. Lives on rocky and sometimes sandy bottoms from 10-15 meters to over 50 meters deep. Grows up to 40 centimeters high when extended.

Dead men's fingers
Alcyonum palmatum

Antozoan with compact colonies and large digiform ramifications which start from a polyp-free basal stem. Color varies from pink to dark red; whitish polyps. Grows on detritus or muddy bottoms from 7-10 meters to over 200 meters deep. Maximum size 20 centimeters.

Cup coral
Caryophyllia smithii ▶

Solitary hard coral with polyps protected by a cup-shape skeleton, narrowed at the base and with enlarged edges. The polyp inside can have up to 80 tentacles with enlarged points. Color varies from white to pink. Lives on rocky or detritus bottoms with little light, from 4-5 meters deep to over 500. Maximum size 2 centimeters.

Cladocora caespitosa ▼

Colonial hard coral which forms colonies made up of the skeletons of polyps, which are similar in appearance to cylindrical little branches. The appearance of these colonies varies according to depth, going from pads close to the surface to branched forms in deep water. Brownish. Lives on hard substrates from 1-2 meters down to more than 600 meters. Maximum size 50 centimeters diameter.

Phosphorescent sea pen
Pennatula phosphorea

◀ Octocoral with characteristic plume shape. Composed of a large primary polyp buried in the sediment, whose elongated, cylindrical upper part produces other lateral polyps. Greyish in color, but it is also phosphorescent. Lives on muddy bottoms from 20 to 100 meters. Measures up to 20 centimeters in height.

Astroides calycularis

◀ Colonial encrusting hard coral which forms extended pads of retractile polyps inside calcareous skeletons of varying prominence. A thermophilic species, it is more frequent in the southern regions of the Mediterranean. Red and orange. Lives on rocky bottoms with little light, from a few meters down to over 50. Maximum size 10 centimeters.

Leptosammia pruvoti ▶

Solitary hard coral with a cylindrical calcareous skeleton, from which the big tentacles of the bright yellow polyps stick out. It is common for several specimens of this species to form groups and live so close together as to seem a colony. Lives on rocky bottoms with little light. Maximum size 8 centimeters high.

Golden zoanthid
Parazoanthus axinellae ▶

Colonial anthozoan consisting of elongated retractile polyps which all start from a common encrusting base. Their are 24-36 long, slim tentacles around the mouth. Yellow. Lives on rocky bottoms and on other organisms (e.g. sponges) from depths of 5-10 meters to over 100. Colonies can cover broad surfaces.

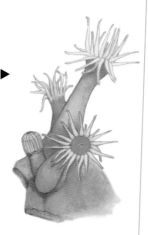

▼ Star coral
Balanophyllia europaea

Solitary hard coral identifiable by its solid oval-sectioned, slightly waisted, skeleton. Whitish-brown. Lives on rocky bottoms with plenty of light, from the surface down to 40-50 meters. Maximum size 2-3 centimeters.

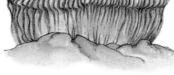

▼ False black coral
Gerardia savaglia

Erroneously called "Mediterranean black coral", this species has fan-shaped colonies with a brown-black skeleton. The covering tissue and the polyps are yellow. Often establishes itself on gorgonians where it covers the branches. Lives on rocky bottoms deeper than 35-40 meters. Maximum height one meter.

Tube dwelling anemone
Cerianthus membranaceus

Anthozoan with elongated body protected by a large tube much of which is buried in sediment. The exposed part has a double crown of long tentacles (more than 200). Color varies from purple to brown. Lives on sandy or muddy bottoms from 5-6 meters to below 40. Maximum size 40 centimeters.

WORMS
Serpula vermicularis

Sedentary worm with a circular- or triangular-section limestone tube, with 5-7 longitudinal ribs. The worm lives inside the tube and only the double horseshoe-shaped crown of retractile tentacles emerges. These are red and white. Found attached to hard substrates at depths of down to 50 meters. Maximum size 12 centimeters.

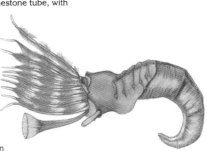

Flat worm
Prostheceraeus giesbrechtii

Flat leaf-like worm, with elongated oval shape. Two small tentacles on the head. Moves with slight wavy movements of the body. Reddish-purple, with white stripes. Found on rocky bottoms to a depth of 50 meters. Maximum size 4 centimeters.

White-tufted worm
Protula tubularia

Sedentary worm with cylindrical limestone tube with an erect terminal section. The retractile branchial tuft is made up of two lobes. The crown of tentacles is white or pink with yellow-orange stripes. Found on hard substrates from 2-3 meters to over 500 meters. Maximum size 5 centimeters.

Bispira volutacornis

Sedentary worm with short, membranous tube. Two equally-sized, spiral branchial tufts. The branchial crown varies in color from white to orange to purple. Lives on substrates of detritus down to 100 meters. Maximum size 15 centimeters.

Bonellia viridis

Unusual worm belonging to the *Echiuridae*, with unusual sexual dimorphism. The female has a sack-shaped body with a long cleft proboscis 2 meters long when fully extended. The male is very small and lives attached to the female. Greenish. The species is found on rocky or detritus substrates with crevices, at depths of 10-100 meters.

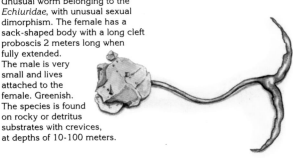

Bearded fire worm
Hermodice carunculata

Polychaete worm with a long cylindrical body divided into numerous segments (more than 100). The branchia and bristles (motor organs) are distributed evenly along the sides of the body. If touched it erects slim white bristles which have a powerful sting. Greenish in color with red and white tones. Found on rocky and detritus bottoms at depths of 1-2 meters to over 20. Maximum size 35 centimeters.

Peacock worm
Sabella pavonina

Sedentary worm with mucous tube encrusted with mud. Branchial crown is composed of two semicircular lobes joined at the base by a membrane. Branchial tuft can be reddish or whitish with dark stripes. Found on sandy or muddy and detritus substrates from 10 to 20-30 meters. Maximum size 25 centimeters.

Lamellated haliotis - *Haliotis lamellosa*

Highly mimetic mollusc with a, ear-shaped shell with a row of holes for the sensory filaments of the mantle. Very pearly inside. Found on rocky substrates from 1-2 meters to 15-20 meters deep, to which it clings tenaciously. Maximum size 7 centimeters.

Shining top shell - *Calliostoma conulum*

Gastropod mollusc with a sharply conical shell made up of ten so slim whorls. External surface is very shiny. Usually reddish-orange with dark and white markings. Found on detritus and hard substrates down to over 40 meters. Maximum size 3 centimeters.

Common cerithe - *Cerithium vulgatum*

Gastropod mollusc with strong, elongated, tower-shaped shell with whorls decorated by spines of varying accentuation. The aperture is slightly off-center towards the outside. Brown and marbled. Found on sandy or detritus beds from 2-3 meters down to 25-30 meters deep. Maximum size 6-7 centimeters.

◀ **MOLLUSCS**
Limpet - *Patella sp.*

Gastropod mollusc found in surface water and the tidal zone where it lives attached to rocks. Flattened, slightly conical shell. It has a large foot which allows the animal to stick hard to the rock during low tide. The biggest specimens reach 5-7 centimeters.

▶

◀ **Turbinate monodon** - *Monodonta turbinata*

Gastropod mollusc with a strong, conical shell with 5-6 convex whorls. Brownish-green with an iridescent opening. Found in the tidal zone and survives exposure well when the tide recedes. Maximum size 2-3 centimeters.

▶

◀ **Rough turbo** - *Astrea rugosa*

Gastropod mollusc with a strong, spiral shell decorated with spiny or warty ornaments. Wide aperture close by an interesting spiraform calcareous operculum which used as a jewel. Found on rocky and detritus bottoms from 10 to 100 meters deep. Maximum size 6 centimeters.

▶

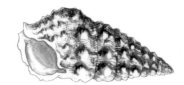

◀ **Cowrie** - *Luria lurida*

One of the few cowries found in the Mediterranean and is immediately recognisable by its oval shape and its shiny mantle. Brownish with dark blotches on both extremities. Found on rocky and sandy beds with poor illumination and in caves, from 4-5 meters down to 40-45 meters deep. Maximum size 5 centimeters.

Mediterranean simnia - *Neosimnia spelta*

Gastropod mollusc parasite, lives on gorgonians. The shell, which is protected by a mimetic mantle, is shiny and tapering with pointed extremities. Color varies according to the parasitic species. Its habits mean it is found on gorgonians and other similar species. Maximum size 2 centimeters.

Knobbed triton - *Charonia rubicunda*

Large gastropod mollusc with a spindle-shaped spiral shell, with a very wide final whorl. Feeds on echinoderms, particularly red stars. Greyish-pink with white and brownish stripes and blotches. Porcelain-like inside. Found on rocky and detrital beds from 15-20 to over 40 meters deep. Maximum size 40 centimeters.

Purple dye murex - *Bolinus brandaris*

The most common murex, characterized by a very long siphon canal and long spines placed in a spiral pattern on the shell. Color is greyish or yellowish-grey. Once use for the extraction of purple dye. Found on sandy and detrital beds from 4-5 meters to over 70 meters deep. Maximum size 10 centimeters.

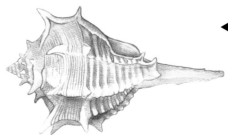

Helmet ton - *Tonna galea*

Large gastropod mollusc with globular shell. The whorls are not well defined and the last one almost envelops the previous spirals. Light brown with a few dark marks. Found on detrital and rocky beds from 15-40 meters deep. Maximum size 25 centimeters.

Red-mouth purpura - *Thais haemastona*

Gastropod mollusc with a thick, egg-shaped shell with conical spirals. Ovoidal opening with a thickened, knurled, outer lip. Tawny-grey with a pinky-orange opening. Found on rocky beds from 3-5 to 30 meters. Maximum size 6 centimeters.

Common whelk - *Buccinulum corneum*

Gastropod mollusc with a very thick, spindle-shaped, shell. Oval opening with sharp lip. Varies from pinky-beige to brown. Found on rocky beds and amongst Neptune grass from 3-5 meters to 30 meters deep. Maximum size 6 centimeters.

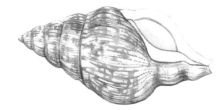

Wooden fasciolaria - *Fasciolaria lignaria*

Gastropod mollusc with spindle-shaped, slightly elongated, shell, with whorls raised by tubercles. Oval aperture with elongated siphon canal. Greeny-brown. Found on rocky beds and amongst Neptune grass down to 30 meters. Maximum size 5 centimeters.

Gastropod mollusc. One of the coat-of-mail shells with several protective overlapping plates which are hinged so that the animal can fold itself up. Olive colored with blotches of different colors. Found on rocky beds close to the surface and in the tidal zone. Maximum size 4-5 centimeters.

Sea hare - *Aplysia depilans*

Large opistobranchiate gastropod mollusc with stout parapodia for swimming. Its thin shell is completely covered by its mantle. Brownish. If touched it defends itself by secreting a pinky-colored liquid. Found on rocky, algae-rich beds from the surface down to 15-20 meters. Maximum size 25 centimeters. ▶

Umbraculum mediterraneum

Gastropod mollusc with an enormously developed foot in proportion to its shell, which is a flattened oval. The surface of the animal is ◀ covered with numerous unequal-length tubercles. Brownish or orange in color with light tubercles and a whitish shell. The species lives on detrital and muddy beds from 15 to over 50 meters deep, where it remains buried during the day. Maximum size 20 centimeters.

Thuridilla hopei

Belongs to the *Saccoglossa* order with a body similar to a snail, with wide, wavy eges to its mantle. The front end of the body has a pair of tentacles. Dark background with yellow, white and blue stripes. Found on rocky beds from 3-5 meters to 20 meters. Maximum size 3 centimeters. ▶

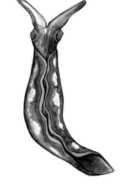

Chromodoris luteorosa

◀ Nudibranch gastropod mollusc with an elongated, flattened body. At the front end of the body there is a pair of tentacles and a plumed branchial tuft at the rear. Violet with yellow blotches. Found on rocky beds from 5-10 to over 50 meters deep. Maximum size 5 centimeters.

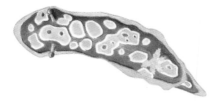

Hypselodoris valenciennesi

Nudibranch gastropod mollusc with a body similar to a snail's, very elongated and with undulated edges. It has a pair of lamellar tentacles on its head and a prominent branchial tuft. Violet to yelowish-green with numerous yellow blotches. Found on rocky and detritus beds from 3-4 to over 40 meters deep. Maximum size approx. 20 centimeters.

▶

Discodoris atromaculata

◀ Nudibranch gastropod mollusc with rounded, flat, body. Easily recognised by its whitish color with dark blotches and because it is nearly always found on the sponge *Petrosia ficiformis*, on which it feeds. Found on rocky beds from 5 meters down to 40-50. Measures up to 15 centimeters.

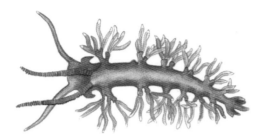

Noah's ark - *Arca noae*

Bivalve mollusc with a symmetrical, sub-rectangular shell. Brownish, but often covered with the red sponge *Crambe crambe* which hides it completely. Found from 4-5 meters to over 70 meters on rocky beds to which it adheres tenaciously with its byssus filaments. Maximum size 10 centimeters.

Fan mussel - *Pinna nobilis*

The biggest of the bivalve molluscs in the Mediterranean. It has symmetrical, triangular valves, red mother-of-pearl inside and strongly encrusted on the outside. Lives stuck vertically into the sand or in the posidonia meadows, from 3-4 meters to over 30. Maximum size 90 meters.

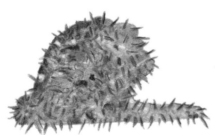

Scallop - *Pecten jacobaeus*

Bivalve mollusc with asymmetrical valves: one flat and the other, which rests on the sea bed, is convex. The surface of the shell is decorated with radial ribs. Reddish-brown. Lives on sandy and detrital beds from 15 meters to over 100. Maximum size 15 centimeters.

Flabellina affinis

Nudibranch gastropod mollusc with slim, elongated body, marked by numerous elongated lateral papillae grouped in tufts. Varying shades of pink. Found on rocky beds from 5 to 50 meters, and is usually found in the company of the hydroids on which it feeds. Maximum 4 centimeters.

Date mussel - *Lithophaga lithophaga*

Bivalve mollusc with tapering, almost cylindrical, shell. Reddish-brown. Lives by drilling into limestone rocks thanks to acid secretions, until it is completely covered by the rock. Found from the surface to 10-15 meters deep. Maximum size 12 centimeters. Protected species.

Winged oyster - *Pteria hirundo*

Bivalve mollusc with unequal valves. At the sides of the hinge the shell has two different-sized lateral "wings". Brownish and often encrusted outside, partly mother-or-pearl inside. Found from 15-20 meters to over 100, adhering to hard substrates and gorgonians. Maximum size 8 centimeters.

Thorny oyster - *Spondylus gaederopus*

Bivalve mollusc with strong, asymmetrical shell with a convex valve and a flat one. Characteristic long, robust spines decorate the shell. Often covered sand hidden by the red sponge *Crambe crambe*, which hides it. Found on rocky substrates to which it encrusted. Maximum size 15 centimeters.

147

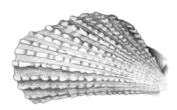

Warty venus - *Venus verrucosa*

Bivalve mollusc with robust, rounded shell with equal valves decorated with raised, concentric stripes. Yellowish-white. Lives buried in sandy and detrital beds from 3-5 meters to over 100. Maximum size 6 centimeters.

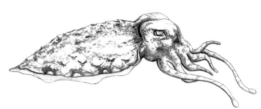

Common squid - *Loligo vulgaris*

Cephalopod mollusc belonging to the *Decapod* order; very tapering body ending in a pair of triangular, lateral fins. Small head with 8 arms and two extendible tentacles with widened extremities. Reddish. Found in coastal waters from 10-20 meters to over 200 meters. Maximum size 40 centimeters.

White spotted octopus - *Octopus macropus*

Cephalopod mollusc belonging to the *Octopods*; very similar to the common octopus, but has longer arms, especially the dorsal ones and is reddish with white blotches. Found on rocky and detrital beds from a few meters deep to over 100. Maximum size 60 centimeters.

Spiny file shell - *Lima lima*

Bivalve mollusc with oval, elongated shell, with equal-sized valves. The outer surface has a series of highly-visible radial ribs with small spines. Yellowish-white. Lives on rocky and detrital beds from 2-3 meters to over 50. Maximum size 7 centimeters.

Common cuttlefish - *Sepia officinalis*

Cephalopod mollusc belonging to the *Decapod* order, oval-shaped with a well-developed head, to which are attached 8 arms and two extendible tentacles. Well-developed shell hidden inside the mantle. Variable coloring due to its exceptional mimetic talents. Found close to sandy or detrital beds, from a few meters' depth to over 100. Maximum size 35-40 centimeters.

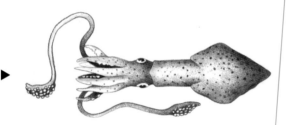

Common octopus - *Octopus vulgaris*

Cephalopod mollusc belonging to the *Octopod* order. Easily recognised by its large, globular head which is distinct from the rest of its body, formed by eight tentacles with double rows of suckers. Coloring is variable due to its mimetic abilities. Found on rocky or detrital beds with crevices, from a few meters to over 100. Maximum size 60 centimeters.

Greater argonauta - *Argonauta argo*

Cephalopod mollusc belonging to the *Octopods*, distinguished by marked sexual dimorphism. The female secretes a kind of pergamon-like shell between two specialized arms, to hold the eggs and part of the animal. The male is smaller and has no shell. Found in the open sea. The female reaches 20 centimeters in size, the male 1.5-2.

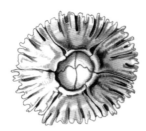

Acorn barnacle - *Balanus perforatus*

Sessile crustacean belonging to the *Cirripedia*. Very similar to the previous species, from which it is differentiated by its large, conical shell with a narrow triangular opening. Found cemented to hard substrates from the surface down to 30-40 meters. Maximum size 3 centimeters.

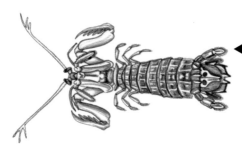

Banded shrimp - *Stenopus spinosus*

Cleaner shrimp with long thin antennae and a third pair of highly developed limbs ending in strong pincers. Reddish-orange with white claw tips and antennae. Found in rocky, poorly illuminated habitats and in caves from 10-15 meters down to 500 meters. Maximum size 7 centimeters.

Common prawn - *Palaemon serratus*

Small prawn with long, notched, upward-curving rostrum. The first pair of limbs has pincers. The abdomen has swimming legs attached to it. The body is transparent with reddish longitudinal stripes. Lives from 2 to 10-15 meters on rocky beds close to Neptune grass. Maximum size 10 centimeters.

CRUSTACEANS

Barnacle - *Chthamalus stellatus*

Sessile crustacean well adapted to a sedentary life. The modified body is protected by a truncated, conical shell, made up of 6 limestone plates which can be closed by mobile opercular valves. Found on hard substrates in surface waters. Maximum size 1.2 centimeters.

Spottail mantis shrimp - *Squilla mantis*

Stomatopod crustacean with a flattened body and a front pair of "limbs" which are extensions of the mouth, for capturing its prey. The rear end of the body has two distinctive ocellar markings. Found on sandy beds from 10-15 meters deep to 100. Maximum size 25 centimeters.

Narval shrimp - *Plesionika narval*

Elegant-looking shrimp with a smooth carapace and a long, lacy, rostrum bending slightly upwards. Pale red with red and gold longitudinal stripes. Lives on rocky and sandy-muddy beds from 10 to over 800 meters deep. Maximum size 12 centimeters.

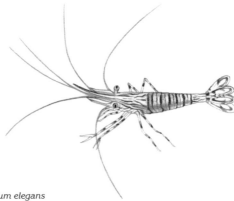

Gnathophyllum elegans

Stumpy, globulous body with short rostrum and limbs which appear to have two points. Head and thorax and abdomen are dark in color with yellow spots. Light yellow rostrum and caudal fan. Lives a few meters below the surface close to Neptune grass. Maximum size 3.5 centimeters.

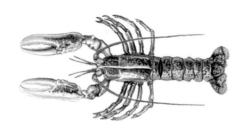

Lobster - *Homarus gammarus*

◀ Large crustacean with two strong asymmetrical pincers, the right is use for breaking and the left for cutting. Bluish-black with yellowish markings. Found on mixed sandy and rocky beds from 10-15 meter up to 60. Maximum size 60 centimeters.

Spiny lobster - *Palinurus elephas*

Large crustacean with convex carapace covered with spines and tubercles. Antennae longer than the body. Dark red with a few white blotches all over the body. White-striped feet. Found on rocky bottoms inside crevices, from 10-15 meters down to 70. Maximum size 50 centimeters.

▶

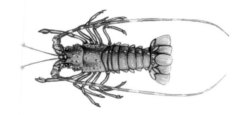

Locust lobster - *Scyllarides latus*

◀ Crustacean with squashed, rectangular body, wider at the front end than the rear. Typical, flattened lamellar antennae with a wavy front edge. Reddish brown with violet antennules. Lives on rocky sea-beds from 10 to 100 meters. Maximum size 45 centimeters.

Small locust lobster - *Scyllarus arctus*

Crustacean which is similar in form to the previous species, from which it differs in size (smaller) and by the shape of its flattened antennae, which have a frilly front edge. Brown, with whitish blotches and blue and red stripes between the abdominal segments. Found on rocky bottoms and amongst Neptune grass, from 5 to 50 meters deep. Maximum size 12 centimeters.

▶

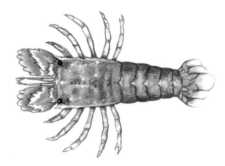

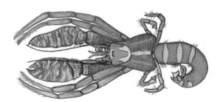

Hermit crab - *Dardanus arrosor*

◀ Large hermit crab with notched asymmetrical pincers covered with light hair. Red, sometimes brighter than others. Found on rocky or detrital bottoms from 15-20 meters to 50 meters. Maximum size 6 centimeters.

Pagurus prideaux

Small hermit crab with well-calcified, wide front end to its carapace. This hermit is always associated with the *Adamsia carciniopados* actinia which grows covering the shell used by the crustacean. Red with salmon pink of yellow pincers. Found on rocky or sandy sea-beds from 5-7 meters down to 400. Maximum size 2 centimeters.

▶

Squat lobster - *Galathea strigosa*

Crustacean flattened back to belly, longer than it is wide. The abdomen is folded ventrally for more than half its total length. ◀ Reddish with bluish hoops. Found on rocky and detrital bottoms from 20-30 meters down to 600. Maximum size 17 centimeters.

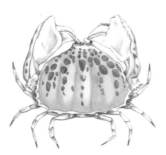

Shamefaced crab - *Calappa granulata*

Crab with very convex carapace and highly-developed pincers, with which it can close the front end of its shell by tucking them underneath. Yellowish with red marks corresponding to the tubercles. Found on sandy-muddy and detrital bottoms, from 15-20 meters down to 400. Maximum size 11 centimeters.

Porter crab - *Dromia personata*

Crab with wider-than-long carapace thickly covered with fine hair which stops before the tips of its pincers. Dark brown with pinkish pincer tips. Lives on rocky bottoms or in grottos from 5-10 meters down to over 100. Maximum size 7 centimeters.

Warty crab - *Eriphia verrucosa*

Crab with flattened shell, with spines (some forked) along the front and sides. A cleft and series of spines between the eyes. Reddish brown with dark markings and black point to the pincers. Lives on rocky bottoms in the tidal zone. Maximum size 7 centimeters.

Marbled crab - *Pachygrapsus marmoratus*

Crab with flattened, virtually square carapace with side edges which are almost straight and parallel. Greeny brownish marbled with yellow. Found in the tidal zone. Maximum size 5 centimeters.

Spinous spider crab - *Maja squinado*

Crab with ovoid carapace, very convex, covered with a large number of spines. Forked rostrum. Very long limbs. Yellowish or reddish brown in color. Found on rocky, algae-rich sea-beds, from depths of 3-5 meters down to 70 meters. Maximum size 18 centimeters.

Herbstia condyliata

Crab with sub-triangular carapace, longer than it is wide. Forked rostrum. Numerous tubercles on the back. Reddish-grey with blue stripes. Found on rocky sea-beds, mainly inside caves, from depth of 5-7 meters down to 50. Maximum size 4 centimeters.

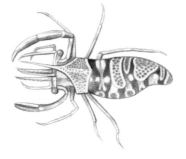

Anemone shrimp - *Periclimenes amethysteus*

Crustacean with elongated, laterally compressed body. Transparent with two Y-shaped blue bands on the back and further marks on the sides. Found on rocky and detrital sea-beds together with anemones, from a few meters to 15-20. Maximum size 3 centimeters.

151

BRYOZOANS

False coral - *Myriapora truncata*

Colonial, arborescent organism with dichotomous ramifications in all directions. Short, round-section branches which appear to have been chopped off. Covered in minute pores which correspond to the individual components which make up the colony. Pinky-red in color, fades when out of water. Found on rocky, weakly-illuminated sea-beds from 2-3 meters to over 90. Maximum height 10 centimeters.

Deerhorn coral - *Pentapora fascialis*

Colonial organism which grows in several shapes, but mainly erect with flattened branches and irregular lobes. Bright pink-orange. Found on rocky or detrital weakly-illuminated sea-bottoms, from 20 to 100 meters. Maximum height 15 centimeters.

Sea lace bryozoan - *Sertella septentrionalis*

Lacy colony made up of expanded, erect laminae with fluted edges. Color varies from bright pink to whitish. Found on rocky, poorly-illuminated bottoms and inside caves, from 10 to 35 meters deep. Measures up to 10 centimeters.

ECHINODERMS

Crinoid - *Antedon mediterranea*

Characteristically-shaped echinoderm, consisting of a small central body with ten thin arms which look feathery due to the lateral pinnules. Color varies from red to yellow to white to pink. Found on rocky or sandy and detrital floors, from 10-15 meters to over 80. Maximum size 25 centimeters.

Sea cucumber - *Holothuria tubulosa*

Cylindrically-bodied animal covered in a thick, leathery integument. The upper part is covered with papillae and the belly is covered with bands of tube-feet. Brownish sometimes with reddish reflections. Found on rocky, muddy and sandy bottoms from 3-5 meters down to 100. Maximum size 30 centimeters.

Sea gherkin - *Cucumaria planci*

Animal with elongated, pentagonal-sectioned body, covered with a thick, hard, smooth, integument. The front end has a corona of long, fringed, retractile tentacles. Brown with dark and light markings. Found on rocky, sandy or muddy, or detrital bottoms from 5 meters to over 200.
Maximum size 15 centimeters.

Astropecten aranciacus

Large star with five flattened, triangular, arms edged with long spines. Reddish or orange with dark blotches. Found on sandy bottoms, where it buries itself, from 4-5 meters down to 20-25. Maximum size 60 centimeters.

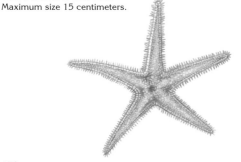

Goose foot star - *Peltaster placenta*

This star is easily recognised by its continuous concave edges, going from tip to tip of successive arms. Color varies from yellow to brownish to red. Found on detrital or sandy bottoms from 10-15 meters down to 1000. Measures up to 17 centimeters.

Ophidiaster ophidianus

Red star with long, flexible, cylindrical arms attached to a small central disc. Crimson or orange-red with dark markings. Found on rocky bottoms from 7-10 meters down to 100.
Measures up to 35 centimeters.

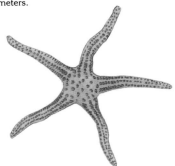

Hacelia attenuata

Starfish with five long, arms which are much thinner at the ends, almost conical. The body is covered with regular longitudinal series of plates. Red to yellow to orange, with plates in a contrasting color. Found on rocky, poorly-illuminated bottoms and in caves, from 5-7 meters to 150 meters.

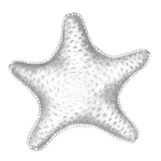

Cushion star - *Asterina gibbosa*

Small star with pentagonal body, with five not very distinct arms, with rounded tips. The surface is rough to the touch because of its plates and prickles. Greeny-grey. Found on rocky, sandy and muddy bottoms, from 3-5 meters down to 150. Measures up to 6 centimeters.

Red star - *Echinaster sepositus*

The commonest red star in the Mediterranean. The central disc is small and has five circular-sectioned, pointed arms attached to it. Granulous surface. Color varies from dark red to orangy-red. Found on rocky, detrital bottoms and amongst Neptune grass, from 2-3 meters down to 250 meters. Measures up to 30 centimeters.

Coscinasteria tenuispina

Irregular starfish with 6-12 different length arms, slightly flattened and pointed. Body covered with prickly plates and spines. Color varies from whitish to reddish with purple or bluish markings. Found on rocky, algae-rich bottoms from 3-5 meters down to 100.
Measures up to 20 centimeters.

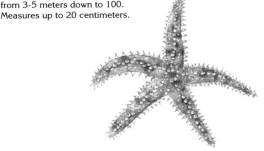

Spiny starfish - *Marthasterias glacialis*

Starfish with large subcylindrical, pointed arms. Body covered with large protuberances set in longitudinal series and strong spines. Color varies from greenish to reddish-brown. Found on rocky and detrital bottoms from 3-5 meters down to 180. Measures up to 70-80 centimeters.

Mediterranean basket star - *Astrospartus mediterraneus*

◀ Unusually-shaped, unmistakable ophiuroid . Central polygonal body to with very mobile, ramified, arms, in every direction. Greyish. Found on rocky or detrital bottoms, often attached to other organisms, from depths of 20-30 meters down to 800. Measures up to 40 centimeters.

Arrow urchin - *Stylocidaris affinis*

Almost spherical sea-urchin with large primary spines surrounded at the base by smaller ones. Reddish. Found on detrital or muddy bottoms, from 30 meters down to 1000. Shell measures up to 5 cm diameter.

▶

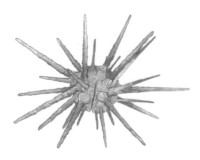

Long-spined urchin - *Centrostephanus longispinus*

◀ Round-bodied urchin with numerous, very long and highly mobile, spines. Purply-brown ; the spines have alternate light and dark hoops. Found on rocky, poorly-illuminated bottoms, from 10-15 meters down to 200. Shell diameter up to 4 centimeters.

Black sea urchin - *Arbacia lixula*

Slightly squashed shell with short spines. Characteristic black color. Lives on rocky bottoms rich in coralline seaweeds, from 1-2 meters to 40. Shell diameter measures up to 6 centimeters.

▶

White tip sea urchin - *Sphaerechinus granularis*

◀ Round shape, easily recognised by its blue-purple spines with white tips. Found on rocky bottoms and amongst Neptune grass, from 3-5 meters to 100. Maximum shell diameter 13 centimeters.

Melon urchin - *Echinus melo*

Large-shelled urchin, semispherical or slightly conical. Small, scanty, spines. Shell is green or yellowish and the spines have alternate light and dark bands. Found on rocky bottoms from 20-30 meters to 100 meters. Maximum shell size 14 centimeters.

▶

Stony sea urchin - *Paracentrotus lividus*

◀ Slightly squashed shell. Not many spines, but strong and sharp. Color varies from reddish through brown through purplish. Found on algae-rich rocky bottoms and amongst Neptune grass from 1-2 meters to 80. Maximum shell size 7 centimeters.

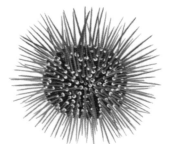

Heart urchin - *Echinocardium cordatum*

Heart-shaped shell, longer than it is wide. Spines and tubercles are fine and uniform. Yellowish-grey. Found on sandy bottoms from 10-15 meters down to 250 meters, where it buries itself.

Purple heart urchin - *Spatangus purpureus*

Heart-shaped shell without the usual radial symmetry, covered in scanty spines and flattened on the back. The top side of the shell has a pattern of lanceolate petals on it. Dark purplish with whitish spines. Found on sandy, detrital bottoms from 15-20 meters to 900. Maximum shell size 12 centimeters.

TUNICATES

Ciona - *Ciona intestinalis*

Cylindrical ascidian, covered with a thick, gelatinous, highly contractile tunic. The mouth and anal siphons are multilobed. Whitish, translucid. Found on hard substrates from 1-2 meters to 500 meters. Maximum size 20 centimeters.

Glass bell tunicate - *Clavelina lepadiformis*

Colonial ascidians, consisting of transparent individuals attached to a single stolon. The individuals are club-shaped and transparent, showing the internal organs. Found on rocky floors, sometimes attached to other organisms, from 3-5 meters deep to 50. Maximum size 6 centimeters.

Sea potato - *Halocinthya papillosa*

One of the common ascidians, shaped like a little barrel from which the mouth and cloacal siphons emerge. Its tunic is rough to the touch. Red and yellow or white. Found on rocky bottoms and amongst Neptune grass from 10-15 meters to over 100. Maximum size up to 12 centimeters.

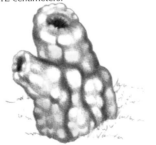

Sea cone - *Phallusia mamillata*

Conical ascidian covered in a thick, cartilage, tunic with large rounded tubercles scattered all over the body. Translucid white with bluish reflections. Found on rocky, detrital and muddy beds from 2-3 meters to 180. Maximum size 15 centimeters.

Aplidium nodiferum

Colonial ascidian with a tendency to form pedunculate colonies shaped like mushrooms. Translucid red-orange. The little red marks visible through the tunic are the individual members of the colony. Found on rocky, poorly-illuminated bottoms from 3-5 meters to 30 meters. Maximum size 4-5 centimeters.

Rock violet - *Microcosmus sp.*

Solid ascidian with thick, very encrusted tunic, making the animal hard to recognise on the sea floor. Greyish-brown with purple-colored siphons internally. Found on rocky and detrital bottoms from 5-7 centimeters to 200. Maximum size 22 centimeters.

FISH

Great white shark - *Carcharodon carcharias*

Large, man-eating shark. Typically greyish in color on the dorsal region and very pale, practically white on the belly. It lives preferably at depths between the surface and 200 meters and is frequently present in coastal waters. Feeds on large pelagic fish (for example, tuna) and cetaceans. Its migrations appear to be linked with temperature changes. Reaches lengths of over 7 meters.

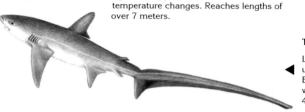

Thresher shark - *Alopias vulpinus*

Large shark easily recognised by its caudal fin, with a very large upper lobe making up almost half the total length of the animal. Bluish-grey on the back and whitish underneath. Lives in surface waters both out at sea and close to the coast. Measures up to 4.5 meters.

Basking shark - *Coetorhinus maximus*

Large shark, easily recognised by its long gill slits which almost meet under the belly. Long snout, especially in the younger individuals. Very small teeth and branchiospines for feeding on plankton. A pelagic fish, it is often found in coastal waters. Measures up to 15 meters.

Lesser spotted dogfish - *Scylliorhynus canicula*

Small, streamlined shark with a short, rounded snout. Large nostrils which in part cover the mouth. The first dorsal fin starts behind the base of the pelvis. Light brown with numerous dark blotches. Lives in coastal waters close to sand and mud or gravel bottoms, from 35-40 meters deep to over 150 meters. Measures up to 80 centimeters.

Nurse hound - *Scylliorhynus stellaris*

Small, slim shark with short, rounded snout. Smaller nostrils than the previous species. First dorsal fin starts in front of the base of the pelvis. Light brown with numerous large, rounded, blotches. Lives close to rocky or muddy bottoms from 20 meters to over 150 meters.

Blue shark - *Prionace glauca*

Streamlined shark with dorsal slightly set back and very developed, crescent-shaped pectorals. Typical blue color on the back. Lives in coastal and deep-sea waters, between the surface and a depth of 150 meters. Maximum size 3.8 meters.

Marbled electric ray - *Torpedo marmorata*

Ray-shaped, with a flattened body, in which the head, trunk and pectoral fins are widened to form a more or less circular disc. The front edge is truncated. There are two transparent electric organs on either side of the head. Dark in color with lighter marbling. Lives on detrital or sandy-muddy bottoms from 20 meters to 200 meters. Maximum size 100 centimeters.

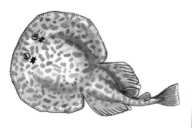

Starry ray - *Raja asterias*

Ray with strongly depressed body, forming a disc joining the head, the trunk and the pectorals. The tail is quite distinct from the body. The center of the back has a row of raised notches. Brownish with numerous dark and yellowish circular blotches. Found on mixed mud and sand and sandy bottoms from 10 meters to 300 meters. Measures up to 80 centimeters.

Thornback ray - *Raja clavata*

Flattened front to back, forming a disc combining head, trunk and pectorals. There are numerous spines on the back and a series of large notches in a row down the middle of the body. Brownish in color, with several marks on the tail. Lives on sandy-muddy and sandy bottoms, from 10 meters to 200. Measures up to 110 centimeters.

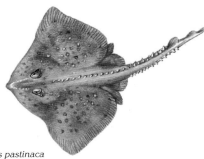

Stingray - *Dasyatis pastinaca*

Ray with a disc-shaped body, slightly wider than long. Pointed snout. No dorsal fin and the tail is 1.5 times as long as the body. Olive-colored with reddish nuances. Found on sandy-muddy and detrital bottoms, from a few meters to 200 meters. Measures up to 2.5 meters.

Eagle ray - *Myliobatis aquila*

Large ray with rhomboid body, wider than it is long. Head is quite distinct from the central disc of the body and the tail is much longer than the body. Dark-colored back with whitish belly. Found close to sandy and mixed sand and mud beds in coastal waters, to depths of 200 meters. Maximum length 2.6 meters.

Moray eel - *Muraena helena*

Eel-shaped body, robust and slightly compressed at the rear end. Short head with a well developed mouth which is almost always held open. No pectoral fins. Marbled and sometimes black. Lives on rocky bottoms from a few meters to 80 meters. Maximum length 1.3 meters.

Conger eel - *Conger conger*

Eel-shaped body with a subcylindrical front end. Elongated snout with a wide mouth and big lips. Well-developed pectorals. Color varies from blackish to whitish. Lives on rocky and sandy-muddy bottoms, from 3-5 meters down to 100 meters. Maximum length 2 meters.

Pilchard - *Sardina pilchardus*

Oval-sectioned, tapering body. Ventral profile has a series of small, protruding, toothed scales. Greenish back, golden white sides with dark marks. A pelagic and coastal fish living in shoals, from 10-15 meters to 180 meters. Maximum size 25 centimeters.

Anchovy - *Engraulis encrasicolus*

Very slim, tapered, body ending in a conical, pointed nose. Upper jaw is more develope than the lower one. Scales tend to fall when the animal is handled. Blue-green back and silvery sides. Lives in banks in pelagic and coastal waters, between the surface and 180 meters. Maximum size 20 centimeters.

Forkbeard - *Phycis phycis*

Tapered, deep, body, compressed back section. One barbel on the jaw. Pelvic fins are thread-like. Dark brown or reddish brown. Found on rocky and sandy-muddy bottoms from 10-20 meters down to 650. Maximum size 65 centimeters.

157

Cling fish - *Lepadogaster candollei*

Small fish with a compressed front end to its body and an elongated head. The mouth is on the underside and there are two suckers between pelvic fins. Reddish or yellowish green. Lives in surface waters on algae-rich rocky bottoms and reefs. Maximum size 7 centimeters.

Blackwing flying fish - *Hirundichthys rondeletii*

Elongated body with flattened belly. Large pectoral fins extending to the dorsal fin. Lower lobe of the caudal fin is more developed than the upper one. Bluish back and light-colored underside. Lives close to the surface, jumping out of the water in long, planing, leaps if frightened. Maximum size 30 centimeters.

Aphanius fasciatus

Stumpy, oval body with a short nose. Small, very oblique mouth. The dorsal and anal fins are almost opposite each other. Brownish back and white belly, with in males alternate silver and dark stripes. Females are light-colored with vertical black stripes and white fins. Lives in brackish water. Maximum size 6 centimeters.

Gar-fish - *Belone belone*

Elongated, subcylindrical body with a pointed nose and jaws which are elongated into a kind of beak. Bluish back and silvery white sides and belly. Lives in coastal waters, from the surface to 20-30 meters. Maximum size 90 centimeters.

Big scale sand smelt - *Atherina boyeri*

Elongated fish with subcylindrical, compressed body. Big eyes. Small, terminal mouth. Back is blue-green flecked with black; the side are whitish with a silver longitudinal lines. Lives in shoals in coastal waters and lagoons. Maximum size 13 centimeters.

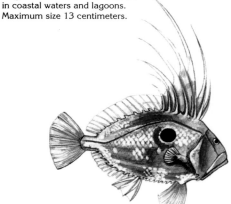

John Dory - *Zeus faber*

Oval shaped, deep, compressed body. Has characteristic long rays on the dorsal fin and the ocellar marking on the sides, which make it easy to pick out. Golden-grey with dark shading. Lives close to sandy or muddy bottoms, from 20-30 meters deep to 400 meters. Maximum size 60 centimeters.

Drumfish - *Capros aper*

Deep, compressed body. Convex area over the eyes. Small, very protractile mouth, which is converted into a tube when capturing prey. Red with yellow transverse bands. Found close to muddy bottoms, from 25 meters to 600. Maximum size 16 centimeters.

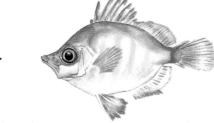

Longspine snipefish - *Macroramphosus scolopax*

Deep, compressed body terminating in an elongated head. Long, tube-shaped snout with a small terminal mouth. Body is rough to the touch. Pinkish red. Lives in bottom waters, from 40-50 meters to over 200 meters. Maximum size 20 centimeters.

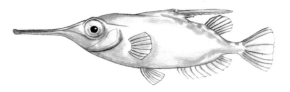

Horse pipe-fish - *Syngnathus typhle*

Pipefish with thin, elongated, body. Has a distinctive high, compressed, nose with a straight profile, with an almost vertically-cut mouth at the extremity. Color varies from brown to greenish-brown. Found close to Neptune grass and zosters from 1-2 meters to 20-30. Maximum size 35 centimeters.

Common sea-horse - *Hippocampus hippocampus*

Unmistakable fish. Distinctive head position, which is set at an angle to the body and the prehensile tail. Brownish or greenish-black. Found close to Neptune grass from 2-4 meters down to 20-30. Maximum size 15 centimeters.

Flying gurnard - *Dactylopterus volitans*

Elongated body, very square at the front. Head covered with strong bones. Distinctive pectoral fins in two parts, the second one being very wide and brightly colored in blue with white blotches. Lives on sandy and muddy bottoms and close to Neptune grass, from 8-10 meters to 80 meters.

Red scorpionfish - *Scorpaena scrofa*

The largest of the Mediterranean scorpionfish, easily recognised by the large number of fringed appendices around the head, the mouth and the sides, Reddish with brownish and black marks. Found on rocky and detrital bottoms and amongst Neptune grass from 3-4 meters to over 300 meters. Measures up to 50 centimeters.

Black scorpionfish - *Scorpaena porcus*

Stout-shaped body, typical of the scorpionfish. Distinctive large fleshy excrescences above the eyes and a marked socket around them. Blackish-brown with darker blotches. Found on rocky and detrital bottoms and amongst Neptune grass, from 3-4 meters to over 100. Maximum size 30 centimeters.

Small red scorpionfish - *Scorpaena notata*

The head of this scorpionfish is virtually free of all cutaneous appendices. Recognise by its brighter red coloring and a black mark in the middle of the dorsal fin. Lives on poorly-illuminated, rocky bottoms, from 5 to 700 meters deep. Maximum size 18 centimeters.

Streaked gurnard - *Trygloporus lastoviza*

Fish with a streamlined body which tapers towards the tail. Large head covered with bony plates. Has characteristic wide pectoral fins with blue marks, the first three rays of which are separate and mobile. Reddish-colored. Lives on detrital and sandy-muddy bottoms, from 20 meters to over 200 meters. Measures up to 40 centimeters.

African armored searobin - *Peristedion cataphractum*

Elongated, octagonal-section, body, entirely covered with large bony scales. The head is plated and has two characteristic rostrum-shaped extensions, one on each side of the head. Red. Lives on sandy-muddy and detrital bottoms, from 30 meters down to 700 meters. Maximum size 40 centimeters.

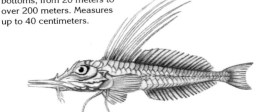

Sea bass - *Dicentrarchus labrax*

Streamlined, tapering body, with powerful head and well-developed mouth. Robust, forward-facing spines on the preoperculum. Double dorsal fin. Silvery-grey. Found close to sandy and rocky bottoms, from 3-5 meters down to 100 meters. Maximum size 1 meter.

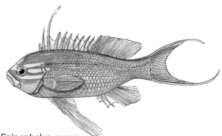

Grouper - *Epinephelus guaza*

Large, oval body with a well-developed head and large mouth. Wide, rounded caudal fin. Brownish with blotches of varying degrees of darkness. Lives on rocky bottoms with plenty of crevices, from 3-5 meters to 100. Measures up to 1 meter.

Painted comber - *Serranus scriba*

Tapered body, slightly compressed, with a pointed head. Reddish-grey with dark vertical bands and a characteristic bluish mark on the sides and variegated patterns on the nose and the opercula. Lives on rocky bottoms and close to posidonia, from 4-5 meters to 100 meters deep. Measures up to 35 centimeters.

Shark-sucker - *Echeneis naucrates*

Elongated, tapering fish. Recognised by its modified forward dorsal fin which has evolved into a sucker (ventose) with transverse lamellae. Whitish with a wide dark longitudinal band from the nose to the tail. Found in coastal waters, where it swims alone or attached to a large fish.
Maximum size 1 meter.

Gurnard - *Trigla lyra*

Elongated body with subquadrangular profile. Large head covered in strong bony plates which are ridged and spiny. The first three rays of the pectorals are free. Reddish with bluish blotches on the fins. Lives on muddy or detrital bottoms, from 40-50 meters to over 400 meters. Maximum size 60 centimeters.

Swallow tail seaperch - *Anthias anthias*

Oval-bodied fish with short nose and pronounced sickle-shaped tail, with elongated lobes. Very developed pelvic fins. Red or bright pink with golden stripes on the head and sides. Lives close to rocky bottoms with plenty of crevices. From 15-20 meters down to 200 meters. Maximum size 25 centimeters.

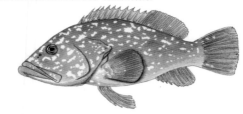

Wreck fish - *Polyprion americanum*

Deep, powerful body with a large head and slight concavity on the back of the neck. Transverse bony crest on the operculum. Rough scales on the body. Brownish-grey. Lives on rocky and mixed sand and mud bottoms, from 30-40 meters down to 400. Young individuals tend to stay close to the surface. Maximum size 2 meters.

Cardinal fish - *Apogon imberbis*

Oval-bodied fish with short head and big eye. Prominent jaw. First dorsal fin is less developed than the second one. Red or pinky body, with white stripes crossing the eyes. Male fish incubates the eggs in its mouth. Found on rocky bottoms with plenty of crevices, from 2-3 meters down to 200. Maximum size 15 centimeters.

Leer-fish - *Lichia amia*

Long, moderately deep body, ending in a pointed nose. Well-developed mouth, opening extending past the eye. Very irregular lateral line. Dark coloring on the back and silvery-white sides and belly. Lives in coastal waters from the surface to 50 meters. Maximum size 2 meters.

Amberjack - *Seriola dumerili*

Robust, tapering body, compressed laterally. Well-developed head. Twin-lobed, well-defined, caudal fin is attached by a slim peduncle. ▶ Silvery-grey, with a dark line from the eyes along the body. Lives in deep-sea waters but comes close into the coast, from 10-15 meters to 70 meters. Maximum size 2 meters.

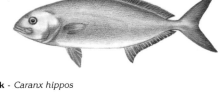

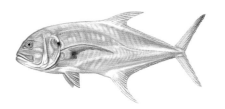

Crevalle jack - *Caranx hippos*

◀ Elongated body, oval and moderately compressed. Convex front profile and short nose. Eyes have adipose eyelids. Caudal peduncle is covered with faired bony plates. Bluish green back with silvery sides. Found in pelagic or coastal waters to depths of 350 meters. Maximum size 100 centimeters.

Pilot fish - *Naucrates ductor*

Elongated body ending suddenly in a blunt nose. Forward dorsal fin ▶ consists of a few separate rays. Caudal peduncle has fleshy keel on either side. Silvery with wide dark transverse bands. A pelagic fish, living with sharks and other large fish. Measures up to 70 centimeters.

Horse-mackerel - *Trachurus mediterraneus*

◀ Elongated, slightly compressed, body. Large eyes protected by a well-developed fatty eyelid. Lateral line is raised on bony shields. Bluish-grey back and light-colored belly. Lives in shoals in pelagic and coastal waters, from the surface to 600 meters. Maximum size 60 centimeters.

Dolphin dish - *Coryphaena hippurus*.

Robust, elongated, compressed body. Head of the adult fish has a convex profile. The dorsal fin begins immediately behind the head. ▶ Metallic greenish-blue with gold and silver reflections and small dark marks on the sides. Lives in pelagic waters, from the surface to 30-50 meters. Maximum size 2 meters.

Bogue - *Boops boops*

Tapering body, subcylindrical at the front. Short nose and large eye. Bluish or greenish on the back and silvery. With golden stripes on the sides. Lives on rocky, detrital and sandy-muddy bottoms ◀ and amongst Neptune grass, from 3-5 meters to 350 meters. Maximum size 36 centimeters.

Dentex - *Dentex dentex*

Robust, deep, compressed body. Large head and wide mouth which has large, canine teeth. Blue-grey with dark marks on the sides. Fins are shaded with pink. Lives close to rocky or sandy bottoms or posidonia meadows, from 15 to 150 meters. Measures up to 100 centimeters.

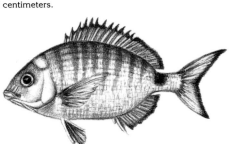

White seabream - *Diplodus sargus sargus*

Oval, very deep, compressed body. Silvery grey, darker on the snout. 8-9 alternating light and dark stripes on the sides. Rear edge ◀ of the caudal is black. Lives on rocky and sandy bottoms close to rocks, from 2-3 meters to over 50 meters. Measures up to 40 centimeters.

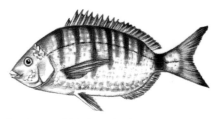

Two-banded seabream - *Diplodus vulgaris*

Oval, deep, compressed body. Slightly protractile mouth. Brownish- or greenish-grey. Characteristic dark band along the neck. Tail peduncle has a dark mark extending along the rays of the dorsal and anal fins. Found on rocky and sandy bottoms and amongst Neptune grass, from 2-3 meters to 130 meters. Maximum size 45 centimeters.

Saddled seabream - *Oblada melanura*

Elongated body, slightly compressed. Short nose and big eye. Silvery grey with bluish reflections on the back. Characteristic big, white-edged, black, saddle-shaped mark on the caudal peduncle. Lives on rocky bottoms and close to Neptune grass, from 3-5 meters to 40 meters. Maximum size 30 centimeters.

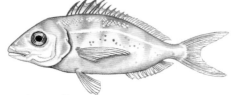

Common seabream - *Pagrus pagrus*

Oval, deep, compressed body. Very convex head profile. Large, canine teeth sometimes revealed. Silvery with pinkish nuances. Reddish eyes. Lives on rocky and sandy bottoms, from 10-15 meters to 200 meters. Maximum size 80 centimeters.

Gilt-head bream - *Sparus aurata*

Oval outline, deep and laterally compressed. Robust head with large molar-shaped teeth in the mouth. Grey with gold and silver reflections. Golden band between the eyes. Lives on sandy and detrital bottoms from 2-3 meters to 40 meters. Maximum size 70 centimeters.

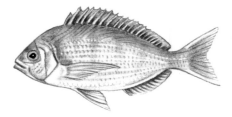

Sharpsnout seabream - *Diplodus puntazzo*

Oval body with pointed nose. Slightly open mouth reveals large, dark, incisors. Silvery grey. 5-7 alternating light and dark stripes on the sides. Dark caudal peduncle. Lives on rocky bottoms from 2-3 meters to 150 meters. Maximum size 60 centimeters.

Striped seabream - *Lithognathus mormyrus*

Elongated, compressed body with a long, pointed, nose. Silvery-grey, darker on the back. 14-15 vertical, dark, lines on the sides. Lives on sandy bottoms close to Neptune grass, from 2-3 meters to 80 meters. Maximum size 55 centimeters.

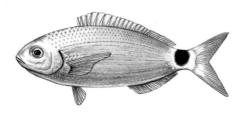

Pandora - *Pagellus erythrinus*

Oval, compressed body, ending in a pointed nose and a straight head. Small eye, bright pink with small blue marks on the upper part of the sides. Rear edge of the operculum is reddish. Lives on rocky, detrital, sandy-muddy bottoms, from 15-20 meters to 300. Maximum size 60 centimeters.

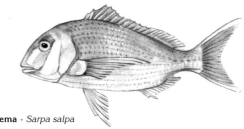

Salema - *Sarpa salpa*

Elongated, compressed body. Small head and rounded nose. Thick-lipped mouth. Blue-grey with 10-11 longitudinal golden stripes. Lives close to rocky and sandy bottoms with plenty of vegetation, from 2-3 meters to 20 meters. Maximum size 50 centimeters.

Black seabream
Spondyliosoma cantharus

Oval, compressed body. Pointed snout, but short. Slightly oblique mouth, pointing upwards. Long dorsal fin, but it can be totally bent along the back. Brownish-grey with metallic reflections and golden, longitudinal stripes. Lives on rocky or sandy bottoms close to Neptune grass, from 10-15 meters to 150. Maximum size 60 centimeters.

Blotched picarel - *Spicara maena*

Elongated, slightly compressed body. Slightly convex on the back of the head. Very protractile upper jaw. Back is blue or greenish-grey; silver sides with a distinctive rectangular black mark. Lives on rocky bottoms or amongst Neptune grass, from 5-7 meters to 170. Maximum size 25 centimeters.

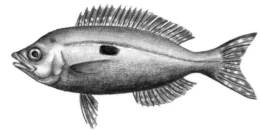

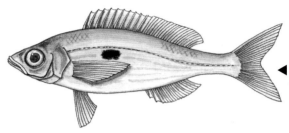

Picarel - *Spicara flexuosa*

Elongated, slightly compressed body. Very protractile upper jaw. Yellowish, blue-grey or green-grey back; dorsal fin has dark margins. Black rectangular mark on the sides. Lives on sandy and muddy bottoms, from 5-7 meters to 130. Maximum size 20 centimeters.

Brown meagre - *Sciaena umbra*

Robust-bodied fish with slightly arched back. Downward-turned mouth, with 5 pores on the front edge of the bottom jaw. Pelvic and anal fins have white front margins. Lives on rocky bottoms close to Neptune grass, from 5-7 meters down to 180. Maximum size 70 centimeters.

Shy drum - *Umbrina cirrosa*

Long, compressed body, with a straight ventral profile. Small, ventral mouth with a short barbel below the bottom jaw. Silvery-grey with dark, slanting stripes on the sides and back. Lives on rocky, sandy and detrital bottoms, from 10-15 meters down to 100. Maximum size 100 centimeters.

Red mullet - *Mullus barbatus*

Slightly compressed body. Short head, with a pair of barbels underneath the lower jaw, which are as long as the pectorals. Almost vertical front profile to the head. Pink- or reddish. Found on muddy or detrital bottoms, from 10 to 500 meters. Maximum size 30 centimeters.

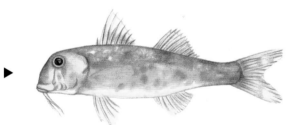

Striped red mullet - *Mullus surmuletus*

Slightly compressed body. Short head with a pair of barbels underneath the lower jaw which are as long as the pectoral fins. Distinctly oblique front profile to the head. Reddish with a dark band from the eyes to the tail. Lives on rocky or detrital bottoms, from 10 to 500 meters. Maximum size 40 centimeters.

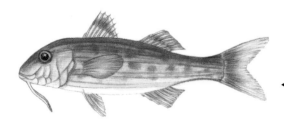

Damselfish - *Chromis chromis*

Oval, compressed body. Short head and small mouth. Adults are brownish, while young fish are an almost fluorescent shade of blue. Lives around rocky bottoms and near posidonia meadows, from 4-5 meters to 50. Maximum size 15 centimeters.

Barracuda - *Sphyraena sphyraena*

Tapering, compact body, laterally compressed. Long head with pointed nose and a prominent lower jaw. The two dorsal fins are quite separate. Bluish-grey topside with numerous dark bands on the sides. Lives in open water from the surface down to 100 meters. Maximum size 165 centimeters.

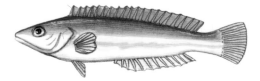

Rainbow wrasse - *Coris julis (male and female)* ▲ ▶

Slim, tapering body. Female fish have brown or dark red backs and a light band on the sides, Males have a greenish-blue back with a red or orange band, edged with blue, on the sides. Lives on rocky bottoms, close to Neptune grass, from 2-3 meters to 120. Maximum size 25 centimeters.

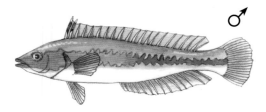

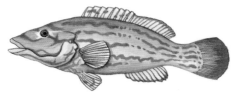

Green wrasse - *Labrus viridis*

Elongated body with long, pointed nose. Generally greenish, lighter on the belly. Often has a white stripe running down the sides from nose to tail. Lives on rocky bottoms, close to Neptune grass, from 4-5 meters to 50 meters. Maximum size 45 centimeters.

Cuckoo wrasse - *Labrus bimaculatus*

Elongated, slightly compressed body. Head is longer than the depth of the body. Young and female individuals are orange or red with three dark marks on the back, male fish are brownish with a ◀ greeny-blue head and blue marks on the sides and back. Lives on rocky bottoms, close to meadows, from 3-5 meters down to 200. Maximum size 40 centimeters.

Peacock wrasse - *Symphodus (Crenilabrus) tinca*

Oval-bodied, slightly-compressed fish. Elongated, flattened snout. Young and female fish are greenish- or brownish-grey with white lips. Males are greenish, bluish or yellowish-green, with rows of small red marks on the sides and a blue upper part of the head. Lives on rocky bottoms and close to posidonia, from 2-3 meters to 80 meters. Maximum size 44 centimeters.

Five-spotted wrasse - *Symphodus (Crenilabrus) roissali*

Stout, oval body, head length equals depth of body, short nose. Female fish are brownish or greenish-brown. Males are reddish-brown ◀ or green with yellow and greenish marks and red lips. Both have a mark on the tail peduncle and five marks on the dorsal fin. Lives on rocky bottoms and close to Neptune grass, from 2-3 meters to 30 meters. Maximum size 20 centimeters.

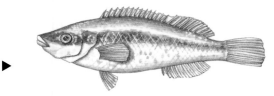

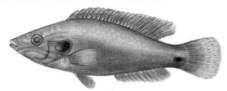

Axillary wrasse - *Symphodus (Crenilabrus) mediterraneus*

Oval, stumpy, fish. Short head and nose. Young and female fish are a yellowish, marbled, brown. Males are bluish-, brownish- or greenish-grey, with lines of small light-colored spots. Both sexes have a mark on the peduncle and one on the operculum. Lives mainly close to posidonia meadows, from 2-3 meters to 40-50 meters. Maximum size 18 centimeters.

Ocellated wrasse - *Symphodus ocellatus*

Oval-bodied fish, very compressed. Short head and nose. Females are yellowish brown with green and pink striped sides. Male fish are green, orange or brownish with two dark longitudinal stripes and ◀ bluish marks. Both sexes have an ocellar mark on the peduncle and one on the operculum. Lives on seaweed-rich rocky bottoms, from 5 meters to 30 meters. Maximum size 15 centimeters.

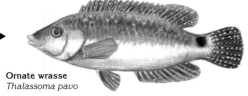

Ornate wrasse
Thalassoma pavo

Elongated, compressed body with oval, pointed, head. Small mouth with big lips. Caudal fin has elongated lobes. Female fish are greenish-brown with a dark lateral band. Males have a red head with bluish stripes and a vertical red band behind the operculum. Lives on rocky bottoms and close to Neptune grass, from 2-3 meters to 150 in the most southern regions of the Mediterranean. Maximum size 25 centimeters.

Pearly razor fish - *Xyrichthys novacula*

Very compressed body, with a very deep head and almost vertical profile in adult fish. Dorsal fin extends along almost the whole body. Curiously, if threatened this fish buries itself. Lives on sandy and muddy bottoms and close to Neptune grass, from 4-5 meters to 50. Maximum size 30 centimeters.

▶

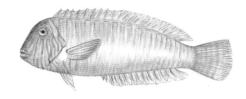

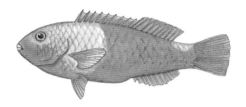

Parrotfish - *Sparisoma cretense*

◀ Ovoid, elongated and slightly compressed body. Terminal mouth with strong jaws and beak-like teeth. Female fish are reddish and males brownish or greenish. Found on rocky bottoms and close to Neptune grass, from 3-4 meters to 40-50. Maximum size 50 centimeters.

Weever - *Trachinus araneus*

Elongated, flattened body. Head is not very large, but the mouth is wide. The dorsal fin and the operculum have dangerous venomous spines. Yellowish-grey with dark blotches of varying sizes. Found buried on sandy or sandy-muddy bottoms, from 2-3 meters to 100. Maximum size 50 centimeters.

▶

Star-gazer - *Uranoscopus scaber*

◀ Solid body, slightly compressed at the rear. Large head, flat back. Has a retractile tentacle inside the mouth which acts as bait for small fish. Greyish-brown. Found on sandy and muddy bottoms, from 15 meters to 250. Maximum size 35 centimeters.

Black faced blenny - *Trypterigion tripteronotus*

Elongated, spindle-shaped body with pointed nose. Dorsal fin is divided into three sections. Greyish-brown. During the mating season males are red with black heads. Found on rocky, poorly-illuminated bottoms, from 1-2 meters down to 8-10. Maximum size 8 centimeters.

▶

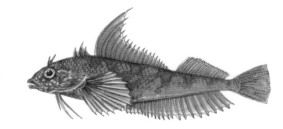

Butterfly blenny - *Blennius ocellaris*

◀ Elongated body, large head with rounded profile. Distinctive marking is a large ocellar mark on the big dorsal fin.
Found on rocky and detrital bottoms, from 30 meters to 200. Maximum size 20 centimeters.

Peacock blenny - *Lipophrys pavo*

Elongated body with short nose; front profile almost vertical. Adult males have a distinctive nuchal crest. Greenish with dark vertical bands edged with blue. Found on rocky or sandy seaweed-rich bottoms from the surface down to 5-7 meters. Maximum size 13 centimeters.

▶

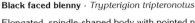

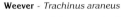

Tompot blenny - *Parablennius gattorugine*

◀ Large blenny with big head and obliquely-profiled nose. Large fringed tentacles over the eyes. Brownish with dark, vertical bands. Found on rocky bottoms and amongst Neptune grass, from 2-3 meters to 30-35. Maximum size 30 centimeters.

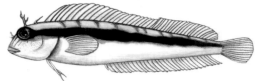

Sand-eel - *Gymnammodites cicerellus*

Elongated body ending in a long, pointed, nose. Upper jaw is protractile. No pelvic fins. Brown back with greenish reflections. Dark blue head and silvery belly. Lives on detrital bottoms, from depths of a few meters down to 120 meters. Maximum size 17 centimeters.

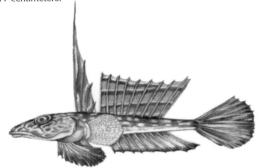

Red-mouthed goby - *Gobius cruentatus.*

Goby with elongated body, large head and wide mouth. Lips and cheeks are bright red. Reddish-brown with irregular blotches. Found on rocky and sandy bottoms and amongst Neptune grass, from 10 meters to 40. Maximum size 18 centimeters.

Buchicchi's goby - *Gobius bucchichi*

Elongated body covered in rough scales. Large head with bulging cheeks. Light yellowish-grey, with small dark blotches, some on the eyes. Found on sandy-muddy bottoms and around Neptune grass, alongside *Anemonia sulcata*. Maximum size 10 centimeters.

Bonito - *Sarda sarda*

Small tunny with tapered body. Very wide mouth. The two dorsal fins are set very close together. Metallic blue with dark stripes on the back and silver sides and belly. Lives in coastal waters from the surface down to depths of 200 meters. Maximum size 90 centimeters.

Striped blenny - *Parablennius rouxi*

Very tapering body, with small head and almost vertical front profile. Feathered tentacle over each eye. Whitish with a dark, longitudinal band. Lives on rocky bottoms from 2-3 meters deep to 40 meters. Maximum size 8 centimeters.

Dragonet - *Callionymus lyra*

Elongated body with wide, flattened, triangular head. Male fish have a very high forward dorsal fin. No scales on the body. Yellowish-brown; females have greenish blotches and males blue during the mating period. Found on sandy and muddy bottoms from 10-15 meters to 400. Maximum size 30 centimeters.

Slender goby - *Gobius geniporus*

Slimline goby covered with rough scales. Large, rounded head with numerous pores on the cheeks. Marbled brown with dark blotches. Green pupil. Found on sandy-muddy bottoms and close to posidonia meadows, from 10 meters to 50. Maximum size 16 centimeters.

Little tunny - *Euthynnus alletteratus*

Robust, spindle-shaped body, without scales except for the front of the body and the lateral line. Bluish back, with an irregular pattern of stripes of blotches, and silvery-grey sides and belly. Lives in coastal waters from the surface down to 50 meters. Maximum size 1 meter.

Mackerel - *Scomber scombrus*

Elongated, rounded, body ending in a pointed nose. Characteristic eyes with a fatty eyelid. Greenish-blue with black stripes on the back and white sides and belly. Lives in shoals in pelagic and coastal waters, from the surface to 250 meters. Maximum size 50 centimeters.

Wide-eyed flounder - *Bothus podas*

Flatfish with eyes on the left-hand side, but set obliquely. Front head profile is almost straight, especially in mature males. Brownish with numerous different colored blotches, from white to bluish to yellow. Found on sandy-muddy and detrital bottoms, from 10-15 meters to 400. Maximum size 45 centimeters.

Turbot - *Psetta maxima*

Flatfish, almost circular in shape, with eyes on the left side of the head. Wide, oblique mouth. Body covered with bony tubercles. Reddish-grey, but changes according to the bottom, as this is a highly mimetic fish. Lives on sandy and detrital bottoms, from 20-30 meters to 100. Maximum size 100 centimeters.

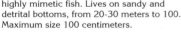

Triggerfish - *Balistes carolinensis*

Wide, oval body, highly compressed and covered in thick, rough, scales. Pointed nose and strong incisors. Forward dorsal fin has large spiny rays which can be blocked in the erect position. Blue-grey and marbled, with blotches on the fins. Found close to rocky bottoms, from 4-5 meters to 100. Maximum size 45 centimeters.

Blue fin tuna - *Thunnus thynnus*

Large fish with robust, tapered, body. Caudal peduncle has a series of dorsal and ventral pinnules. Bluish back and silvery white sides and belly. Lives in pelagic waters in shoals, from depths of a few meters down to 40-50 meters. Maximum size 3 meters.

◀

Swordfish - *Xiphias gladius*

Robust bodied-fish; the nose terminates with an elongated rostrum shaped like a sword. Brownish-black back and light-colored belly. Lives in pelagic and coastal waters, from the surface to over 600 meters. Maximum size 4.5 meters.

Sole - *Solea sp.*

Oval flatfish with eyes on right side of head. Small, slightly curved, mouth. Varies in color due to its mimetic ability, but is usually grey-brown or reddish. Measures up to 70 centimeters.

Sunfish - *Mola mola*

Unmistakable fish with oval, compressed and very deep body. Highly developed dorsal and anal fins which join in the rear like a kind of caudal fin. Brownish with light and silvery-grey blotches on the sides. Lives in pelagic waters to a depth of 360 meters. Maximum size 3 meters.

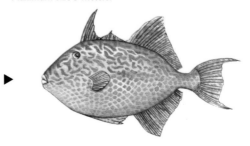

Cover
Enormous branches of yellow and red gorgonians emerge from a rocky wall surrounded by the blue waters of the southern Mediterranean.
Photograph by Franco Banfi

Back cover
Top The Spiaggia Rosa (Pink beach) of the island of Budelli, in the Archipelago of the Maddalena, owes its name to the unmistakable color of the sand: a fine mixture of granite, shells and marine microorganisms.
Photograph by Marcello Bertinetti/ Archivio White Star

Center The brown Mediterranean grouper (Epinephelus guaza) can grow to one metre in length and fifty kilos in weight.
Photograph by Roberto Rinaldi

Bottom Rocky bottoms habitat.
Drawing by Monica Falcone and Roberta Vigone/ Archivio White Star

168 A small blenny peers out from its hole and, seemingly with interest, observes the outside world.

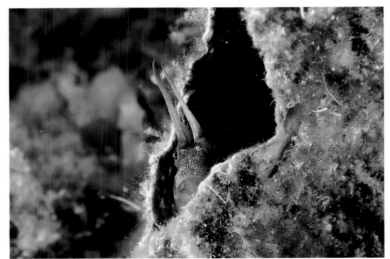